Working with High-Risk

A Relationship-based Practice Framework

Peter Smyth

 Routledge
Taylor & Francis Group

LONDON AND NEW YORK

First published 2017
by Routledge
2 Park Square, Milton Park, Abingdon, Oxon OX14 4RN

and by Routledge
711 Third Avenue, New York, NY 10017

Routledge is an imprint of the Taylor & Francis Group, an informa business

© 2017 Peter Smyth

British Library Cataloguing-in-Publication Data
A catalogue record for this book is available from the British Library

Library of Congress Cataloging-in-Publication Data
A catalog record for this book has been applied for

ISBN: 978-1-138-23447-5 (hbk)
ISBN: 978-1-138-23449-9 (pbk)
ISBN: 978-1-315-27004-3 (ebk)

Typeset in Sabon
by Apex CoVantage, LLC

This book is dedicated to the many youth with whom I have crossed paths over the years. It is also dedicated to my parents, Terry and Laurie Smyth, who taught me what a privilege it is to serve others.

Contents

Acknowledgements

This book was a labour of love, but just like good practice in the helping professions, this did not happen in isolation. My first big thank you is to my daughter Kiara Smyth who, using her amazing teaching skills, came along on this journey with me and edited the first draft of the book. We agonized over commas, argued over what did and did not make sense, laughed, got unfocused and silly, and stayed up way too late on many occasions. I will remember these days very fondly. Thanks so much to my wife, Cheryl, and other three kids, Conor, Braden, and Jenna, who supported me through this process and were probably more patient than they needed to be. I love you all. I was also blessed with the support and encouragement of my sisters Geraldine, Catherine, and Clare, and my brother Kevin.

Thanks to my good friend, Arlene Eaton-Erickson. You were with me through the earliest days of the High Risk Youth Initiative starting in 1999, and you continue to give to me the gift of your wisdom, ideas, and time. Our chats continue to inspire my thinking and evolve my practice. The concepts in this book would not have developed without your input, openness, and thoughtfulness. A big thanks also to my many colleagues who were part of the early days in the High Risk Youth Unit I supervised for seven years. Breaking new ground with such dedicated professionals was a brilliant experience and the memories will stay with me forever. Being surrounded with like-minded people, working in the government or in the community, made this tough work not only worthwhile, but it felt like we could actually change practice in our child welfare system. It has been a blessing to have you journey with me over these many years: Heather Peddle, David Rust, Frank Wingrove, June Emery, Jean Lafrance, Karen Bruno, Karyn Schultz, Renee Sullivan, Brianna Olson, Wallis Kendal, Diane Conrad, Catherine Broomfield, Marliss Taylor, Rebecca Edwards Rabiey, Mandy Halabi, Karen Drynan, Larisa Jeffares, Fayanne Perry, Mark Cherrington, Barb Dewalt, Sherrie Young, my sister Clare Smyth, and so many others. Thank you to all of the workers, supervisors, and managers in the bigger High Risk Youth Initiative in Edmonton, again whether you work for the government or with one of the many dedicated community agencies. Your passion for working with youth, your ongoing support, and your willingness to take risks is always inspiring and appreciated.

Thank you to the managers who supported me and had faith, in particular Al Failing, who gave the go-ahead for the first high-risk youth caseload; Cheryl Hartshorne, who pushed to expand the initiative; Michelle Sandquist, who helped the initiative through some tough times; Sheli Steil, who was a genuine ally; and Lisa McDonald, who truly understood the bigger picture and pushed me to keep writing. Thank you to the many others who were open to trying new things and learning with me.

I am indebted to all of the youth I have known over the years, whether working with them directly or indirectly. In particular, I want to thank those of you who contributed to the book in different ways, including Alysha, Melissa, Meagan, Sonja, Aimee, Kathryn, Little Nicole, Lori, Kyla, Leanne, Candace, Jen, and Cory. You will never know how much you taught me and just how truly grateful I am.

Thanks to Michael Ungar for being a generous and wise ally in our work with the youth. Your work on resiliency in complex and troubled youth has proven to be very important in helping all youth and changing practice perspectives in workers. Being the first keynote speaker at the first High Risk Youth Conference (now called the Allies for Youth Connections Conference) was inspirational and very fitting. Thank you Annie-Marie McLaughlin for the encouragement to learn, write, and teach, and for your support and interest in my work with youth.

Thank you so much Shannon Kneis from Routledge for your guidance and support through the whole process from manuscript to publishing, and for believing that this book is important. Also to your colleague Clare Jarvis and former colleague Lianne Sherlock for making this book a reality. The ability of all of you in answering all of my questions thoroughly and patiently was amazing, and you provided me with a wonderful learning experience. Much appreciation to Sally Keefe Cohen for your advocacy and guidance too. I am indebted to author Joan Galat; you were not only a brilliant editor when we were involved with a magazine for the Alberta College of Social Workers, but you also believed in me as a writer and you were generous in sharing your passion for writing and convincing me my book needed to be written and published.

To Cory Nicotine: you are a leader, a mentor, and an inspiration to so many people. Thank you for supporting the use of the photograph on the cover of the book.

Chapter 1

Introduction
A relationship-based practice framework

"I can make it on my own . . . don't need no one else"
I know you think it's safer to be by yourself
"Leave me in my darkness; this is the way I want to be
Protected by my walls, I'll survive . . . you'll see"
You won't take the chance of again being rejected
It's safer being lonely than it is to be connected[1]

As the writing of this chapter begins, an article in the *Edmonton Journal* appears that is prophetically relevant to the subject matter of this book. Journalist Darcy Henton (2010) tells the story of Christopher Crane, age 19 and a member of a gang at troubled Maskwacis Cree Nation,[2] near Edmonton, Alberta. In 2008, he fired the gun in a drunken drive-by shooting. A stray bullet found an innocent toddler. The child survived but for the rest of her life will have to live with this trauma, as well as a bullet that is lodged in her spine and the scars from her surgery.

Crane also had to survive trauma in his childhood and he will also have to live with those scars for the rest of his life. Henton reported that Crane never really had a father and a step-father died a violent death. His alcoholic mother abandoned him and his grandfather who helped raise him was charged with sexually assaulting young girls. He bounced around from his mother to various relatives and along the way was physically, sexually, and verbally abused. By age 11 he was smoking marijuana regularly. He dropped out of school at age 12, as he felt no one cared whether or not he attended. He lived in poverty, had no education, and had no job prospects. Crane's mother died in a car accident in December 2009, while he was in jail.

Earlier, his mother had described her son to a psychologist as "always angry." The psychologist further told the court that Crane was "moody, sad, and despondent," and added that he thought the teenager has been exposed to trauma, as he showed post-traumatic symptoms. The psychologist testified that "violence was never far from this man. . . . He saw it and he partook in it." Crane had been taking medications for anxiety most of his life. He has had a common-law spouse since he was 14 and they have a 3-year-old son. He has been violent toward his spouse. However, the psychologist does not see Crane as "decidedly anti-social," but rather as immature and rebellious. While he is seen to be a moderate risk for re-offending, much of this depends on whether he can wean himself from alcohol and drugs, which he has used to self-medicate his anxiety and depression. Other barriers to Crane, throughout his life, have been the fact he had undiagnosed vision and hearing problems. According to a psychologist, he possibly has organic brain damage, as well as limited comprehension skills and a limited vocabulary.

Henton asks whether Crane can be saved or should be saved. After such a tragic start, can Crane turn his life around? Since his mother was buried, he has apologized for his actions and vowed to be a better father to his son. He has hopes and dreams but the psychologist says that whether he has the ability to see a positive future these remains to be seen. He has dropped his gang colours and Crane said he was never into being a gang member and never really played the role. He told the judge, "I am not what people think I am."

It is unclear if Crane knows who he is at all. While not excusing his role in the shooting, he had no one to trust, no one to look out for him, and was abused and abandoned by the very people who should have been keeping him safe. He tuned out at age 11 and drifted. Perhaps it can be different now, but who does he turn to? Can he emerge from his dark, unsafe world, or is he destined to be the next generation in his family whose troubles are too overwhelming and consuming?

While not all who experience a similar childhood as Crane end up involved in such serious violence (Schore, 2003), they often do lead high-risk lifestyles. They are very often intensely angry, trust no one, self-medicate, dissociate, break the law, and quite possibly don't believe that they will ever have hope, let alone achieve their goals. It's not that youth coming from such trauma don't have goals and dreams, but there is a disconnect, as most of these youth do not ever expect their goals will be realized. Given their poor self-worth and the barriers they face in life, goals and dreams tend to remain in the realm of fantasy. The lack of caring they have experienced "marks a youth who has learned to live without hope, to truly believe in his or her guts that he or she is alone and always will be" (Kagan, 2004, p. 47).

A shift in practice

This tragic story illustrates the obvious – that high-risk youth do not come out of nowhere. Of all of the youth who have come into the High Risk Youth Initiative (a child protection unit within Edmonton and Area Child and Family Services Region)[3] since its inception in November 2005, *all* have struggled with family problems from childhood. *All* of the youth have issues around abandonment and rejection, which psychologist Richard Kagan (2004) calls "the greatest curse" given "the feeling of being unwanted eats away at his or her inner being" (p. 46). *All* of the youth struggle, on some level, with building relationships and developing trust. This is not to say all of the youth are, or would be, diagnosed with Reactive Attachment Disorder, but all do have some level of difficulty in this area. Based on the experience of the High Risk Youth Initiative (HRYI) in developing specialized programming for high-risk youth, the problems start very early. Relationship issues faced by the youth are a challenge to overcome and without intervention they can chart a destructive journey throughout their whole life (Maté, 2008; National Scientific Council on the Developing Child, 2010a). A vast majority of the literature on attachment theory, and Reactive Attachment Disorder, focuses on the onset of attachment from in utero to 36 months, and then up to about age 12. There is comparatively little written about how youth and young adults continue to manage with their attachment issues and how it impacts so many areas of their lives. This is surprising given we humans are such social creatures and our survival as a species is dependent on our ability to form and maintain successful relationships with others (National Scientific Council on the Developing Child, 2004b; Perry & Szalavitz, 2006) and, further, that we all will have difficulty loving others if we are unable to love ourselves (Szalavitz & Perry, 2010). As Kagan (2004) notes, attachment to a caring parent means survival. Abandonment to a young child means an emotional trauma at minimum and death at the extreme. By the time an unattached child is an adolescent, they have learned to keep people at a distance and accept they are on their own in the world because they cannot rely on others (Batmanghelidjh, 2006; Howe, 2005; Smyth & Eaton-Erickson, 2009). Their walls are castle thick and outside of this protective barrier lies a frightening existence. This is a lonely and dark place to be, but a place with which high-risk youth are familiar.

Getting connected

Readers will be introduced to the *Get Connected* practice framework that has been incorporated into child welfare and community practice with youth, and high-risk youth in particular, over the past decade through the HRYI. This model is a relationships-based, anti-oppressive practice framework and philosophy. It is informed by attachment theory and neuroscience related to how trauma impacts the brain (Chapters 2 and 3); a harm reduction philosophy (Chapter 4); resiliency and strength-based approaches (Chapter 5); as well as the importance of community collaboration (Chapter 6). Drawn from this theoretical base, strategies are presented to engage, build relationships, and work with youth in ways they hear, see, and feel as meaningful, allowing them to take the risk of having a caring person come into their isolated world (Chapters 7 and 9). This is a break from traditional approaches to child welfare work, which is focused on personal deficits and punishment-consequence perspectives.

A focus of this book will be on how youth cope, or do not cope, when they have no healthy connections to others, but also on how they make their lives work, develop resiliency, create their identities, and strive toward surprisingly mainstream goals in their lives. This book will also go beyond the struggles high-risk youth face because of their early childhood experiences and shattered relationships to focus on how the child welfare system – and indeed other systems, whether government, agency, or community organizations – interact with the youth.

In the Western world, the human services field continues to be driven by risk-management (Lonne, Parton, Thomson & Harries, 2009; Wharf, 2002a), deficit-based, or problem-saturated systems (Lonne et al., 2009; Luckock & Lefevre, 2008; Madsen, 2007; Saleebey, 1997; Ungar, 2004). Government ministries, in particular, are prone to working in isolation instead of drawing from the wisdom of professionals from other government ministries, non-profit organizations, outreach agencies, and informal supports (Mullaly, 2010; Wharf, 2002a). Interestingly, while maintaining we are in social work, or child welfare, to help families and keep children safe, we cling to oppressive, punishment-consequence orientations based on power and control (Lonne et al., 2009; Luckock & Lefevre, 2008; Strega & Sohki Aski Esquao, 2009). Despite the challenges – or perceptions of challenges from an adult point of view – youth have with the various systems, they actually do want connections with safe and healthy adults (Siegel, 2013). However, instead of drawing them in, we tend to push them away, reinforcing that the world is an unsafe and lonely place, and that one cannot trust adults. Therefore, the youth typically remain marginalized and excluded from mainstream society (Gaetz, 2004; Mullaly, 2007, 2010) and are seen as what Ungar (2006, p. 11) refers to as "dangerous, delinquent, deviant or disordered" adolescents. This is magnified even more so for Aboriginal[4] youth, as well as those who may be part of the LBGTQ+ community, immigrant youth, or those pregnant and parenting. Such labelling and societal attitudes serve to create more barriers to youth accessing services and having the opportunity to build safe relationships so they can actually get to the place that we, ironically, *demand* of them in the first place – feeling safe, coping, and managing their lives.

However, more recently, practice has been changing, and while change is slow and painful, there is more empathy and compassion being brought into working with children, youth, and families. This allows for more of a focus on building relationships first and building support teams in partnership with the youth. This is not to say that many workers have not been putting their hearts, souls, and minds into their work with children, youth, and families, but a relationship-based focus has clearly not yet been embraced fully in the Western world of child welfare (Lonne et al., 2009; Luckock & Lefevre, 2008; Mullaly, 2010). Notably, however, the shift has started, so as momentum builds, hopefully it will become harder to return to traditional methods and oppressive practice. This book will hopefully contribute to taking this more compassionate model of practice to a tipping point, leaving little room for traditional practices that youth see as ineffective and frustrating.

The 'high-risk youth' label

Of course, the fact the term 'high-risk youth' is a label is not lost on those of us involved in the HRYI in Edmonton, Alberta. Admittedly, it has been uncomfortable to be talking about an anti-oppressive practice framework and philosophy while calling the youth 'high risk.' This goes back to 1999, when the first 'high-risk youth caseload' was created within Edmonton and Area Child and Family Services Region as a response to comments from youth who felt disengaged with the child welfare system. It was a term to reference a separate group of youth who needed more help, rather than leaving them at the bottom of the priority list due to being "defiant, uncooperative and manipulative." Their behaviours were certainly putting them at risk to harm themselves or be victims of violence or sexual exploitation. Though the youth had no input in deciding a name for the caseload, the name stuck. The caseload existed for four years before leaving for another position within Child and Family Services. The 'high-risk youth' tag continued when the caseload was expanded to become the HRYI in November 2005.[5]

The 'high-risk youth' label became the reference point for a designated group of youth who required a program to better serve them. People have rightly questioned the name and some youth have reacted to it as well. Some asked what they had done to be labelled a 'high-risk youth.' Some asked why they were still a high-risk youth even though their circumstances had changed. Others, unfortunately, took it as a badge of honour. A vast majority, however, accepted it, acknowledged it, or simply didn't have an opinion. Many discussions have taken place as to how this term might help or hinder youth from getting services, as well as how public perceptions are reacting to this identified group of youth, especially given youth are already marginalized and often feel excluded in the community (Gaetz, 2004).

The consensus within government and the community was that it would be a good idea to change the 'high-risk youth' label to something more positive. It turned out that this was a challenge in itself, as suggested names said very little about the population of youth; suggested the outcome we, as service providers, desired; or would have little meaning to the youth. The next obvious step, then, was to canvass the youth. This proved even more troublesome. Initially, the youth attending feedback sessions asked what was wrong with 'high-risk youth.' They had difficulty coming up with names, thus youth forums yielded very little. Consensus among the youth, whether in a group format, or individually, was not to change the name. What we learned, at least, was that 'high-risk youth' had become a positive tag for them. It was a place where things were different, where 'people actually cared,' and where a youth could get help. It appears that we as services providers were having more difficulty with the name than the youth were, leaving us with the dilemma of deciding whether to abandon the label when the youth have given no such direction, and to which they have a positive association. However, we remain the *High Risk Youth Initiative* for now. This is our reference point and the term that continues to be used by the government, community, and, indeed, the youth. This is a long explanation simply to say that the term, 'high-risk youth' will be used throughout this book!

Honouring the voices of youth

If youth were not initially engaged in naming the initiative, efforts have since been made to incorporate their voices into developing the larger initiative. Intentional steps continue to be taken to incorporate the voices of youth into the practice framework and philosophy as it evolves. In general, youth are not averse to sharing their thoughts and opinions, as blunt and harsh as they may be at times. When we are able to avoid justifying our position and becoming defensive, their comments are valuable in helping us think critically and acknowledging that, while some aspects of our work make sense for us, it is irrelevant if it does not make sense for the youth.

To incorporate the needs and voices of the youth, there needs to be built-in flexibility and adaptability. There needs to be questions asked as to whether we are building programs and services to meet the needs of the system or the needs of the youth. When youth are questioning what we are doing and why we are doing it, this must be our red flag to stop and incorporate some self- and system-reflection as to who is actually being served. As Luckock and Lefevre state: "children were not just objects of any intervention but subjects with important views and feelings about what was happening to them" (p. xiii). This means making ourselves available as a "personal resource" for the child (Luckock & Lefevre, 2008, p. xxix) so they feel comfortable enough to participate in the system rather than simply being the object of policies and procedures.

Leading up to the development of the HRYI, the youth-serving agencies that provide placements for children and youth who are in the care of the government expressed frustration that there were a relatively small number of youth using a high number of beds and who were not engaging or buying into services. They would leave the group home, though often returned before the magic 48 hours, at which time their bed would be closed. Having eaten and cleaned up they would be off again. This frequently played-out scenario prompted the creation of the High Risk Youth Task Force to conduct an in-house study[6] to get the youth's perspective as to how resources were meeting their needs.

In March 2005, this task force released 'The Word On the Street: How Youth View Services Aimed at Them' (Smyth, Eaton-Erickson, Slessor & Pasma, 2005).[7] Most of the youth who fit into the category of 'high-risk youth' reported that they had had negative experiences with 'the system' and believed it either did not help them or made their situation worse. These experiences included a lack of meaningful relationships with social workers and service providers, a lack of support during life transitions, and not feeling heard by the system. They too referenced programs being developed in the best interests of the system rather than them. Youth expressed feeling constricted by rules and expectations. While they saw basic rules as important to avoid chaos, they did not think that they had any input into developing such rules, thus their relevance became suspect. They believed child welfare workers did not have time for them, did not hear them, and did not understand them. Most youth were not familiar with service plans, and, therefore, did not appear to feel connected to the helping process. This made them suspicious of the system and, while they acknowledged that they needed help, they generally did not see Child and Family Services as a viable provider of such assistance (Smyth & Eaton-Erickson, 2009).

Despite this, an overall theme of the report was one of opportunity and hope. As the youth spoke, it became clear that if they had a positive relationship with their case worker, they appeared to view the whole system in a positive light. Conversely, if they believed that they had a negative relationship, they saw the whole system as negative. This was also true for youths' relationship with caregivers (foster parents and group home or residential staff) and service providers such as youth workers, family workers, and therapists. This illustrated how important it is for youth to have a positive connection with an adult even if it is difficult for them to take such a risk. Secondly, by focusing on building relationships with youth, not only would youth be tentatively open to engaging, they may also attain a level of buy-in that could initiate a process of healthy change (Smyth & Eaton-Erickson, 2009).

Relationship-building also demonstrates to youth a collaborative *working with* stance (Madsen, 1999; Strega, 2007; Turnell & Edwards, 1999), rather than *doing to* or *doing for* (Luckock & Lefevre, 2008; Saleebey, 1997; Wharf, 2002a), which youth have identified as a barrier to feeling connected to the system (Smyth & Eaton-Erickson, 2009). Of course, there have been many examples in my practice to show that when youth are told what to do, where to stay, and how to behave, especially before any kind of positive relationship has been developed, youth do not 'buy in.' This often results in power struggles, typically leaving the youth facing barriers that prevent them from accessing the services they need.

A follow-up, in-house study was completed in 2007, appropriately titled, 'More Words from the Street: A Follow Up Report on How Youth View Services Aimed at Them.'[8] This research compared youth who were part of the HRYI, youth who had status with child welfare services but who were not in the HRYI, and youth who had no status at all. Youth involved with the HRYI were positive about the services that were provided, whether through the case workers or community partners. For the most part, they appreciated being involved in the decision-making process, the availability of case worker, and the support they received. For youth with status but not in HRYI, some reported getting services but, in general, relationships with their case workers were more strained, meaning the youth did not feel the same level of support. In addition, they were not typically involved with their case plans. Some blamed 'the system' rather than their case worker (caseloads being too high, too much paperwork, case workers being overworked). The non-status youth talked about the many barriers to getting supports and services, and also stated that they were not heard and were essentially on their own, even if they were getting emotional support from community agencies. All three groups saw the value in having a positive relationship with an adult who would support them. Not surprisingly, the youth still wanted a connection with someone trustworthy, caring, respectful, and non-judgemental.

While the youth responded positively to the HRYI with respect to having a connection to their workers, being heard, and feeling supported, there have also been rewards for workers. Being able to break out of the traditional child-welfare mould has been a liberating experience, providing the opportunity to work in partnership with the youth, take risks together, be flexible, bend rules, be creative, be in the community, and build support teams with community partners. This practice framework demands a heightened level of self-awareness (understanding the impact you have on a youth, and how the youth impacts you as a worker); critical reflection (do I practice in anti-oppressive ways and in the best interests of the youth regardless of what I think is best?); thoughtfulness around ethics and boundaries (maintaining healthy worker-client boundaries, discouraging dependency, and finding a balance between being realistic and hopeful; discussed in detail in Chapter 10); and the worker accepting the role of youth ally (Bishop, 2002). In short, this intentional, relational way of working with youth not only is a benefit to them, but makes us better practitioners. It is also humbling because – using anti-oppressive and harm reduction language – it becomes clear that we are not the experts in the lives of the youth but rather we learn to appreciate that they are the experts in their own lives. We can guide, advise, advocate, and engage in discussions, but we don't *do* to them, or *for* them, we journey *with* them.

The *Get Connected* practice framework does not have all the answers, but we can help them find answers that work for them. Is this not why we got into this field in the first place – to help others? I am amused at times because people will say that the practice framework of the HRYI is cutting-edge practice or a radical approach to working with youth. I believe it is simpler than that. As a social worker I believe this is basic practice! This is building relationships, being a safe person for others, wanting to give people hope. When in school studying to be in the helping profession, not many people had a vision that one day they would be in a position of having control over clients or service users,[9] having the authority to tell them what to do, and punishing them if they don't comply. Yet, how did we stray so far from our ethics and values and our purpose for entering the helping profession in the first place? The *Get Connected* practice framework helps pull us back to our roots. It is the youth that can help guide us back to what is important if only we are open to truly hearing and honouring their voices.

A challenging population

At the risk of presenting this work as child welfare nirvana, I must acknowledge that it comes with challenges as well. Working with high-risk youth is intense and requires a lot of patience. It is not for everyone, as not everyone is cut out for working with youth, let alone those youth whose first words to you may be "fuck you, I don't need anybody telling me what to do." My experience is that it may take a while for them to buy in, but if workers are genuine and non-judgemental, and are respectful and good listeners, they may very well risk engaging in a relationship (Batmanghelidjh, 2006; Brendtro & du Toit, 2005; Herbert, 2007; Lemma, 2010; Luckock & Lefevre, 2008; Ungar, 2004). Experience has demonstrated that when they do buy in, they buy in hard. The youth who are most resistant initially often end up making the most solid connections, perhaps because they put the most energy into the relationship, whether negative (initially) or positive (once past the testing phase). However, once they have taken the risk of allowing a healthy adult into their lives, they want contact and lots of it! Whether face-to-face, texting, Facebook, or email, they want connection.

Workers commit to being available so as not to repeat the youths' experiences of rejection and abandonment, which can be a juggling act with a caseload of up to 15 high-risk youth.[10] With that comes the challenge of finding a work-life balance, the secondary and vicarious traumatization that can result from hearing about the adverse experiences of so many youth, the fear of a tragic incident given the high-risk lifestyles of the youth, the need to be constantly vigilant about maintaining limits and boundaries given the youth have typically experienced such profound boundary violations throughout their lives (Reamer, 2012), and finding a balance between attending to the needs of the youth and maintaining the administrative duties that are part of the child welfare system.

So who are these youth who require much attention and provide workers with rewards and challenges? Smyth and Eaton-Erickson (2009) asked the question and defined 'high risk':

> We refer to high-risk youth as 'the disconnected': They rarely have family to rely on. They rarely have a healthy support network to help guide them. . . . They live risk-filled lifestyles characterized by such things as drugs, sexual exploitation, violence, living on the streets and family breakdown. They typically have difficulty trusting adults and perceive they are alone in the world. . . . They are not 'at-risk' youth; they are 'high-risk youth.' They are not heading in a bad direction or on a path of self-destruction; they are already there. . . . They are hard to engage, slow to change, test frequently, and challenge one's practice, ethics, and boundaries. Many youth have shared that they expect the relationship with their child welfare worker to be problematic. Despite this we have come to believe that all youth want connection, but attempting to connect with high-risk youth is a risk-filled journey that requires patience.
>
> (p. 119)

I have also learned this population of youth demonstrate resiliency and have many strengths. This may not be evident if practicing from a deficit-based or problem-saturated perspective (Luckock & Lefevre, 2008; Madsen, 2010; Saleebey, 1997), but does become apparent once efforts have been made to engage youth in a meaningful way.

However, explaining why a youth is high risk, as opposed to at risk, can be problematic. High-risk youth would fall under the umbrella of 'hard-to-serve youth.' While some these subgroups can be challenging to serve, they are not necessarily street-involved youth struggling to make safe choices. For example, a 17-year old with Asperger's Syndrome may also have trouble making connections with others, perhaps is prone to acts of aggression, and has trouble following through with service plans. Indeed, a service provider is faced with challenges, though the youth would not fall under the label of 'high-risk youth.' A caregiver may also be challenged in meeting the needs of a severely mentally and physically handicapped youth, but again, while definitely a hard-to-serve youth, he or she is not a high-risk youth. An 'at-risk' youth may be making poor choices, as opposed to engaging in a high-risk lifestyle. They might be experimenting with drugs, but not using to escape their painful existence. The at-risk youth might swear at his teacher, but is not packing a knife for protection. They may be couch surfing with friends without telling their parents, but is not engaging in survival sex to avoid sleeping in a dumpster. They may blow off a meeting with a youth mentor, but is not trashing a caregiver's house out of fear they are getting too emotionally close.

As the HRYI has expanded in Edmonton and area (with a population of over one million[11]), it is estimated that there now well over 250 youth (14–21 years old) who would fit the criteria for 'high-risk youth' (see Box 1.1) and who have status[12] with Child and Family Services. In addition, with the emergence of younger children showing up on the street who are involved in, or being coerced into, high-risk behaviours, and who are very challenging to engage, it is estimated that there are dozens of high-risk children between the ages of 11 and 13 who have government status (Eaton-Erickson, Campbell & Smyth, 2011). Of course, this does not include many more from both age groups who are experiencing similar challenges in their lives but have no child welfare status. However, these youth are likely to be getting some of their basic and emotional needs met through community agencies and outreach services.

Box 1.1   Criteria for high-risk youth

This definition is intended to be a guide for Edmonton and Area Child and Family Services Region staff. For a youth to be defined as 'high risk' there is no condition that they have to meet a certain number of criteria. This is part of an assessment to determine the needs of the youth, also taking into account how disconnected they may be from having supportive people in their lives, their struggles with being able to form healthy relationships, and whether they could benefit from the overall philosophy of the High Risk Youth Initiative given previous challenges with compliance, finding appropriate placements, and avoiding help.

- Defined by the level of risk regardless of age.
- The use of drugs and/or alcohol appears to be interfering with day-to-day functioning.
- The choices they are making may jeopardize their safety (including where they are living and with whom they are associating).
- They cannot identify a healthy adult in their lives outside of the professional community.
- The youth struggles with authority figures and has few, if any, people they can trust.

- There have been multiple placements or the youth is unwilling to stay in an "approved placement."
- There have been multiple file closures due to lack of follow through by the youth.
- The youth is involved with, or at-risk for, sexual exploitation including survival sex.
- Multi-generational involvement with child and youth services.
- He/she is a sexually exploited youth within the definition of the Protection of Sexually Exploited Children Act (PSECA).

Definition updated and approved by the High Risk Youth Operations Committee in January 2012.

A snapshot of 55 high-risk youth with government status in late 2011 provided the following interesting, and somewhat surprising, statistics (while the number of youth now involved with the HRYI has greatly expanded, the percentages in each of the categories has remained constant):

- Nineteen per cent of the youth were permanent wards of the government, while 80% were voluntary. This is significant given a vast majority of the youth state they have not had good experiences with the child welfare system but now want ongoing services past the age of 18.
- Consistently, since starting the high-risk youth caseload in 1999, 85% of the youth are female.[13]
- At any given time almost 25% are pregnant and/or parenting and many do very well during their pregnancies. Many have become successful parents (Chapter 8).
- Also consistently, close to 70% are Aboriginal youth. This is close to the proportion of Aboriginal children in care, at 68% (Office of the Child and Youth Advocate, 2012), despite Aboriginal children making up only 9% of the children in the province. The over-representation of Aboriginal young people actually increases with the severity of the intervention (Office of the Child and Youth Advocate, 2012).

In addition, the LGTBQ+ (lesbian, gay, transgendered, bisexual, and questioning), or queer,[14] population of youth require an enhanced level of support, as historically they have not been served well by child welfare services due to ignorance, discrimination, or homophobia (Abramovich, 2013a; Luckock & Lefevre, 2008; Quinn, 2002). Research shows that LGTBQ+ youth are over-represented in numbers of youth who drop out of school and who are struggling with addictions, homelessness, suicide, and mental health issues (Abramovich, 2013a; Berger, 2005; Dame, 2004; Quinn, 2002).

Further statistics relating to the 2011 analysis of 55 youth highlight the complexity of the youth and the challenges they face:

- Almost 100% struggle with attachment and trauma (including transgenerational trauma).

- Over 90% struggle with addictions. Case workers and services providers need to understand that a vast majority of these youth are using drugs and alcohol to self-medicate or numb out as a way to escape reality.
- Addictions are typically connected to mental health concerns and over 90% struggle with mental health issues, whether diagnosed or suspected. Diagnoses include depression, anxiety, attachment disorder, Post-Traumatic Stress Disorder, Bipolar Disorder, Obsessive-Compulsive Disorder, schizophrenia, drug-induced psychosis, dissociation, and a combination of the following cluster of disorders: Attention Deficit Disorder, Attention Deficit Hyperactivity Disorder, Oppositional Defiant disorder, and Conduct Disorder. Other diagnoses may include Fetal Alcohol Spectrum Disorder, pica, various learning disorders, and Tourette's Syndrome.
- Over 90% have been involved in the justice system to some degree ranging from accumulating and failing to pay fines for riding the transit system without a ticket to assault, robbery, attempted murder and murder, possession of weapons, drug trafficking, stealing vehicles, public drunkenness, assaulting a police officer, making death threats, and more. Close to half of the youth have spent time in youth and/or adult jail. Others may spend time in residential treatment services, hospital psychiatric wards, or in addictions treatment programs.

In addition, many live unstable lifestyles moving from place to place (couch surfing), living in shelters, engaging in survival sex (trading sex activity for a place to stay, food, drugs, and alcohol), or are homeless. For many high-risk youth, their physical health suffers as well (Gaetz, O'Grady, Buccieri, Karabanow & Marsolais, 2013), though given their issues with trust, body image, shame, poor self-esteem, and sitting patiently in a hospital emergency room for an average of eight hours, they are typically reluctant to deal with their health issues and often feel unwelcome at hospitals (Nicholas et al., 2015).

Many of these transient youth are 'graduates' of the child welfare, youth justice, and educational systems. A high percentage of youth have spent time in foster homes as children but they typically did not make it in foster care past the early teen years due to 'out-of-control behaviours.' In short, their attachment issues re-emerge, they are unable to regulate themselves, testing behaviours escalate, and a vast majority of foster parents do not have the understanding or capacity to cope with a youth still dealing with the trauma they have experienced and the resulting impact on their brain development. Some youth have been in 30–50 placements by the time they hit 16 years old. They are very skilled in sabotaging placements and in keeping people at a safe emotional distance. These are kids who walk away from caregivers like it is water off their backs. Not only do they have a view of the world as an unsafe, lonely, and frightening place in which adults inevitably give up on them (i.e., a repeat of rejection and abandonment), but this is reinforced time and time again. How are they supposed to see the world, and the people in it, as safe and caring? This is not to blame the foster parent, or adoptive parents, as they are typically devastated and confused when the placement breaks down. Their dreams of providing a child from tragic circumstances an opportunity for a stable and loving home are shattered and there are feelings of guilt, exasperation, and betrayal. For the youth, they may see this home as simply the next stop. Caregivers learn the harsh reality that, for these youth, love alone is not enough.

Youth this complex seem beyond the training and expectations of all but the rare foster home, and they typically do not have an understanding or the training to be

tuned in to the emotions and the needs of the youth in their care. Many turn to punitive measures or threats to end the placement or gain control, or some may become
verbally and/or physically abusive as they see their control slip away. Traditional
group homes are even more challenging for the youth given the propensity for a standard rule-based, punishment-consequence orientation from which they often practice.
As Perry (2010) tells us, the tough love and three-strikes mentality does not fit for
these traumatized youth. Such traditional thinking can create power struggles and
potentially an 'us versus them' dynamic, which is hardly conducive to establishing
supportive and nurturing relationships. The goal with children and youth should be to
draw them in through understanding and kindness, rather than adopting punishment-
consequence tactics that are short-sighted and harmful and can serve to alienate the
youth even further (Brendtro, Mitchell & McCall, 2009; Neufeld & Maté, 2004;
Reamer & Siegel, 2008; Szalavitz & Perry, 2010).

While there are many good people in the helping profession making a difference in
the lives of many youth, the structures in place do not always support the relational
approaches, and this contributes to youth being kicked out of placements or being disillusioned enough that they choose to leave even when they have nowhere else to go. Of
course, with each placement breakdown, the sense of being rejected and abandoned, of
being let down, and of being marginalized and alienated is reinforced. The basic need to
have a sense of belonging somewhere, with someone, becomes an even more elusive goal.

We can make a difference

What we, as social workers, child and youth care workers, youth workers, caregivers, family workers, teachers, psychologists, and counsellors need to understand and
appreciate is that despite their defiance and anger towards us, youth are searching for
connections with safe adults (Howe, 2008; Kagan, 2004; Luckock & Lefevre, 2008;
Ungar, 2004, 2006). I have learned, working with this population, that their resistance is more about their capacity to take a risk and allow people into their dark and
lonely world than it is about not wanting people in their lives. On the surface people
often see resistance and negative behaviours. The youth are shrugged off as dangerous, delinquent, deviant, and disordered by the dominant forces of a neo-liberal
society that reinforces a punishment mentality (Lonne et al., 2009; Mullaly, 2010;
Ungar, 2004). However, digging deeper, we can start to understand that when youth
are not feeling a sense of belonging and cannot find their place in the community, such
behaviours "make a satisfying substitute" (Ungar, 2009, p. 19). Ungar further states:

> They want to know they count. . . . So much of what they want can only be found
> when adults who care for them are part of their lives . . . our children need their
> attachments with adults to create a secure sense of who they are. . . . they want
> real connections.
>
> (2009, p. 19)

Likewise, Brendtro et al. (2009) tell us that rather than punishment, "these children
need adults who will walk with them through the storms of life until they break free
of the pain of the past" (p. 109).

The youth demonstrate this need for connection and help every day, but are the
conditions right for the youth to risk connection? Some youth, in the time they are

involved in the HRYI (which may be years), may not be able to develop the capacity to trust given the damage that has been inflicted on them. We must, however, be available to at least give them the opportunity and encouragement to make a connection, as the alternative is that they continue to be lonely, sad, bitter, and angry throughout life. This can serve to maintain their isolation and loneliness. Having experienced a dearth of attachment figures, these children and youth simply don't know how to manage relationships in a competent manner, causing people to keep them at a distance (Howe, 2008). If we can truly understand this population of youth and appreciate how their traumatic experiences have shaped their brains and their relationships, we can help offer them new experiences. These can challenge the youth to see positive exceptions in people who genuinely treat them with dignity and respect, and who help them to feel included instead of marginalized. It is, indeed, in our grasp to give these high-risk youth a sense of belonging and a different view of the world. Like Howe (2008) tells us, "If poor relationships are where things emotionally go wrong, healthy relationships are where things can be put right" (p. 161).

As discussed in the closing chapter of the book (Chapter 11), as practitioners we need to be very self-aware, thoughtful, and critical when working with high-risk youth. We must stop finding excuses to avoid building relationships. This means we too need to be vulnerable and reach out. It is heavy work. These are very damaged people. But, if we are open to making a difference and we are open to learning and becoming better practitioners, we will discover that these wonderful youth are also wonderful teachers. I continue to be educated, and I must give much credit to the youth for this and for allowing me the privilege of being part of their lives. They have helped make me a better social worker and a better person. They have taught me to be much more patient and appreciate the fact that years of maltreatment from birth cannot be undone in a matter of months or years, despite systemic pressures. I have learned that when connections are not happening, it often has more to do with the way a worker approaches a youth than it has to do with the youth resisting or not wanting help. I have learned that despite the use of drugs and alcohol to numb out and cope with trauma, many young women have enough respect for their unborn baby that they do stop using. Sadly, I have also learned that when youth still have connections with their parents who have their own issues and they cannot get off of the rejection and abandonment treadmill, they are the most likely to be extremely self-destructive. These learnings will be explored throughout this book.

I trust this book does indeed reflect the wealth of information that the youth have given me. I hope that it helps others who work with youth, or are interested in working with youth, to be open to learning from the life experiences the youth present. I hope it helps workers to embrace relationship-based practice. If we cling to the punishment-consequence orientation, we will not be able to give youth the opportunity to see the world in a new light. We will simply continue to fail them and reinforce their very low expectations of adults. As we have typically done, we can continue to persist in doing things the same old way. However, this presents us with an ethical challenge if evidence is suggesting traditional interventions are not effective and the youth are telling us as much (not to mention it fulfils Einstein's definition of insanity – doing the same thing over and over and expecting different results!). Like Perry writes (2006):

> It is sad reality that all of our best efforts – all of our governmental programs, our not-for-profits, our public and private institutions, our child protection systems,

and our education, mental health, and juvenile justice systems – fail these highest-risk children. We recreate the chaos, fragmentation, trauma, and neglect these children have experienced in their homes.

(p. 29)

Or, we can honour the voices of the youth, be more intentional and critical in our practice, appreciate that these youth are a big deal and deserve better, and acknowledge that without a relationship with these youth, we really have nothing to work from.

My goals for you reading this book are:

- To better meet the needs of the youth we serve.
- To appreciate doing work within a meaningful and genuine relationship.
- To always consider the experiences that have impacted the lives of these youth.
- To learn to become more patient than you ever thought possible.
- To be very thoughtful and intentional in all aspects of practice.
- To be a partner/collaborator rather than the expert.
- To be able to reconnect with why you wanted to be in the helping profession in the first place.
- To think anti-oppressively.
- To be passionate about being involved in the lives of high-risk youth.

Please feel free to discover many more.

While this shift in practice is exciting, there inevitably will be times when you will be challenged, question yourself, and feel like you are swimming upstream. However, it will be a journey from which you will not want to return. Change can be hard, but, like we encourage the youth to do, it's about taking risks and letting go. As John Maynard Keynes wisely told us: "The difficulty lies, not in new ideas, but in escaping the old ones."[15]

Notes

1 Taken from the poem 'Disconnected' by Peter Smyth (2006, unpublished).
2 Maskwacis was formerly known as Hobbema but the name change came into official use in October 2013. The area which has traditionally been known as Maskwacis (meaning Bear Hills) by the Plains Cree was changed to Hobbema in 1891, by the president of the Canadian National Railway, in recognition of a Dutch landscape painter (www.samsoncree.com/name-change).
3 The High Risk Youth Initiative is an initiative within the Government of Alberta, Human Services, Children and Youth Services, Edmonton and Area Child and Family Services Region.
4 The term "Aboriginal" is used to refer to the population of indigenous youth who may be First Nations, Metis, or Inuit in Canada. According to government of Canada statistics from 2011, 65% of Aboriginal peoples are First Nations, 30% are Métis, 4% are Inuit. Over half of Aboriginal people live in urban centres (Statistics Canada, National Household Survey, 2011). *Aboriginal peoples:* The descendants of the original inhabitants of North America. The Canadian Constitution recognizes three groups of Aboriginal people – Indians, Métis and Inuit. These are three separate peoples with unique heritages, languages, cultural practices and spiritual beliefs. *First Nation:* A term that came into common usage in the 1970s to replace the word "Indian," which is widely considered offensive. Although the term First Nation is widely used, no legal definition of it exists. Among its uses, the term "First Nations peoples" refers to the Indian peoples in Canada, both Status

and non-Status. Some Indian peoples have also adopted the term "First Nation" to replace the word "band" in the name of their community. *Métis:* People of mixed First Nation and European ancestry who identify themselves as Métis, as distinct from First Nations people, Inuit or non-Aboriginal people. The Métis have a unique culture that draws on their diverse ancestral origins, such as Scottish, French, Ojibway and Cree. *Inuit:* An Aboriginal people in Northern Canada, who live in Nunavut, Northwest Territories, Northern Quebec and Northern Labrador. The word means "people" in the Inuit language – Inuktitut. The singular of Inuit is Inuk. (Retrieved from: Aboriginal Affairs and Northern Development; http:// www.aadnc-aandc.gc.ca).

5 The High Risk Youth Initiative was one unit from 2005–2012 and then was expanded to cover Edmonton and area in 2012.

6 These 'in-house' studies indicate that this was not rigorous research that could be generalized to other child welfare jurisdictions, but rather the aim was to get a sense of what youth were thinking about the services that were being offered to them, give them a voice, and prompt discussions on how services could be improved.

7 The report was completed by the High Risk Youth Task Force, which was a subcommittee of the Edmonton and Area Child and Family Services, Group Care Sector and made up of Child and Family Services and agency staff. A series of youth forums were held around Edmonton targeting areas in which higher-risk youth were known to hang out and access services on a more street-level basis (see also 'References' for author information).

8 This study was produced by the Steering Committee of the High Risk Youth Initiative in Edmonton, Alberta.

9 The term 'client' is generally not used in this book, with a preference for 'service user.' Karen Morgaine and Moshoula Capous-Desyllas, in their book, *Anti-Oppressive Social Work Practice: Putting Theory into Action (2015)*, write that 'client' implies inequality as well as separateness and passivity, while 'service user' implies a sense of power and having the right to object if the standard of service is inadequate (although this also suggests passivity). Morgaine and Capous-Desyllas use the word 'participant,' reflecting the participatory nature of social work practice. In this book, as not all workers involved with youth are social workers, the term 'service users' is used most frequently. The term 'participants' is used, but more to reflect youth involved in research.

10 Caseloads within the High Risk Youth Initiative have ideally been capped at 15. There is no scientific formula to explain this number, but rather it was a number that seemed reasonable as compared to regular caseload sizes of between 20–30 children, youth, and families. It was thought that at 15 youth, this would allow for more time to spend with the youth, which would enhance relationship-building. This would also move away from doing so much crisis intervention work and seeing the youth, typically, when things were going wrong. More time was needed to celebrate the things that were going right! Once a connection has been made, the youth want time with their case workers and 15 youth has shown to be very busy indeed. It has proven difficult to maintain this number and caseloads have often risen into the low 20s, meaning, potentially, a return to a crisis-management practice rather than putting more energy into building relationships.

11 This number is from the City of Edmonton for 2012 (retrieved from: http://www.edmonton. ca/city_government/news/2012/chief-economist-report.aspx).

12 Status with Alberta Child and Family Services means they are under one of the following orders or agreements: Permanent Guardianship Order, Temporary Guardianship Order, Custody Agreement with Guardian (child is in care but no court orders are involved), Enhancement Agreement with Guardian (child is not in care but the family is receiving support), Custody Agreement with Youth (youth is voluntarily in care and 16–17 years old); Enhancement Agreement with Youth (youth is not in care, is 16–17, and is voluntarily receiving services); Support and Financial Assistance Agreement (youth is 18–21 and is still wanting/needing services under a young adult voluntary agreement).

13 As there is little literature that discusses high-risk youth specifically, the reasons that females make up 85% of caseloads is hard to say. Speculating, it could be traditional societal attitudes that girls need protection while boys are more able to find their way without being as vulnerable to harm and exploitation; that girls might be more open to reaching out for help

and taking risks in making connections; that their vulnerability to being sexually exploited brings them to the attention of authorities; that boys might be able to find people to stay with without being expected to trade sex for a place to stay as frequently; girls are less resistant to services over time; and/or perhaps that some girls may be more mature and see that they need support. Girls may also be more willing to accept help if they become pregnant.

14 LGTBQ+ refers to lesbian, gay, transgendered, bisexual, questioning/queer *plus* others such as 'T' for transsexual, 'I' for intersex (or what used to be called hermaphrodism), '2S' for Aboriginal term of two-spirited, and 'A' for non-LGBTQ+ allies). 'Queer' will honour those who have reclaimed this word rather than being seen in the traditional derogatory sense.

15 John Maynard Keynes (1883–1946), British economist.

Chapter 2

Where do high-risk youth come from?

Part A: the attachment perspective

> The most powerful rewards and the most intense pain come from relational experiences.
> Bruce Perry[1]

Some youth tell me that they are doing well and do not need to rely on anybody else. They do not need family, as they just let you down, and they certainly do not need social workers, youth workers, counsellors, teachers, and anybody trying to help because those people just "fuck with your head." They may see themselves as independent and they do not need anyone to mess it up – thank you very much. They have learned through their adverse childhood experiences that the only person they can truly rely on is themselves. Interestingly, however, the youth who have been most resistant – the ones who tell me they "hate fucking social workers" – have often been the ones who have eventually bought in the most intensely; the ones who end up actually taking the risk of allowing workers into their world. They are the ones who end up asking for services on a voluntary basis past the age of 18.

This is no longer surprising, and probably should never have been because I have come to learn that *all* youth want a connection with a healthy adult regardless of their initial resistance. It is not uncommon to hear professionals say that these youth do not want any help or complain that they are uncooperative, defiant, and manipulative. My experience, however, has shown me that this speaks more to the youths' fear, shame, anxiety, and the risk of further rejection and abandonment (Howe, 2005; Kagan, 2004; Szalavitz & Perry, 2010). It is far less about indifference or wanting to be independent, or even isolated, than we may believe. This basic need for humans to attach and have emotional needs met starts in utero and lasts through our lifetime. Indeed, to survive as humans, we depend on our ability to form and maintain successful relationships (Perry & Szalavitz, 2006). Therefore, it should not be surprising that even youth who display what appears on the surface to be a negative attitude need attachments, much like they need air, water, and food. This is particularly true if we hope to help children and youth, and particularly high-risk youth, heal from their traumatic childhood experiences. As Perry and Szalavitz tell us, "The more relationships a child has, the more likely he [or she] will be to recover from trauma and thrive" (2006, p. 230).

Attunement and attachment

[T]he most powerful rewards we can receive are the attention, approval and affection of the people we love and respect. Similarly, the most powerful pain we experience is the loss of that attention, approval and affection.

Bruce Perry and Maria Szalavitz[2]

Bonding to the parent before and after birth forms the blueprint for all future relationships, as such care and nurturing allows for the building of trust (Kagan, 2004). Attachment is the deep and critical connection established between a child and caregiver that starts in the womb. If a mother is chronically depressed, angry, anxious, dissociated, or exposed to continuous stressors during pregnancy, the experience has an effect on the baby, including low birth weight and hyperarousal (Heller & LaPierre, 2012; Levy & Orlans, 1998). In the words of Dr. Gabor Maté, "stressed mothers have stressed babies."[3] Heller and LaPierre (2012) expand:

The fetus reacts to the mother's state of distress with its own distress. The only way a fetus can cope when a mother experiences chronic distress states is by going into contraction, withdrawal, and freeze. Instead of an expansive nurturing environment, the womb becomes a toxic, threatening place in which the fetus is trapped. Biological distress lies at the foundation of psychological distress. *Early chronic physiological distress undermines subsequent psychological development, creating psychological symptoms that may not become apparent until later in life.*

(authors' emphasis) (p. 133)

Maté (2012, video) adds that in stressful situations, such as domestic violence, the mother will have a higher level of cortisol (a stress hormone) in the placenta, making it more likely they will have children who will later exhibit behaviour problems. There is evidence that pre-natal alcohol or cocaine use can result in disorganized/disoriented attachment (discussed below) and, of course, this can be continued after birth since the post-natal environment of a mother struggling with addictions can impact the connection and bonding process between the mother and child (Schore, 2003).[4] Thus, these issues of stress, mental health, and substance abuse "can leave a deep scar on the unborn child [as] the fetus can sense and react to love and hate, as well as ambivalence and ambiguity" (Levy & Orlans, 1998, p. 29).

Attachment influences every component of the human existence: mind, body, emotional relationships, and values (Boyd Webb, 2006; Levy & Orlans, 1998). The goal of attachment is protection (Boyd Webb, 2006; Howe, 2005) but this is profoundly influenced by whether one experiences kind, attuned parenting or whether one receives inconsistent, frequently disrupted, abusive, or neglectful care (Perry & Szalavitz, 2006). *Attunement* (see Box 2.1) is the quintessential component of a larger process called *attachment* (Maté, 1999) (see Box 2.2). Healthy attachments have been associated with development of a conscience, impulse control, self-esteem, getting along with others, self-awareness, thinking skills, and age-appropriate developmental abilities. Strong attachments also help children self-soothe and calm themselves (i.e., self-regulate), accept responsibility for what they do wrong, set limits on their own behaviours, plan ahead, understand consequences, and work to achieve their goals. They can give and receive affection and do not have to be in control of all situations (Kagan, 2004). In short, in order to function, children depend on attachments (Maté & Neufeld, 2004).

Box 2.1   Attunement/serve and return

Attunement is also referred to as "serve and return" in attachment and neuro-scientific literature.

Attunement: As the infant looks into the parent's eyes, the child sees that he or she is recognized. The child coos, sighs, or cries and the parent responds with a caress, a smile, or mimics the infant's sound or gesture. With each response, the infant feels validated and real.

Richard Kagan, PhD (2004, p. 19)

Attunement: The attentive care that a mother gives to her child not only shapes the brain systems involved in forming and maintaining relationships, but also the baby's capacity to "self-regulate."

Maia Szalavitz and Dr. Bruce Perry, MD, PhD (2010, p. 15)

This sharing of emotional spaces is called attunement. . . . Attunement is necessary for normal development of the brain pathways and neurochemical apparatus of attention and emotional self-regulation.

Gabor Maté, MD (1999, pp. 22–23)

Serve-and-return interaction with adults . . . forms the foundation of brain architecture upon which all future developments will be built. It helps build neuroconnections between different areas of the brain building emotional and cognitive skills children need in life.

Center on the Developing Child, Harvard University,
'Serve and Return Interaction Shapes Brain Circuitry' (video, 2011)

Box 2.2   Attachment

Attachment is the enduring emotional connection between caregivers and child, in the first several years of life, characterized by the development of trust, security, and the desire for closeness, particularly when the child is under stress. It profoundly influences every component of the human condition – mind, body, emotions, relationships, and values. Attachment is not something parents do to their children; rather it is something that children and parents create together, in an ongoing reciprocal relationship.

Terry M. Levy and Michael Orlans (1998, pp. 1, 224)

Attachment is an interactive process, brain to brain, limbic system to limbic system, a synchronicity of parent and child.

Richard Kagan, PhD (2004, p. 7)

Some use the term bonding interchangeably with attachment, and it has been described more specifically as referring to the mother's feeling for her infant.

Rosemary Farmer (2009, p. 53)

Emotional self-regulation and loss

Secure attachment helps children regulate their emotions so feelings they experience are not overwhelming. Infants have no ability to regulate their own stress apparatus. A responsive, predictable, and nurturing adult – most often the mother, at least initially – plays a key role in the development of a healthy stress-response neurobiology (Maté, 2008). Anything that threatens the mother's emotional security may disrupt the developing electrical wiring and chemical supplies of the infant's brain's emotion-regulating and attention-allocating systems. A calm and consistent emotional milieu throughout infancy, therefore, is an essential requirement for the wiring of the neurophysiological circuits of *self-regulation* (Maté, 1999) (see Box 2.3). The ability to attain a sense of calm after a period of being upset is essential in keeping the infant from feeling consistently over-stimulated and overwhelmed (Boyd Webb, 2006). Infants whose parents are not attuned to comforting their infants in this way, and are not able to teach them affect regulation, have children who learn very early that they cannot rely on adults (Boyd Webb, 2006), something commonly verbalized by high-risk youth. Those who find it difficult to recognize and regulate their emotions rapidly get into social difficulty later in life (Howe, 2005). Howe (2008) elaborates:

> [I]f we are not exposed to good quality socio-emotional experience, the brain will either develop in the light of the social emotional experience to which it has been exposed, no matter how disturbed, or, in the case of extreme emotional neglect and deprivation fail to develop the relevant neurological architecture even to begin to handle social and emotional experience in anything like a competent fashion.
>
> (p. 74)

Box 2.3 Self-regulation

Self-regulation: Because trauma in infancy occurs in a critical period of growth of the emotional-regulating limbic system, it negatively affects the maturation of the brain systems that modulate stress and regulate affect, including aggressive affective states. In other words, infants who experience abuse and/or neglect and little interactive repair are at high risk for developing aggression dysregulation in later stages of life.

Allan Schore, PhD (2003, p. 127)

Self-regulation: This very close connection between the infant's and the mother's right [brain] hemispheres allows the infant to use the mother's more mature emotion-regulating right hemisphere as the model for imprinting (i.e., attaching to the mother) and hard wiring of brain circuits. This connection eventually allows the infant or young child to manage his or her own affective abilities.

Rosemary Farmer (2009, p. 58)

Abuse, neglect, violence, and disruption of secure bonds evoke terror and utter helplessness in children who totally rely on adults to calm their emotions. Only as their brains mirror comforting caregivers can children gradually learn to calm

---

themselves. But traumatized children have not yet developed such emotional self-regulation. They experience pervasive distress shown by anxiety, fear, rage, guilt, depression, attention deficits, impulsivity, explosiveness, oppositional behaviour, and conduct problems.

Larry Brendtro et al. (2009, p. 108)

Jeremy's stress system didn't mature past the low frustration tolerance and the lack of regulation of infancy. He couldn't regulate himself – and he couldn't begin to recognize the needs of others. Without self-regulation, he wouldn't be able to fully develop the capacity to empathize.

Maia Szalavitz and Dr. Bruce Perry, MD, PhD (2010, p. 15)

Mental health is based on the ability to recognize, understand, and regulate emotions. The lack of such capacity can cause physical illness and invoke many psychosomatic problems including eating disorders, panic attacks, and substance abuse (Howe, 2005; Maté, 1999, 2008) all of which are common among youth involved with the High Risk Youth Initiative. These youth can be struggling with emotional dysregulation and symptoms of Post-Traumatic Stress Disorder (PTSD) even though they have no conscious memory of traumatic abuse and/or neglect. Dr. Gabor Maté (2012, video) states that "they can't recall it, but they remember it" given the trauma is stored in *implicit memory* – "the emotional imprint of early experiences for which there is no recall." Memory for which there is recall is *explicit memory* and develops with the hippocampus in the brain, which is responsible for consolidating memory from short-term into long-term memory (Maté, 2012, video). This can be confusing for the youth who cannot remember such experiences, or may believe they are responding to a situation in the present, when in fact it is from the past. Research has come a long way from the days in which the belief held that children did not have memory until 18 months of age and thus would not remember the trauma they may have experienced (Heller & LaPierre, 2012).

Parents or carers who are poor readers of their infant's emotional cues compromise the child's healthy psychosocial development (Howe, 2005). Abusive and neglectful parents or carers react negatively when their infants cry, which can result in traumatized infants remaining in a state of hyperarousal and fear. These children never know from one minute to the next whether they will receive care, be ignored, or be abused. They experience the world as unpredictable and unsafe; their attachment relationships reflect this uncertainty and therefore are characterized as "anxious" or "insecure" (Boyd Webb, 2006). Abuse, neglect, violence, and disruption of secure bonds, from which most high-risk youth emerge, evoke terror and utter helplessness in children who totally rely on adults to calm their emotions (Brendtro et al., 2009; Howe, 2008), thus prompting such anxiety and insecurity. Parents or carers who cause great distress in their children, and then fail to regulate the ensuing turmoil, do their children particular psychological harm. Survival for such children is under threat, as they have no control over their environment. They have no choice but to be hypervigilant, or in survival mode, all of the time – watchful and frightened, with stress levels remaining permanently high (Howe, 2008). For these insecurely attached children and youth, without this last shred of control in an otherwise chaotic life, there is a belief they could die (Kagan, 2004).

Alternatively, those who have been guided to self-regulate have been found to be more secure, empathetic, and flexible in their behaviour options. Without this gradual process of learning how to regulate their affect, children grow up at the mercy of their emotions and also without a sense of trust in the ability of adults to help them when they are afraid (Boyd Webb, 2006), even though as youth they rarely admit, or even recognize, they are afraid. When the youth come to the High Risk Youth Initiative, their inability to regulate their emotions and their lack of trust in adults is evident. It takes time and patience for the youth to allow somebody into their world, where the fear then does become self-evident. Often by this time these youth have some awareness of what they never had – families that have loved and protected them. This can bring with it a painful sense of loss and a deep and tragic sense of deprivation, which may be dealt with through rage or the beginnings of a deep depression (Boyd Webb, 2006). Gabor Maté, in his landmark book on addiction, *In the Realm of Hungry Ghosts* (2008), challenges us to "imagine the shock, loss of faith, and unfathomable despair of the child who is traumatized not by hated enemies but by loved ones" (p. 36). Brendtro et al. (2009) echo this sentiment: "The most destructive abuse comes not from stranger danger but from the very individuals children have learned to love. No brain program exists to deal with the terror of abuse from a trusted person" (p. 109).

Sandra Bloom, a psychiatrist specializing in trauma-related emotional disorders, with her colleagues, discovered in the 1980s, to their astonishment, that when they started asking about trauma, over 80% of patients presenting with depression, self-mutilation behaviours, addictions, eating disorders, panic anxiety, dissociative disorders, and character disorders had histories of prolonged, severe, and repeated experiences of trauma in their background, usually beginning in childhood and compounded in later life. This prompted her team to start asking different questions. Instead of asking, "What is wrong with you?" it became, "What happened to you?" (Bloom, 1993, p. 1). This is a good place to start for all of us working in the child welfare system, especially given the multi-generational impact of trauma, and given children and youth who are struggling in their family environments are being raised by parents who never had the opportunity to bond with their own parents or by alternate caregivers who do not appreciate the trauma and lack of attachment that has marked the early lives of the youth.

Despite their childhood trauma and lack of attachments, these youth rarely shut their parent(s) out of their lives. If the parents who have lost connections with their children do re-engage, the children often return having built up a fantasy image that their parent(s) have changed and they will now find the love and protection they have been missing. This often results in bitter disappointment and the youth will travel through the agonizing cycle of rejection. Their spirit is crushed once again. Troubled foster children, as well as troubled youth, do not stop yearning for their birth families, and many eventually find their way home as teenagers, even if permanent wards of the government (see Box 2.4). Repeated rejections delay, or more likely prevent, future attachments. Such compromised attachments continue to leave "scars on their souls" (Levy & Orlans, 1998).

Box 2.4   Jenny's story: the capacity to connect

'Jenny' was 15 when she came to the High Risk Youth Initiative (HRYI). She had already been in the system a few years but had not been able to connect with her previous case worker. By the time I met Jenny, she was no longer the pleasant, compliant child of the past, but rather defiant and demanding.

This change in Jenny largely began at age 13, when she started arguing with her foster parents and challenging the decisions they made for her younger sister. Jenny started running away and losing placements because her foster parents could not handle her behaviour. She began to use alcohol and drugs, likely to escape her trauma and her current circumstances. She would get into fights, sometimes blacking out and not remembering the damage she had inflicted.

The 'revolving door' process had started in earnest by the time Jenny was 14. Wherever she was placed, she found a way to sabotage. Jenny would be great for the first week or two, but then would become increasingly defiant. She would not take responsibility for her actions, try to lie her way out of any situation, and then, when kicked out again, she would leave devoid of any positive or negative emotion. The sweet, baby-faced child had become a terror. Even when leaving her sister behind in the foster home, she left as if she had no care in the world. This is devastating to foster parents who often give so much of themselves to try and make a home for children in their care, only to see how little the child had reciprocated emotionally. It appeared as if Jenny had walked out smugly feeling she had won the battle and got what she wanted. In some sense it had been a victory, as she would avoid showing any vulnerability and was able to control her environment in order to survive.

While on the surface Jenny's actions appeared to be rebellious and defiant, a look at Jenny's past painted a more complex picture. Jenny was the fourth child of five. She had only known her mother as physically frail and struggling with alcohol and drugs. She drank when pregnant and consequently Jenny was diagnosed with Fetal Alcohol Spectrum Disorder. While her younger sister continued to do marginally well in foster care, Jenny and her older siblings all struggled with addictions, homelessness, and criminal involvement. Jenny was also sexually abused on a number of occasions, starting when she was eight. She had to learn to raise herself and ended up being passed around to different relatives who either were indifferent to her given their own issues, were abusive, or could not handle her.

Despite being stuck in the cycle of rejection and abandonment, Jenny still clung to any attention given to her by her mother, as if she had convinced herself that one day her mother would want to look after her and nurture her as a daughter. One day when Jenny was 16, she left me a telephone voice message. Jenny was sobbing deeply and said her mother had asked her how she was doing for the first time in her life. This was not her mother telling Jenny she loved her, but just asking her how she was doing!

Though transferring Jenny's file to the HRYI was difficult for the worker, it was another day in the system for Jenny. It became clear that behind the pleasant exterior there was a cold detachment – her safe place. As a symptom of her past, it was doubtful that Jenny would learn to really trust anyone in the HRYI, but *that did not stop me from trying! After five years only small gains has been made and our connection remained shallow. Jenny did get to the point of understanding that she would not be harmed or deceived. This allowed her to reach out for help when she was in a crisis, though this was far from actually trusting anyone.*

Three years after her file closed, I happened to see Jenny at a community agency. She was glad to see me and we were able to spontaneously hug each other. She was free of addictions, had her daughter in her care, and looked healthy. I was struck by the warmth in her eyes, as this had not been there before. While I don't know if she is able to trust others, I am satisfied that the years of effort in trying to make a connection with Jenny were worth it. Time appears to help, but five years of working with Jenny had not allowed for being able to undo the damage of not feeling attached to her primary caregiver, and often feeling unsafe in the world. She still faces challenges, and has not always been the caregiver for her daughter, but hopefully Jenny will be able to avoid the same struggles her mother faced in being emotionally available for her.

The new relevance of attachment theory

Neuroscience should be linked to attachment theory.

Rosemary Farmer[5]

Over the years attachment theory has been in and out of vogue, at times being the source of much discussion and being adopted in practice and assessments, while at other times there has been cynicism in that Reactive Attachment Disorder[6] was being over-diagnosed at the exclusion of other factors that may be at play. In fact, the actual condition is relatively rare (Perry & Szalavitz, 2006). Indeed, this would appear to follow the pattern of fad diagnoses over the years, such as in the 1990s and 2000s with Tourette's Syndrome, Attention Deficit Hyperactivity Disorder (ADHD), and Attention Deficit Disorder (ADD), which has been referred to as the "flavour of the nineties" (Maté, 1999, p. 21). This has brought speculation about children being misdiagnosed with a number of disorders, particularly ADHD (Heller & LaPierre, 2012; Levy & Orlans, 1998). More recently children come with a cluster of diagnoses given to children and youth who display behaviour issues – Attention Deficit Disorder/Attention Deficit Hyperactivity Disorder, Oppositional Defiance Disorder, *and* Conduct Disorder. This may come with anxiety disorders, depression, and possibly symptomology of obsessive-compulsive disorder, bipolar disorder, Borderline Personality Disorder, psychosis including schizophrenia, and indications of psychopathology, among others. This is not to say there is no validity to these, but, as Perry (2014, lecture) states, this cluster of diagnoses doesn't get to the "heart of the issue": lack of attachments.

Assessments can certainly report different, or even contradictory, mental health issues over time. For example, a youth may be assessed by a psychologist in the community, then shortly after hospitalized and seen by a psychiatrist and hospital psychologist or clinic social worker. A youth may later be placed in a non-medical secure setting[7] and seen by a psychiatrist and psychologist there, and the result is three different pictures emerge with different and contradictory recommendations (e.g., the main issue is: behaviour related not to a mental health issue *versus* the youth may benefit from medications due to a specific diagnoses; or the youth should be placed in a very structured setting *versus* the youth needs to be empowered by making their own decisions).

Upon reviewing the history of these youth, it does remain consistent that, whatever the assessments state, they are struggling with a lack of and/or broken attachments, and that this critical history is not always addressed in reports of children and youth. It is in this history of high-risk youth where one often learns of trauma, repeated rejection and abandonment, exposure to violence and substances, physical and emotional neglect and abuse, and sexual abuse. Even when case workers come to the High Risk Youth Multi-Disciplinary Consultation Team, the history of the youth is requested and, again, there are repeated stories of adverse childhood experiences. Perry (2010) states that 90% of children involved with the child welfare system have some level of attachment disruption/dysregulation, though with the high-risk youth population, this comes much closer to 100%. The issues are further compounded when the youth see no improvement in their caregiving environment and end up going from placement to placement, whether in and out of care or bouncing from foster care to group care, to residential care, to youth jail, to hospital psychiatric wards, to living on the streets.

Many high-risk youth have burned out placements because foster parents, group home or residential staff, extended family, or other caregivers do not understand trauma, attachment, and brain development, and associated behaviours; or because they rely on punishment-consequence approaches which are ineffective with this population. Many of these youth have been in 30–50 placements before ending up on the streets, which, needless to say, reinforces their attachment issues. Thus, the cluster of diagnoses noted above would appear to speak to the symptomology of significant attachment behaviours rather these disorders being the root concern. Indeed, children and youth who feel unloved and uncared for, who experience what Dr. Bruce Perry calls a "poverty of relationships," and who see the world as a dark, hostile, and lonely place, do act out. They can be aggressive, have trouble focusing, may not care about their physical and emotional wellbeing, and are likely to be resistant and push people who show concern away rather than risk further abuse and rejection. Therefore, being defiant, oppositional, and uncooperative can be a coping strategy and a way to manage fear and frightening relationships rather than a mental illness. In fact, this may be a demonstration of their resilience and will to survive rather than a demonstration of deviant or disordered behaviour (Ungar, 2004, 2005, 2006).

Of course, there is also evidence that serious mental illness can result from adverse life events, though these also have a connection to the ability to make and maintain relationships (American Psychiatric Association, 2013; Levy & Orlans, 1998; Regehr & Glancy, 2010). These might include psychotic illnesses, personality disturbances including Borderline Personality Disorder and narcissism, mood disorders such as bi-polar disorder, and obsessive-compulsive disorders and dissociation. In particular, one close link to attachment disorder is Borderline Personality Disorder (BPD), of which one theory is that this diagnosis is the adult manifestation of Reactive Attachment Disorder, as studies have shown that unresolved trauma/disorganized attachment, as well as fearful/preoccupied attachment, are linked with BPD (Fonagy, 2000; Holmes,

2004; Levy, 2005). Sadly, a number of high-risk youth – but certainly not all – with severe attachment issues have been diagnosed as having BPD as young adults. Much like that which is found in children with RAD, those who suffer with BPD report childhood physical abuse, sexual abuse, emotional abuse, emotional neglect, and/or physical neglect (Fonagy, 2000; Howe, 2005; Perry & Szalavitz, 2006; Regehr & Glancy, 2010, Winston, 2000).

What this all ultimately points to is the need to help them heal by helping them build attachments so as to be able to deal with the behaviour issues, depression, and anxiety that often arise out of not having a sense of belonging and of having a view of the world that it is unsafe and frightening, and that it is one in which adults cannot be trusted (Brendtro & du Toit, 2005; Howe, 2005, 2011; Levy & Orlans, 1998; Maté, 1999, 2008; Szalavitz & Perry, 2010). Of course, while one person can make a significant difference, helping traumatized children and high-risk youth takes a team working collaboratively, as often the youth typically face a multitude of issues, including Fetal Alcohol Spectrum Disorder, learning challenges, poverty, or other diagnoses possibly brought on as a result of significant substance misuse (Batmanghelidjh, 2006) or a genetic pre-disposition triggered by negative environmental circumstances. (Farmer, 2009; Regehr & Glancy, 2010; Siegel, 2003). As Siegel (2003) discusses:

> The mind develops throughout life as we interact with others in our environment. The genetically influenced timing of the emergence of specific brain circuits during the early years of life makes this time a time of exquisite importance for the influence of interpersonal relationships – with parents or other caregivers – on how the structure and function of the brain will develop and give rise to the organization of the mind.
>
> (p. 8)

Attachment theory, once again, is particularly relevant in the discourse of troubled children and youth given that the technological advances of the past 30 years have permitted neuroscience researchers to confirm Bowlby's belief that attachment has a biological link (Farmer, 2009). Attachment theory emerged in the 1950s with John Bowlby and was expanded upon by Mary Ainsworth over the following 20 years. They sought to explain and measure the responses of infants to separation from their mothers (Washington, 2008), revolutionizing the thinking about a child's tie to the mother and its disruption through separation, deprivation, and bereavement (Bretherton, 1992). Bowlby (1969, 1973, 1980) described the infant as actively involved in developing the relationship with the mother in order to increase their proximity to each other to ensure safety and security, and to maximize the chances of getting their basic and emotional needs met. In her well-known 'strange situation' test, Ainsworth developed the standard method of assessing attachment. During such tests, children are observed experiencing the separation and return of a primary caregiver, or 'secure base,'[8] and then classified into one of four attachment categories: insecure-avoidant (Type A); secure (Type B); insecure-ambivalent (Type C); or insecure-disorganized/disoriented (Type D)[9] (described in Table 2.1) (Bretherton, 1992; Howe, 2005, 2011; Kagan, 2004; Levy & Orlans, 1998; Washington, 2008).

Sadly, recent research suggests that, approximately, just 62% of infants display a secure attachment pattern, while 15% exhibit an insecure-avoidant, 9% an insecure-resistant,

Table 2.1 Patterns of attachment

Attachment	Overall caregiving	Key behaviours of child	Internal working model	Perception of others	Organization of attachment behaviour
Secure (Type B)	Consistently responsive: Caregivers respond appropriately to the distress and upset being experienced by the child.	Approach caregivers directly and positively knowing that their distress and upset will be recognized and responded to *unconditionally* with comfort and understanding.	Feels loved, lovable, and loving. The child feels effective, autonomous, and competent.	Experienced as attuned, loving, available, co-operative, predictable, and dependable.	Organized (see Table 2.2): Children feel understood and in tune with their parents and feel safe and relaxed.
Avoidant (Type A) Also referred to as: *anxious-avoidant; fearful-avoidant*	Consistently unresponsive: Caregivers rebuff overtures of need and attachment behaviour. Caregiving feels rejecting and controlling. Dismissive and unavailable.	Avoids displaying need and overt attachment behaviour. Children can be tolerated by otherwise rejecting caregivers as long as they do not make too many demands. Children learn to contain their feelings – over-regulated affect. They contain their need and mask their distress.	Unloved and unlovable, although it is seen as self-reliant.	Cognitively represented as rejecting, unloving, and intrusive, and predictably unavailable at times of need.	Organized (see Table 2.2): Young children behaviourally adapt to the characteristics of the caregiving environment. The strategy to contain their need and mask their distress allows them to remain reasonably close to, or accepted by, attachment figures who may otherwise reject them.
Ambivalent (Type C) Also referred to as: *ambivalent-resistant; anxious-ambivalent*	Inconsistently responsive: Caregivers are uncertain, insensitive, and unreliable. Sometimes the parent responds appropriately to the child's needs and attachment behaviour and is protective and comforting. At other times, the response is anxious, flustered, or irrelevant, or there may be no response at all.	Maximize displays of attachment behaviour. By overplaying their needs and distress, they increase the chances of getting a response from an otherwise under-responsive caregiver. Little stress can produce intense displays of protest, demand, and upset. Children are prone to whine, cling, fret, and shout. These strategies might be defined as fighting for attention, pleading for protection.	Low worth, ineffective, and dependent.	Insensitive, depriving, neglecting, unpredictable, and unreliable.	Organized (see Table 2.2): Young children behaviourally adapt to the characteristics of the caregiving environment. There is a set goal of psychological proximity to an otherwise insensitive, inconsistent caregiver.

(Continued)

Table 2.1 (Continued)

Attachment	Overall caregiving	Key behaviours of child	Internal working model	Perception of others	Organization of attachment behaviour
Disorganized (Type D) Also referred to as: disorganized-disoriented; avoidant-ambivalent;	*Frightening and dangerous:* Parents can be confusing and dangerous (abusive), emotionally unavailable (psychotic, depressed, heavy drug or alcohol abusers), or fail to offer protection in times of danger (neglect).	Attachment behaviours can sometimes appear incomplete, contradictory, or odd. Children's attachment behaviour becomes increasingly incoherent and disorganized, showing confused, alternating mixes of avoidance, angry approach responses, behavioural disorientation, apprehension, or inertia. In cases where the fear escalates to traumatic levels, children might freeze, physically and psychologically.	Frightened, alone, ignored, dangerous, and even bad.	Unavailable and unpredictable, confusing and contradictory, frightening and frightened, hostile and helpless, dangerous and unreliable.	*Disorganized* (see *Table 2.2*): Children find it difficult to organize any attachments strategy that results in either increased caregiver availability or increased responsiveness.

Adapted from David Howe, *Attachment Across the Lifecourse: A Brief Introduction* (2011).

Table 2.2 Organized/disorganized attachment

Organized attachment	Young children behaviourally adapt to the characteristics of the caregiving environment. "[S]ecure, avoidant and ambivalent infants have developed a set of coherent and organized rules based on experience that predict and guide their future behaviour. Bowlby ... stressed that as the representational system is *organized*, individuals are capable of maintaining functional relationships with others.... Despite their anxiety, avoidant and ambivalent infants have been able to adapt to their parents and select, evaluate and modify their behaviour in a manner that allows them to achieve proximity to and contact when needed" (Howe quotes George, 1996, p. 414).
Disorganized attachment	The attachment figure is actually the cause of the child's initial fear and distress, and having frightened the child, the parent also fails to recognize or do anything about the child's fearful state. Attachment systems remain chronically activated and their arousal goes unregulated. Whatever behavioural strategy the children use, it fails to bring proximity, care, or comfort. As a result their attachment behaviour appears to lack a strategy, direction, or focus. However, when stress levels are lowered, otherwise *disorganized* children can, and do, show some signs of organization in their attachment behaviour such that their strategies might be recognized as either avoidant, ambivalent, or even secure. Thus children might be classified as disorganized-secure, disorganized-avoidant, or disorganized-ambivalent.

Taken from David Howe, *Attachment Across the Lifecourse: A Brief Introduction* (2011).

and 15% an insecure-disorganized pattern (Allen, 2011). Research shows that 80% of children with a history of parental maltreatment would fit the disorganized classification (Cunningham & Page, 2001). Ungar (2009) writes that "it is estimated that 30 to 45 per cent of children are insecurely attached, meaning they're not confident that someone will be there to meet their needs" (p. 109).

Attachment theory has indeed gained new relevance given advances in neurobiology. As stated earlier, attachments are essential and it is the first three years of the child's life that are crucial with respect to the bonding process (Bowlby, 1969; Howe, 2005; Kagan, 2004; Levy & Orlans, 1998), with the short window of 8 to 18 months being particularly critical (Kagan, 2004). In 2013, the *Diagnostic and Statistical Manual of Mental Disorders, Fifth Edition (DSM-5)* was released and changed the diagnostic criteria for Reactive Attachment Disorder. While the DSM-IV discussed two subtypes for Reactive Attachment Disorder – emotionally withdrawn/inhibited and indiscriminately social/disinhibited – in DSM-5, these subtypes are defined as distinct disorders: *Reactive Attachment Disorder* and *Disinhibited Social Engagement Disorder*.[10] The DSM-5 does address the consequences of neglect as a common requirement to both disorders:

> Social neglect – that is, the absence of adequate caregiving during childhood – is a diagnostic requirement of both reactive attachment disorder and disinhibited social engagement disorder. Although the two disorders share a common etiology, the former is expressed as an internalizing disorder with depressive symptoms and withdrawn behavior, while the latter is marked by disinhibition and externalizing behavior.
>
> (American Psychiatric Association, 2013, p. 265)

While the DSM is the bible of the world of psychiatry, there are limitations and cautions. Psychiatrist Gabor Maté (1999) writes that the DSM commits the faux pas of calling external observations *symptoms*, whereas that word in the medical language denotes a patient's own felt experience, which is not considered in making a diagnosis. "External observations, no matter how acute, are signs. . . . The DSM speaks the language of signs because the worldview of conventional medicine is unfamiliar with the language of the heart" (p. 8). Perry is also critical of DSM diagnoses using symptoms, as the brain is very complex. "As a result it seemed to me that the same 'output' might be caused by any number of different problems within it. But the DSM doesn't account for this" (Perry & Szalavitz, 2006, p. 11). Despite such limitations, this is the standard reference in the medical world and is applied to high-risk youth.

While there will continue to be challenges with diagnosing children with Reactive Attachment Disorder and Disinhibited Social Engagement Disorder (DSED), attachment disorder or attachment difficulties will continue to be used to describe children in less formal terms than described in the DSM. For example, Levy and Orlans (1998) have a definition of 'attachment disorder' that addresses the state of the child lacking a trusting bond (see Box 2.5), while Kagan (2004) outlines the behavioural challenges that children with 'attachment difficulties' face, and incorporates both internalizing and externalizing behaviours that would be associated with RAD and DSED in the DSM-5 (see Box 2.6).

Box 2.5 What is attachment disorder?

Attachment disorder is developed when children, for a myriad of reasons, do not form a trusting bond in infancy and early childhood. A lack of trust generates feelings of aloneness, being different, pervasive anger, and an inordinate need for control. A trusting bond is essential in continued personality and conscience development, and serves as the foundation for future intimate relationships.

There are a variety of conditions that place a child at risk for attachment disorder. They include, but are not limited to, the following: neglect; physical, sexual, or emotional abuse; painful or undiagnosed illness or injury; sudden separation from primary caregiver; pre-natal abuse including alcohol and/or drug abuse, and poor nutrition; frequent foster placements and failed adoptions; pathological or inadequate childcare; physical or psychological abandonment by mother; and premature birth.

Taken from: *Attachment, Trauma, and Healing: Understanding and Treating Attachment Disorder in Children and Families,* Terry M. Levy and Michael Orlans (1998, p. 247).

Box 2.6 Behavioural symptoms of children with significant attachment difficulties

A compulsive need to control others, including caregivers, teachers, and other children; intense lying, even when 'caught in the act'; poor response to discipline: aggressive or oppositional-defiant; lack of comfort with eye contact (except when lying); physical contact (wanting too much or too little); interactions lack mutual enjoyment and spontaneity; body function disturbances (eating, sleeping, urinating, defecating); increased attachment produces discomfort and resistance; indiscriminately friendly and charming; easily replaced relationships; poor communication; many nonsense questions and chatter; difficulty learning cause/effect; poor planning and/or problem-solving; lack of empathy, little evidence of guilt and remorse for others; ability to see only extremes (all good or bad); habitual dissociation or hypervigilance; and pervasive shame, with extreme difficulty reestablishing a bond following conflict.[11]

Taken from: *Rebuilding Attachments with Traumatized Children: Healing from Losses, Violence, Abuse and Neglect,* Richard Kagan, PhD, (2004, pp. 17–18). Kagan is using a list compiled by psychologist Daniel Hughes in *Facilitating Developmental Attachment,* 1997, pp. 30–31.[12]

Secure and insecure attachment

Siegel (2003) tells us:

> Secure attachment is generally associated with a child's development of emotional competence, a sense of well-being, and interpersonal skills. Security of attachment

enables children to feel secure and be able to explore the world around them . . .
it may never be "too late" to begin to offer children these basic elements of secure
attachment.

(p. 37)

Children require safe, stable, responsive, consistent, predictable, and loving environments, and to know their physical and emotional needs will be met. This will help
them develop emotional intelligence and social competencies necessary in developing healthy intimate relationships, navigating various social situations in flexible and
open ways, and having the capacity to trust. With such positive experiences, children
generally see people in a positive light, reducing the need to be guarded and suspicious
of the motives of others. They tend to develop high self-esteem and feel confident and
effective (Howe, 2005). Such caregiving situations in childhood do not need to be perfect, but sufficient or 'good enough' (Howe, 2011, 2014; Winnicott, 1988). Parents
may not attend to the everyday needs or overtures of children in a timely fashion, but
"if this diminished attention occurs on an intermittent basis in an otherwise loving
environment, this is not a big concern" (National Scientific Council on the Developing
Child, 2012, p. 3). The child does need to know, however, that he or she is valued and
must have a parent who can regulate their own emotions and demonstrate problem-
solving skills (Kagan, 2004). Indeed, as developmental psychologist Urie Bronfen-
brenner stated, "Somebody's got to be crazy about that kid. That's number one. First,
last, and always" (National Scientific Council on the Developing Child, 2004a, p. 1).

Attachment disorders are related to trauma in the life of an infant. Boyd Webb
(2006) references Terr (1991) in discussing two types of traumas. While Type I
trauma consists of a single event (e.g., witnessing someone close being killed or
harmed, or being in a car accident), it is the Type II trauma that fits with the experiences of high-risk youth. Type II consists of "numerous frightening events taking
place over time, and lead to long-term symptoms" (p. 14). The chronic situation
under Type II can drastically impact the child's emotional functioning and ability to make attachments, particularly if the experiences start in the early bonding
years. Also making a difference for future emotional development is the source of
the trauma and whether it was due to an accident or an intentional act. When the
person who inflicts the trauma is a caretaker on whom the child depends, and to
whom the child feels some form of attachment, the response will tend to be more
complicated and more resistant to treatment than the reactions of a child who was
traumatized by a stranger as the result of a random event (Boyd Webb, 2006). For
example, a youth (age 20) who was participating in a workshop planning group[13]
talked about his experiences growing up. He was around much alcohol and drug
abuse, violence, and sexual activity from his earliest memories. While he saw many
people passed out throughout his childhood, one picture is etched onto his brain.
He remembers getting up in the morning and seeing his naked mother passed out on
the living room floor. He shook his head and commented that at 10 or 11 years of
age, "no kid should ever have to see that."

It is these children and youth that so often come into the child welfare system
and, indeed, into the High Risk Youth Initiative (see Box 2.7). As Boyd Webb (2006)
confirms, many youth enter the child welfare system for similar reasons: They are
born to poverty-stricken adolescent mothers who lack the knowledge, skills, and/or

motivation to care adequately for their infants and dependent young children. Some mothers' haphazard parenting often results in periodic or chronic neglect of their children, which may be interspersed with occasional eruptions of abusive behaviour when the children cry, misbehave, or otherwise make demands for attention. This is certainly not to engage in mother-blaming. Through no fault of their own, many young mothers, as we see in the HRYI, come from traumatic childhoods themselves, in which their circumstances cause them to struggle with depression and/or anxiety. Many such mothers have their own attachment issues, may have other mental health diagnoses (such as FASD), may be struggling with addictions, and may be involved in unhealthy relationships that involve violence. Attachment issues are very often multi-generational, giving the child such a tragic and difficult start in life.[14] However, it should be noted that some young mothers who have fallen under the 'high-risk youth' label have done well as mothers, particularly if they have been able to accept help and allow people into their world to help them care for their children. It is also recognized that not all mothers who have experienced chronic childhood trauma struggle with attachment, bonding with their own children, or raising their children in healthy environments, especially if they have a support network and adequate material resources (Ungar, 2011).

Box 2.7   Tammie's story: disconnected for protection

The first time I met 'Tammie' (16) was at her sister's apartment. They were prone to fighting and as a result Tammie had to move out. Tammie was indifferent and uninterested in my presence. I didn't push; the meeting didn't last long. The second time we met was when moving her to a shelter/group home. She was frustrated with her circumstances, angry at her sister, and alone and moving yet again. She was not in the mood for talking, or stopping for a coffee, or having lunch. We hauled boxes and bags in silence except for the odd time I would ask how she was doing, which was met by a stare or her rolling her eyes. The third time we met I went to the shelter, as she had physically fought with a male resident after being a victim of sexual insults. Tammie was immediately hostile toward me, making it clear that social worker's "don't do shit for anybody." For her, they "fucked over me and my family." I didn't defend the track record of the system with her family. I told her I was not here to tell her what to do, but to learn what she wants, and to see if she has any goals she wants to work towards. This got her attention as she related that previous workers – from as far back as she could remember – had told her what they wanted her to do and never asked what she wanted. While telling her I hoped things could be different, she was far from convinced and would not fall for me manipulating her. I reminded her she was a permanent ward (though she didn't need reminding as she is painfully aware of her status) and that we might be stuck together at least until she turns 18. She definitely planned to rid herself of the system as soon as she could. Tammie had had many social workers involved in her life. She reported some never cared and rarely saw her; some tried to control her, which made her more defiant; and others she saw as weak and easily intimidated. A couple seemed okay but they never stayed around long enough or couldn't handle her. It was clear that Tammie was going to keep her walls up and not risk letting anyone into her world. Her anger and hostility was effective in keeping people at a safe emotional distance. This unsettled service providers who didn't know what words or actions would trigger a sarcastic or insulting response.

Through gently pushing Tammie to talk on this third visit, I learned that she assumed she would be kicked out and went on to say that "nothing has ever gone right in my life." Having reviewed her files, and seen the litany of childhood trauma and relationship breaks throughout her life, including abuse in care, it was hard to tell her different or find exceptions to her statement. Tammie's first few involvements with child welfare came well before her first birthday due to alleged drug use by her parents and being left with inappropriate caregivers. Shortly after, the family moved to another province and she was left in the care of her grand-mother, who was found dead from a drug overdose when Tammie was two. Back with her parents, she was exposed to alcohol and drug use as well as domestic vio-lence. She was showing signs of emotional trauma and, by the time she came into care at age three, she showed little affect and was physically aggressive. Tammie went through over 30 placements over the years, including foster homes, group homes, residential treatment centres, and psychiatric units. When 12, Tammie was introduced to drugs and alcohol; she also started to run away.

By 16, Tammie's anger was typically on the surface, while her ability to trust was deeply buried. This made sense given her life experiences and, while I knew I needed to be patient, the verbal abuse and criticism was wearing on me. I had to push myself to keep meeting with Tammie, as she was also very demanding, believing the system owed her for "the shit and abuse I have been put through." After working with youth for many years, self-doubt started to creep in and my pride took a hit. I couldn't make a connection with Tammie. She appeared to pick up on this vanity, reinforcing that social workers are all the same and the system will never change.

Time to push back. One afternoon, Tammie was really testing and being abu-sive. I told her she needed to stop as her attitude was starting to become so chal-lenging, I didn't know if I should be working with her at all. I added that after four months, I had done my best, refused to give up, and hoped that even a little part of her life could turn around. I explained that I understood why she pushed me away, how adults had been letting her down all of her life, and that risking a rela-tionship would be very difficult. To go down this road was a gut reaction rather than a planned, intentional confrontation. There are times when such conversa-tions can be powerful, but typically only when a worker has a lot more credibility in the eyes of the youth than I had with Tammie. It can come across as getting into the head of the youth, which can give them a sense of losing control and becom-ing vulnerable. When a youth has no connections and has to rely on their own intuition to survive, this is not a place they want to go. With such comments, some youth act like they have been exposed; that someone has exposed their secrets. If they are ready and open to making a connection, this can be a breakthrough step. If the youth is not ready, there is the risk they will pull away further and commu-nication could be lost permanently. It's like telling a youth, "you can trust me," when they have no capacity to trust anyone. Why should they?

> *Fortunately, Tammie's response was, "why the fuck do you think I push people away?" I again said I thought I knew why letting anybody into her world would be very risky. I told her we need to find a way to work together because she needs to experience life in a different way. She sobbed, while I tried to hold myself together. It changed our relationship and it went from strength to strength after that moment. Through all of this Tammie demonstrated her resilience by completing high school, getting jobs, and building up her social and material resources. She started letting people into her life who were willing to help her. She gained some control over her addictions to periodic marijuana usage, overcame her resistance to attending medical appointments, and started seeing a therapist (after vowing this would never happen). Tammie wants to be a social worker and has a vision how some changes to the system would benefit youth. Tammie also joined a group with other high-risk youth who used Forum Theatre and their personal experiences as a way to teach professionals how to work more effectively with youth.*
>
> *After working together for a few years, Tammie and I were able to reflect on the early days of our relationship. She feels badly, but I tell her that this needed to happen to get us to a better place. I can tell her it challenged me and was frustrating, and she can say she didn't know what else to do other than test me to see if I would give up on her too. Tammie still has struggles, and relationships are still very hard, but she is more open to giving people a chance now. I am indebted to Tammie for teaching me so much and allowing me to tell her story to others.*

The attachment process

Levy and Orlans (1998), discuss how John Bowlby and others applied the idea of interplay between instinct and environment to the mother-infant relationship. This concept suggests that infants are "hardwired to connect" (Fontana & Gonzales, 2006; Maté, 1999) or "neurologically wired" (Perry, 2010, lecture)[15] for attachment/relationship, but this process only unfolds when activated by certain cues or conditions from primary caregivers. Bowlby concluded that infants possess instinctual behaviours (sucking, clinging, following, crying, smiling, and gazing) that serve to keep the mother close, promoting a feeling of security.

Ainsworth later described five phases of attachment (Levy & Orlans, 1998): 1) *Undiscriminating:* no specific social response, baby responds to anyone; 2) *Differential responsiveness:* baby knows and prefers mother; 3) *Separation anxiety:* baby cries when mother leaves and is calmed when she returns; 4) *Active initiation:* baby protests when separated from mother and actively pursues her by approaching, following, and greeting her upon reunion; 5) *Stranger anxiety:* between six and eight months, baby is uncomfortable with strangers. The brain interprets new experiences based on templates (see Chapter 3) of previous experiences so unfamiliar people coming into their lives are perceived as threatening even if they are caring and nurturing (Perry, 2010, lecture).

Howe (2005) defines *attachment figures* as the people whom children seek as a source of protection and comfort at times of need and distress. Securely attached children have relationships with their attachment figures that are relaxed and friendly, with a warmth and intimacy that is natural, but not clingy.

Internal working model

According to Bowlby, by the time babies reach their first birthday, they have a rudimentary *internal working model* (the templates that babies develop, according to Perry, 2006) of their attachment relationships based on their experiences of caregiving (see Table 2.1). The internal working model includes perceptions about the self and of the attachment figure(s) that are encoded on the procedural memory, based on sensorimotor experiences (preverbal, not conscious). These securely attached infants are able to develop a positive internal working model (caregivers are trustworthy and reliable, sensitive, appropriately responsive to my needs, and caring; I am good, wanted, lovable, worthwhile, and competent; my world is a safe and happy place, and life is worth living) and are emotionally and cognitively competent (Levy & Orlans, 1998). In short, caring and nurturing builds trust (Kagan, 2004) and, as such, children with attuned caregivers demonstrate many advantages, as referenced earlier, including a high level of self-esteem and a solid and positive sense of self; healthy relationships with caregivers; stable friendships with peers; the ability to control impulses and emotions; a sense of pro-social values and morality; a belief in their independence and autonomy; positive core beliefs; and a high level of resilience (Howe, 2005; Kagan, 2004; Levy & Orlans, 1998). Children with strong attachments are able to feel guilt, shame, or anxiety after doing something hurtful to others, and they can also accept responsibility for what they do wrong. They develop self-awareness and, most importantly, they learn empathy (Kagan, 2004; Szalavitz & Perry, 2010). They can set limits on their behaviours, plan ahead, understand consequences, and work to achieve their goals. They are more likely to see others as a potentially available resource (Howe, 2005) rather than seeing people as a threat. They do not have a need to be in control of everything in their lives (Kagan, 2004), nor do they have to rely on manipulation and 'crazy lying' to get their way. In addition, such securely attached and 'blessed' children usually do not end up in the child welfare system (Boyd Webb, 2006), unlike the youth in the High Risk Youth Initiative who typically have had a long history in 'the system' (as the youth refer to child welfare services).

As we will see later, young people categorized as 'high-risk youth' struggle with these areas. It follows, then, that a key area in helping such youth to be able to make positive changes in their life requires building a relationship, something most of our youth have been missing or fighting all of their lives. While a relationship to a healthy adult who will spare them the hurt of rejection and abandonment is what, deep down, these youth crave most, it is also the one thing they will put a lot of energy into resisting. For them, this profound human condition of needing to belong (Brendtro, Brokenleg & van Bockern, 1990; Ungar, 2009) is juxtaposed with the intense fear of further rejection and abandonment (Howe, 2008; Smyth & Eaton-Erickson, 2009). This comes from their experiences of abuse and neglect, not just by anybody, but by those who were the ones whom they needed to care for them the most – their parents (Boyd Webb, 2006; Howe, 2005; Kagan, 2004). This hurt can establish a negative internal working model, leaving a nagging sense that one is unlovable and unworthy, and this will impact the way they perceive future relationships (Howe, 2008; Levy & Orlans, 1998; Maté, 2008). Sadly, they may never feel a true sense of connectedness or a sense of being loved and feeling safe. While the goal of attachment is protection (Howe, 2005), this is a feeling that they likely have never had the opportunity to experience.

We hear songs and see movies and we like to believe love can conquer all. While love is, indeed, powerful, it has disappointed many foster parents, adoptive parents, and caregivers who have taken in children with adverse backgrounds. Love in itself is not enough for these damaged children and youth. Love in itself cannot heal children and youth from rejection and abandonment. Children are not blank slates that can start over in a new environment. They will not simply accept love, and certainly will not give it in return, as they have no foundation upon which to understand or accept love (Kagan, 2004; Levy & Orlans, 1998). Rather than responding to stability and love, young people with attachment issues are "bent on maintaining chaos, perpetuating hostility, and avoiding closeness" (Levy & Orlans, 1998, p. 218). This is what they know and this keeps caregivers at a distance, reducing the risk of allowing caring people, who they may later lose, into their world. Kagan (2004) points out that children need a past as well as a future. They are still grieving the loss of their parents and struggling with their trauma, and the kindness of alternative caregivers cannot fill the void and help them heal, at least initially (and by this time many have given up). Kagan (2004) expands: "Paradoxically, children can only begin to grieve within a safe and secure relationship" (p. 70).

In short, while nurture and love are essential to working with children and youth whose early life experiences have caused issues around attachment, there is a need for a deeper understanding of these issues. Like case workers and service providers, they need to be educated as to just how deeply attachment issues and trauma do influence the lives of children and youth. So deep, in fact, they influence the circuits of the brain, release stress hormones that impact on the mind and body and all future relationships, and leave a genetic imprint that can reach into future generations. However, there is also an increasing level of hope as we learn more about the science of brain development and how to better counter negative experiences. This is the subject of the next chapter.

Discussion questions to consider for Chapter 2

1 Can children who experience so much rejection and abandonment, neglect and abuse, truly be able to develop healthy relationships?
2 How do we ensure babies attach to their mother when the mothers have had such negative bonding experiences themselves?
3 Would you support maternity/paternity leave for three years since this generally mirrors how long it takes to complete the bonding process?
4 If we were able to ensure that all children having healthy relationships with adults was the top priority of governments, how do you think this

would impact society? How does capitalism enhance or hinder relationships between child and youth and their parents?

5   *How much do 'systems' – child welfare services, health, mental health, justice (i.e., young offender services), and education – help build positive connections or serve to reinforce negative attachment behaviours?*

Notes

1 From the article, 'Applying Principals of Neurodevelopment to Clinical Work with Maltreated and Traumatized Children: The Neurosequential Model of Therapeutics' (2006, p. 45).

2 From the book, *The Boy Who Was Raised as a Dog and Other Stories from a Child Psychiatrist's Notebook* (2006, p. 85).

3 This quote was taken from the video of the presentation 'Attachment and Brain Development' by Dr. Gabor Maté, published on May 29, 2012, and uploaded to YouTube. Presented by TVOParents.com.

4 Of course, alcohol can introduce a host of issues, including Fetal Alcohol Spectrum Disorder. Cocaine was also thought to do permanent damage, but more recent research has shown that the short-term concerns can be overcome. In addition, the long-term outcomes can be more to do with poverty than cocaine use (for more information of this research, see ' "Crack Baby" Study Finds Poverty Is Worse for Child Development than Exposure to Drug in Womb,' David Knowles, New York Daily News, July, 13, 2013).

5 From the book, *Neuroscience and Social Work Practice* (Farmer, 2009, p. 52).

6 The *Diagnostic and Statistical Manual of Mental Disorders, Fifth Edition (DSM 5)* states: "The prevalence of reactive attachment disorder is unknown, but the disorder is seen relatively rarely in clinical settings. . . . Even in populations of severely neglected children, the disorder is uncommon, occurring in less than 10% of such children" (American Psychiatric Association, 2013, p. 266).

7 Secure Services is one such secure setting. It is a non-voluntary, non-hospital setting under Alberta's Child, Youth, and Family Enhancement Act. It requires court involvement to either place, or justify, why a child or youth has been placed in Secure Services. It is time limited but further confinement can be requested to complete an assessment or if it is determined through an assessment that more time is warranted to address the safety concerns. The criteria for using this part of the Act are: *a) the child is in a condition presenting an immediate danger to the child or others, (b) it is necessary to confine the child in order to stabilize and assess the child, and (c) less intrusive measures are not adequate to sufficiently reduce the danger* (Section 44(2)).

8 'Secure base' was a term coined by Mary Ainsworth referring to the attachment figure, or primary caregiver, from which the child could explore the environment without experiencing anxiety (Levy & Orlans, 1998).

9 The insecure-disorganized category was added in the 1980s by Mary Main and colleagues who were expanding the ideas of Mary Ainsworth with respect to attachment patterns (Levy & Orlans, 1998).

10 For further discussion see: American Psychiatric Association (2013), *Diagnostic and Statistical Manual of Mental Disorders*, 5th edn. (pp. 265–270) Arlington, VA: American Psychiatric Association, trauma- and stressor-related disorders.

11 In working with many children and youth over the years, it is observed that with children and youth exhibiting the behaviours listed by Levy and Orlans, there is much overlap with other diagnoses such as ADHD, ADD, Oppositional Defiance Disorder, Conduct Disorder, PTSD, bi-polar disorder, and even FASD. This brings into question the accuracy of many diagnoses and speaks to the importance of gathering as much about early family history in the assessment in the assessment phase. Gabor Maté (1999, p. 81) states that, "people's life histories should be given at least as much importance as the chemistry of their brains."

Levy and Orlans state that attachment disorder is one of the most easily diagnosed and yet commonly misunderstood parent-child disorders. The authors add that diagnosis rests on four pillars: 1) signs and symptoms; 2) early history; 3) previous diagnoses; and 4) parent's attachment patterns. Many child welfare reports and psychological assessments will discuss many of the outlined behaviours, and even report chaotic lives before and after birth, without considering attachment disorder. In their book *Attachment, Trauma, and Healing: Understanding and Treating Attachment Disorder in Children and Families*, Levy and Orlans include a symptom comparison chart for ADHD, bi-polar disorder, and Reactive Attachment Disorder. More often than not children have many issues to cope with and will have multiple diagnoses. The authors state that the onset of Reactive Attachment Disorder is up to 36 months and that if the bond is secure at that point, and behaviours emerge, the condition cannot be RAD.

12 Hughes, D. (1997). *Facilitating Developmental Attachment*. Northvale, NJ: Jason Aronson.

13 This workshop planning group is called *High Risk Youth Uncensored: An Educational Experience*. This participatory research project is now a project within iHuman Youth Society but started as a partnership between the not-for-profit, arts-based community youth organization (co-founder and outreach worker, Wallis Kendal), the University of Alberta (Dr. Diane Conrad), and Edmonton and Area Child and Family Services–High Risk Youth Initiative (Specialist for High Risk Youth Services, Peter Smyth). Based on a need identified in the community, the project involves a number of youth from iHuman Youth Society as key collaborators working at developing a series of arts-based workshops to educate service providers about how to best meet the particular needs of the high-risk youth populations they serve. Youth are involved in identifying issues, developing curriculum materials, and presenting the workshops. As well as educating service providers (educators, social workers, law enforcement, health practitioners, students, etc.), the project benefits the youth involved in the community at large. https://www.ualberta.ca/~dhconrad/ResearchProjects Pages/HighRiskYouthUncensoredPage.html.

14 Over the years, the attitude toward young mothers has been to pathologize them and blame them for their circumstances. This has left them without adequate help and support, and leaves them struggling with their own issues. In short, with adequate support and resources, the multi-generational cycle could be broken, but arguably has been left to repeat due to inadequate government policy and reinforcing stereotypes.

15 Referenced from notes taken at a presentation by Dr. Bruce Perry in Edmonton, Alberta, on November 15, 2010.

Chapter 3

Where do high-risk youth come from?

Part B: the neuroscience perspective

A neurobiological understanding of attachment, trauma, and brain development

The importance of this point cannot be overstated: Emotional nurturance is an absolute requirement for healthy neurobiological brain development.

Gabor Maté[1]

Long before we see the youth who are struggling and putting themselves at risk, before they are fighting authority and pushing caring people away, and before they are labelled as *high-risk youth*, for most of them there was a predictability about their behaviours based on events that were shaping them even before they were born and right after their birth. Dr. Bruce Perry (child psychiatrist, neuroscience researcher, and expert in childhood trauma and brain development) pointed out, in a 2003 workshop, that 85% of children who are in care have attachment issues. He further stated that as a baby's brain develops, attachments will be the *template* (see Box 3.1) for that person's whole life as they process all incoming information and as they try to make sense of their relationships. Kagan (2004) expands on this theme, stating that attachment forms the foundation for a child's future relationships, learning, and expectations (the internal working model discussed in the previous chapter). The strength of the child's attachments shapes his or her emotional regulatory system and fosters exploration and mastery of feelings of confidence, empathy, language development, reasoning processes, and the ability to manage and resolve conflicts. The consistency of care, empathy, and commitment of a parent allows the child to progress steadily through development stages and build competency. To succeed in these areas, children need to learn that their relationships will be re-affirmed no matter what happens. With inconsistent relationships, kids give up easier. In short, a child's behaviour signals what kind of attachment he or she has experienced.

Box 3.1   Templates

If the first impression for a child is that a person is safe, a template is developed and this becomes difficult to give up. So, even if that person later proves to be unsafe, the child's brain defaults to the template that they are safe. It's the same if the initial experience is unsafe. Even if overwhelming evidence suggests they

> *are safe, the child's brain will not adapt easily (e.g., a traumatized child in a safe foster home cannot feel safe).*
>
> Taken from: Notes from presentation by
> Dr. Bruce Perry in Edmonton, Alberta, November 15, (2010)

This parent-child attachment shapes a child's neurobiology, which, in turn, impacts the child's relationships in an ongoing cycle throughout his or her life (Kagan, 2004). Without safe, secure, and non-stressed attachments, the brain cannot develop optimally (Maté, 2008). Maté (1999) discusses three conditions for healthy growth, both inside and outside of the womb: nutrition, a physically healthy environment, and an unbroken relationship with a safe, ever-present maternal organism. He further states that healthy brain development requires emotional security and warmth in the infant's environment: "A calm and consistent emotional milieu throughout infancy is an essential requirement for the wiring of neurophysiological circuits of self-regulation. When interfered with brain development is adversely affected" (p. 68). This is echoed by Fontana and Gonzales (in Boyd Webb, 2006), who state that infants require consistent connections with loving, caring, and sensitive caregivers for the healthy development of their brains. Abuse, neglect, and other adverse environmental factors can cause neurological damage that interferes with the child's future ability to reason, feel, and regulate their emotional behaviour. Even without abuse, a distressed mother who cannot provide a consistent connection can disrupt a much-needed predictable and safe environment and cause significant distress for a child. As Perry (2006) explains, there are nerve cells called *mirror neurons* in the brain which respond in harmony with the behaviour of others (see Box 3.2). This capacity for mutual regulation provides a basis for the present and future capacity to form attachments. However, if the primary caregiver is frightening to the child and cannot self-regulate, this will also be mirrored. Given the child will mirror the attachment figure's anxiety, stress, and lack of ability to self-regulate, anything that threatens the mother's emotional security may disrupt the developing electrical wiring and chemical supplies of the infant brain's emotion-regulating and attention-allocating systems (Maté, 1999). Without resolution and renewal of safety, the child's social and emotional development is blocked. The child keeps growing physically, but inside, the clock remains fixed on the time when the child's core sense of nurture ended (Kagan, 2004).

Box 3.2 Mirror neurons

There is the class of nerve cells in the brain known as "mirror" neurons, which respond in synchronicity with the behaviour of others. This capacity for mutual regulation provides a basis for attachment. For example, when a baby smiles, the mirror neurons in the mother's brain usually respond with a set of patterns that are almost identical to those that occur when the mom herself smiles. This mirroring ordinarily leads the mother to respond with a smile of her own. It's not hard to see how empathy and the capacity to respond to relationships would

originate here as the mother and child synchronize and reinforce each other,
with both sets of mirror neurons reflecting back each other's joy and sense of
connectedness. However, if the baby's smiles are ignored, if she's left repeatedly
to cry alone, if she's not fed, or fed roughly without any tenderness or without
being held, the positive associations between human contact and safety, predict-
ability and pleasure may not develop [as] not enough repetition occurs to clinch
the connection. People are not interchangeable . . . it is the template memory
of this primary attachment that will allow the baby to have healthy intimate
relationships with an adult.

Taken from: *The Boy Who Was Raised By a Dog*
and Other Stories from a Child Psychiatrist's Notebook,
Bruce D. Perry, MD, PhDE and Maia Szalavitz (2006, pp. 90–91).

Disrupted and anxious attachment not only leads to social and emotional problems, but also results in biochemical consequences in the developing brain. While, as noted earlier, infants are prewired or hardwired for attachment, this only unfolds when activated by certain cues or conditions from attuned primary caregivers (Howe, 2005; Levy & Orlans, 1998; Maté, 1999). When this does not occur, this trauma can cause a baby or infant to be diagnosed as failure-to-thrive (Heller & LaPierre, 2012; Levy & Orlans, 1998; Perry & Szalavitz, 2006). For mistreated children, their brains have been shown to be smaller than normal by 7 or 8%. In a further study on depressed women who had been abused in childhood, the hippocampus (the memory and emotional hub) was found to be 15% smaller than normal (Maté, 2008). Infants raised without loving touch and security have abnormally high levels of stress hormones (cortisol), which can impair the growth and development of their brains and bodies (Howe, 2005; Levy & Orlans, 1998; Maté, 1999, 2003; Schore, 2003). Maté (2008) cites Perry in discussing early childhood stress. A child experiencing such stress will be more over-reactive and reactive. The child is triggered more easily and is more anxious and distressed. After traumatic events end, the brain will be 'reset' to a state of hyperarousal rather than returning to a baseline calm state; thus there is a sense of being under persistent threat. Simply stated, traumatic and neglectful experiences during childhood cause abnormal organization and functioning of important neural systems in the brain (Perry, 2006, 2009).

Children do not have to be reared in physical isolation to suffer deprivation; emotional isolation will have the same effect (Heller & LaPierre, 2012; Maté, 2008). The neurobiological consequences of emotional neglect can leave children behaviourally disordered, depressed, apathetic, slow to learn, and prone to chronic illness. Neglect starves the developing mind of stimulation; it denies the child information and interest about the self and others. In some cases, "neglect slowly and persistently eats away at children's spirits until they have little will to connect with others or explore the world" (Howe, 2005, p. 111).[2] Some parents may not understand that this disconnection is occurring, as often they did not experience attuned caring as small children; they may not notice their difficulty in attuning to their own infants. The parents themselves may be overwhelmed, depressed, anxious, and unable to self-regulate. It is hard to be an attuned young parent if their own minds are racing and hyperaroused as well. In such situations, the void is not in the parent's love or commitment, but in the child's perception of being seen, understood, empathized with, and 'gotten' on the emotional level (Maté, 2008). This becomes evident among many of the high-risk youth who have children of their own. While they do care deeply and set out to do the best for their children, even with supports, they can be lost as to how to connect and be emotionally in tune with their babies.

Building the brain

In many of his works, Dr. Bruce Perry discusses the four major parts of the brain: the brainstem, the midbrain, the limbic system, and the cortex.[3] The brain is organized in a hierarchical fashion – bottom to top and inside to outside. The *brainstem* and *midbrain* evolve first and develop first as the child grows. Moving upward and outward, the brain gets increasingly complex with the *limbic system* and this is followed by the intricate *cortex*. While interconnected, each of these four main areas controls a separate set of functions. The brainstem (also referred to as 'reptilian' brain) is the most primitive and is responsible for automatic functions such as body temperature, respiration, and blood pressure, as well as the critical areas of breathing and heartbeat, which require moment-to-moment monitoring and immediate correction.

The next to develop is the midbrain, which contains key areas involved in regulating sleep, appetite, pleasure, motivation, and attention, areas that also typically operate without conscious control. This is also the area in which many of the stress response systems originate (see Figure 3.1). This is a particularly significant area for babies and toddlers, who do not have an attuned caregiver and who are experiencing abuse and neglect. This will result in a very active stress response system, as the midbrain focuses on survival functions such as safety and responses to threats.

A region called the limbic system surrounds the midbrain. This area is critically involved with relationships and emotional responses that guide our behaviour, including fear, hatred, love, and joy. Our highest, outermost, and uniquely human region of the brain is the cortex, which controls executive functions such as reasoning, planning,

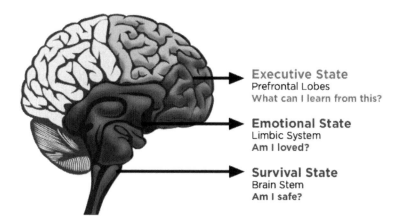

Figure 3.1 Key areas of the brain and what they can mean for children and youth

anticipating, and predicting. The cortex allows language, as well as abstract thought and deliberate decision-making.

These sections of the brain, at the time of birth, are made up of over one hundred billion neurons that will chart paths and make connections based on the social experiences they encounter. By the age of two and a half, approximately 85% of the baby's neurological growth is complete, meaning the foundation of their brain's capacity is in place. The executive functions of the cortex will continue developing most rapidly during adolescence and early adulthood, though the brain continues to develop throughout life, dispelling old beliefs that the brain is static. In short, the brain is 'plastic' (*neuroplasticity* of the brain is described below) and while change can be slow, new learnings can create new neural pathways. This can give hope to those who experience childhood trauma and attachment issues, who have developed negative templates of people and their world, who have a compromised sense of safety, who question their right to exist in the world, and who live with a constant sense of dread and terror (Brendtro et al., 2009; Heller & LaPierre, 2012; Howe, 2008; Perry, 2006, 2009).

Attachment is an interactive process, brain to brain, limbic system to limbic system; a synchronicity of parent and child. Attachment in the child's first three years centres on communication between the right brains[4] of both parent and child, especially visual, face-to-face images of one another, touch, and tone of voice. These experiences form indelible memories in the child's limbic system long before the child develops the capacity for language, including expectations as to whether the parents will respond to distress, whether the child will be soothed, and whether the parents can modulate their own emotions in times of stress (Kagan, 2004). Maté (2003) writes that parental love is not simply a warm and pleasant emotional experience, it is a biological condition essential for healthy physiological and psychological development. Parental love and attention drive the optimal maturation of the circuitry of the brain. Emotional interactions stimulate or inhibit the growth of nerve cells and circuits by complicated processes that involve the release of natural chemicals.

Dopamine – the reward or 'feel-good' chemical – is connected to a sense of desire and 'wanting,' pulling the mother toward the child (Szalavitz & Perry, 2010). Another category of natural chemicals associated to reward are *endorphins*,[5] which enable the emotional bonding between mother and infant, encouraging the growth and connections of nerve cells, and producing the pleasure, contentment, and relaxation that mother and baby enjoy together, thus lowering stress and restoring a sense of calm. Endorphins have been referred to as 'molecules of emotion.' They are the brain's natural opioids, helping create 'highs' that "can be one of the natural rewards of motherhood" (Maté, 2008, p. 154). A third natural chemical, *oxytocin*, is a protein that is necessary for mammals to make the connection between a particular individual and pleasure. Essentially, it "allows us to get *hooked* on our babies" (Maté, 2008, p. 154). Failing to experience normal bonding changes the oxytocin system, "and this can have terrible consequences, particularly with the ability to find comfort and pleasure in loving and being loved by others" (Szalavitz & Perry, 2010, p. 133). All of these 'feel-good' chemicals play an active role in the bonding process (Maté, 2008; Szalavitz & Perry, 2010) and in calming the baby as their emotional needs are fully met.

Emotions are states of physiological arousal, either positive or negative. For example, when *happy* events are experienced by the infant, endorphins are released. It is such positive environments built by parents that regulate the infants' chemical balance in the brain since children do not have the capacity to regulate their own emotional states. Hence infants are physiologically at risk for exhaustion and even death if not regulated by the interaction with the parent. Closeness with the parent, therefore, allows for the achievement of "a fundamental goal of human development; the emergence of a self-sustaining, self-regulated human being who can live in concert with fellow human beings in a social context" (Maté, 2003, p. 205).

The orbitofrontal cortex (OFC) is part of the prefrontal cortex and most involved in social intelligence, impulse control, and attention. Disturbances in the OFC are implicated in disorders of impulse inhibition and emotional self-regulation. It is here that neurophysiological effects of stressed attunement and attachment are most pronounced (Maté, 1999). Maté (1999) further explains that,

> The orbitofrontal cortex . . . has connections with virtually every other part of the cortex. It has rich connections with the lower brain structures, where the body's internal physiological states are controlled and monitored, and where most primitive and powerful emotions such as fear and rage are generated. It is at the centre of the brain's reward and motivation apparatus and contains more of the reward chemicals associated with pleasure and joy – dopamine and endorphins – than almost any other area of the cortex. . . . The OFC has a major role in the control of attention . . . and helps pick out what to focus on. . . . [T]he right OFC interprets the emotional content of communications – the other person's body language, eye movement, and tone of voice. . . . It is deeply concerned with the assessment of relationships between self and others. According to a number of studies, it is "dominant for the processing, expression, and regulation of emotional information."[6] The OFC also functions in impulse control. . . . When it is working properly, it can delay emotional reactions long enough to allow mature, more sophisticated responses to emerge. When its connections are disrupted, it lacks this capacity. At such times primitive, unprocessed emotions will flood our minds, overwhelm our thinking processes and control our behaviour. Finally, the OFC records and stores the emotional effects of experiences, first and foremost the infant's interactions with his or her primary caregivers during the early months and years. Its imprinting of the earliest interactions with the primary caregivers is the unconscious model from which all later emotional reactions and interactions will be formed. Groups of neurons in the OFC encode the emotional footprints of these important experiences. . . . Researcher, Donald Hebb showed that groups of neurons that have fired together once are more likely to fire simultaneously in the future; the principle expressed as *neurons that fire together, wire together.*

(pp. 78–79)

In addition, the circuits responsible for the secretion of important neurotransmitters such as serotonin (mood messenger), norepinephrine (arousal and motivation; fight or flight response), and dopamine – all of which mediate secure attachment through complex interactions – are stimulated and become co-ordinated in the context of the child's relationship with his or her caregivers (Kagan, 2004; Maté, 2003; Neborsky, 2003). When the child experiences a lack of response, the regulatory system in the child fails and the infant may die (Kagan, 2004; Maté, 1999). Maté (2008) further states that sensory stimulation is so necessary for the human infants' healthy biological development that babies who are not picked up can stress themselves to death. This is how fundamental attunement and touch are from the earliest days, as "whoever we are, without connection, we are empty" (Szalavitz & Perry, 2010, p. 3).

Given, then, that humans are hardwired to attach, and depend on it to survive, the brain will fight and adapt to ensure this happens. Even when coming from terrible circumstances, children still want connections with those who are unwilling or unable to love them, and who abuse them. This places children in the 'impossible dilemma' of managing their own rage toward the neglectful and abusive parent(s) they also love and on whom they are dependent (Heller & LaPierre, 2012, p. 138). To accommodate this, children may use a form of dissociation called *splitting* in which the child tries to maintain a secure attachment by splitting off negative feelings into a 'bad self.' Reacting with fear and rage is seen as *bad*, increasing the chance of being further abused, rejected, and abandoned. Reacting by presenting as powerless and gentle is seen as *good* and is a self-preservation way to avoid or reduce the chance of further abuse and neglect. While this can potentially be a life-saving mechanism at the time, in the long run it increases dysregulation and distress and leads to self-blaming and self-hatred. They cannot appreciate that they are 'a good person in a bad situation' but see themselves as unworthy of being loved, or even existing. Splitting also inevitably complicates the process of *individuation* (see Box 3.3), creating vulnerability, an inability to stand up for oneself, and an assumption that people will judge and act in a rejecting manner. Splitting represents *acting in*, or aggression against the self, but, over time, can manifest itself as *acting out*, or aggression toward others, resulting in them becoming the abuser (Heller & LaPierre, 2012, pp. 278–283).

Box 3.3   Individuation

Self-regulation is intimately connected with a process developmental psychology has called individuation, or differentiation. *Individuation – becoming a self-motivating, self-accepting person, a true individual – is the ultimate goal of development. As individuation unfolds, children are able to move more and more independently into the world, impelled by their own interests and needs. Less and less do they require that another person see exactly what they see in order to feel validated, or that another person feel exactly what they feel. They may have needs and a desire for closeness, warmth and mutual support with another human being, but they do not need to be emotionally fused with the other person – they can function on their own if need be.*

Taken from: *Scattered Minds:*
A New Look at the Origins and Healing of
Attention Deficit Disorder, Gabor Maté (1999, p. 166)

This early dissociation may explain why high-risk youth rarely detach from wanting or needing their parent(s) to be an attachment figure. Most never give up that hope and, even if under permanent guardianship status with the government, they eventually find their way back to their parent(s). Occasionally this may have favourable results if time and formal and informal supports have helped heal some wounds but, most often, the parent(s) are still unable to cope with their own lives, thus setting their children up for further heartbreak. Quite possibly, these youth re-enter the treadmill of emotional and/or physical neglect and abuse, and rejection and abandonment. Certainly high-risk youth have been noted to be *acting in* by putting their parent(s) on a pedestal and blaming themselves for their past, and entering into superficial and destructive relationships. They can also be seen as *acting out* by raging against the world and finding identity, status, and belonging in negative peer groups such as gangs.

Genetic potential and the environment

These interactional experiences not only shape brain circuitry but also modulate genetic development. This is radically different from the traditional view that genes play a decisive role in the way a person's brain develops; that they hardwire and blueprint our destiny (Kagan, 2004; National Scientific Council on the Developing Child, 2008). Maté (2008) states that "the expression of genetic potentials is, for the most part, contingent on the environment" (p. 181). He concedes that genes do dictate the basic organization, developmental schedule, and anatomical structure of the human central nervous system, but emphasizes that it is left to the environment to sculpt and fine-tune the chemistry, connections, circuits, networks, and systems that determine how well individuals function. In effect, genes are turned on and off by the environment. Genes tell our bodies how to work, but the environment leaves its signature that authorizes or prevents those instructions from being carried out (National Scientific Council on the Developing Child, 2008, 2010a). Maté (2008) elaborates on how the brain grows in the first year of life and how the brain is wired to its environment:

> There are times in the first year of life when, every second, multiple millions of nerve connections, or synapses, are established. Three-quarters of our brain growth takes place outside the womb, most of it in the early years. By three years of age, the brain has reached 90 per cent of adult size, whereas the body is only 18 per cent of adult size. . . . Outside the relatively safe environment of the womb, our brains-in-progress are highly vulnerable to potentially adverse circumstances. . . .
>
> The dynamic process by which 90 per cent of the human brain's circuitry is wired after birth has been called "neural Darwinism" because it involves the selection of these nerve cells (neurons), synapses and circuits that help the brain adapt to its particular environment, and discarding of others. In the early stages of life, the infant's brain has many more neurons and connections than necessary – billions of neurons in excess of what will eventually be required. This overgrown, chaotic synaptic tangle needs to be trimmed to shape the brain into an organ that can govern action, thought, learning, and relationships and carry out its multiple and varied other tasks – and to co-ordinate them all in our best interests. Which

connections survive depends largely on input from the environment. Connections and circuits used frequently are strengthened, while unused ones are pruned out . . . *synaptic pruning*. "Both neurons and neural connections compete to survive and grow. Experience causes some neurons and synapses (and not others) to survive and grow."[7]

Through this weeding out of unutilized cells and synapses, the selection of useful connections and the formation of new ones, the specialized circuits of the mature brain emerge. The process is highly specific to each individual person. . . . In large part, an infant's early years define how well her brain structures will develop and how the neurological networks that control human behaviour will mature. Our genetic capacity for brain development can find its full expression only if circumstances are favourable.

(pp. 182–184)

A recent study by McGill University and the Douglas Mental Health University Institute discovered that "childhood trauma can actually alter one's DNA and shape the way one's genes work."[8] The study is seen as the most convincing evidence yet that childhood abuse permanently modifies genes. Healthy development of all organs, including the brain, depends on how much and when certain genes are expressed – turned on or off (National Scientific Council on the Developing Child, 2008, 2010b). As a result of life events, even during gestation, chemicals attach themselves to DNA, a process called *methylation*, and direct gene activities or change the activity of any gene. Behavioural traits associated with those genes are likewise changed and can be transmitted across generations (Howe, 2014; Hurley, 2013). In the McGill study, large numbers of chemical – or epigenetic – marks, which inhibit a key mechanism for dealing with stress, were discovered in the brains of young men who were physically or sexually abused as children and later committed suicide. McGill University researcher Michael Meaney states that, "The function of our DNA is not as fixed as previously believed. The interaction between the environment and DNA plays a crucial role in determining our resistance to stress. . . . Epigenetic[9] marks are the product of this interaction" (Douglas Institute, 2009, p. 2). The National Scientific Council on the Developing Child (2008, 2010b) similarly states that there are many non-inherited environmental factors and experiences that have the power to chemically mark genes and control their function. Repetitive, highly stressful experiences, as many high-risk youth have known from their earliest years, can cause epigenetic changes that play particular key roles in brain and behaviour development and damage the systems that manage one's response to adversity later in life.

Multi-generational trauma

As I know from working with high-risk youth, family issues are very typically multi-generational and the youths' parents and grandparents likely experienced the same issues around self-regulation, stress, and trauma. Thus, the tragic inability to bond from one generation to the next continues. How does a young mother, whose mother was never able to bond with her, know how to bond with her own child? Szalavitz and Perry (2010) reinforce this idea, stating that if we want a kinder, more caring society, people need more experiences and places in which they feel safe. To do this we need to nurture the mothers (Maté, 2008; Szalavitz & Perry, 2010) so they can help their babies effectively develop the capacity to modulate stress. An isolated mother is a stressed mother.

Individuals must also be aware of how colonialist government policies, including residential schools and the Sixties Scoop in Canada, in which children were separated from their families, created trauma that has been passed on for generations and continues to impact Aboriginal communities today. As one generation that was torn away from their families struggles to cope, there is an absence of protective relationships for the next generation. It is not uncommon to hear Aboriginal peoples talk about never hearing their parents tell them they loved them, and these parents talk about their shame and guilt, and their inability to tell their children they loved them given their experiences in residential schools. The attachment histories of parents influence their ability to form relationships as well as their parenting practices. Not surprisingly, these parents who were victims of government policy and abused by school personnel, beyond the reach of their own parents who could keep them safe, could very well become dismissive toward their children. As they become preoccupied with trying to cope with their fear and anxiety and struggle to make sense of their lives, the chances of having children with attachment issues increases (Levy & Orlans, 1998). It is such negative environmental influences that can actually alter the genetic plan for the brain, and these epigenetic changes that occur in the foetus during pregnancy can be passed on to later generations (National Scientific Council on the Developing Child, 2007, 2010b). Schore (2003) writes:

> In the light of the fact that many of these parents have suffered from unresolved trauma themselves, this spatiotemporal imprinting of terror, rage, and dissociation is a primary mechanism for the intergenerational transmission of violence. This imprinting, the learning mechanism of attachment, is 'burnt into' developing right prefrontal circuits, and thereby inscribed into long-term implicit memory.
>
> (p. 130)

It is no accident that 70% of high-risk youth are of Aboriginal heritage. With these challenges, and the continued over-representation of Aboriginal children in care of the government in Alberta, sadly, when they have their own children, there is a significant chance that their child will be involved with child protection services as well (Lafrance & Bastien, 2007; Trocmé, Knoke & Blackstock, 2004). Such circumstances can also be exacerbated by the depression that accompanies poverty, potentially compromising the bonding process (National Scientific Council on the Developing Child, 2005).

Living in chaos

The child who does not develop the ability to regulate his emotions in the first two years of life may fail to develop this ability later; as a result, this child may resort to hostile, aggressive behaviour to deal with his or her own over-reactivity to stress (Boyd Webb, 2006). The child continues to rely upon more primitive responses to perceptions of risk, rather than developing neural connections that foster a greater perception of what is happening and consequently greater possibilities and flexibility for coping. Trauma impairs encoding and integration of sensory, emotional, and perceptual experiences into verbal memory and the conceptualization of the child's identity. The child will mould their identity and their very being to survive in a desolate world.

In addition, traumatized children can have difficulties in school and in developing social relationships (Howe, 2005; Kagan, 2004). Developmental impairments mean such relationships are difficult, stressful, or even puzzling (Howe, 2005). Survival for these children means reacting quickly to any gesture or tone of voice that may mean danger, which may give them some sense of control. The signs and symptoms of disorganized attachment and trauma become a way of life and each recurrence of violence and loss confirms for the child that his or her world is chaotic and dangerous. When their primary caregiver has been violent, children will often numb themselves and avoid thinking about, or forget, the worst incidents (Kagan, 2004). According to Kagan (2004), "Their interests become diminished. Time comes to only mean the present. The past is too painful to think about and the future is impossible to imagine as more than just the same chaos and violence. Hope fades away. Children shut down" (p. 39). In short, "the essence of trauma is feeling terrified and alone" (Howe, 2005, p. 167).[10]

For these children fear is always near and very much a part of everyday life. They are hypersensitive to anything new that may be a perceived as a threat, even if it is not. Any stimuli that is novel or threatening is noticed by the amygdala, the almond-shaped set of neurons that controls emotion and aggression, which then mobilizes the appropriate emotion (Brendtro et al., 2009). The concern for traumatized children is that, once the amygdala is activated, it magnifies arousal and floods the cortex with messages of danger. As a result, "the cortex now becomes hyperfocused on the perceived source of the anxiety, initiating a cycle: anxiety – arousal – more anxiety – more arousal in the midst of which all other information is blocked out"; thus there is no ability to concentrate (Maté, 1999, p. 123). This becomes a terrifying pattern and, with no intervention, it can become the way life is – a terrifying existence.

Consequences to individuals; consequences to society

As previously stated, the responsiveness of the human brain to changing conditions is greater earlier in life (plasticity) and, with age, although not completely lost, plasticity does decline. Therefore, as life goes on, change is harder and old patterns of behaviour can become more ingrained. Even with the youth and young adults with whom I work, their responses to relationships, authority figures, physical and emotional threats, fear, and trauma can appear well rehearsed and automatic, which speaks to the many years of practice they have had in learning they cannot rely on the people they need most to meet their emotional needs. These young people can be easily triggered and escalate quickly, often disproportionately to the situation. Howe (2005) explains how "traumatic experience is stored in non-verbal, emotional memory [i.e., implicit memory] where it remains unprocessed, disconnected, and integrated with other developmental experiences, but ready to be activated whenever an event feels like a precursor to the original trauma" (p. 167). He further states that those who suffered early abandonment and abuse can lead chaotic and highly problematic lives:

> Their emotions explode in an infant-like and unregulated manner, producing powerful feelings of fear, rage, hostility and shame, triggered by events, however

innocuous, to the observer, that seem to echo old hurts and dangers. . . . One way to try and defend against such fear and despair is to not reflect, think and mentalize, because they threaten catastrophically to flood the mind with memories and feelings of hurt, emotional abandonment and incoherence.

(Howe, 2005. p. 167)

As if this were not enough, children who have attachment issues and neurodevelopmental challenges due to trauma often suffer also from a sad plethora of physical health issues, including heart disease, cancer, and other stress-related diseases and illness (Howe, 2005, 2014). Dr. Gabor Maté (2003) references a 1996 study reviewing the role of the psychoneuroimmunology (PNI) system in health and disease. He notes:

"In healthy people, neuroimmune mechanisms provide host defence against infection, injury, cancer, and control immune and inflammatory reactions, which pre-empt disease."[11] Disease, in other words, is not a simple result of some external attack but develops in a vulnerable host in whom the internal environment has become disordered. . . . Chronic stress creates an unnatural biochemical milieu in the body.

(Maté, 2003, p. 92)

Having lived with anxiety and frustration throughout their lives, such chronic stress can reduce the ability of the immune system to mount a response to everything from infectious diseases like tuberculosis and flu to cancer (Szalavtiz & Perry, 2010). In addition, stress hormones can result in rising blood pressure and 'gumming up arteries.' Childhood trauma is also a critically overlooked factor in the obesity epidemic – and in virtually every other major cause of death studied. The risks for heart disease, stroke, diabetes, and asthma are all affected by trauma-related changes in the stress response system. But the destructiveness of chronic stress does much more than create physical illness; it also increases the risk for virtually every mental illness known (Szalavtiz & Perry, 2010). This list includes Bipolar Disorder, schizophrenia, Post-Traumatic Stress Disorder, Borderline Personality Disorder, depression, sleeping difficulties, and suicide. Furthermore, pervasive, or toxic, stress will alter the biology of the brain (Howe, 2005; Maté, 2008; National Scientific Council on the Developing Child, 2005; Szalavtiz & Perry, 2010).

Toxic stress

Maté (2003) references researchers who have discovered that maternal care influences hypothalamic-pituitary-adrenal (HPA) function. In humans, child abuse alters the HPA stress response, and this can also increase the risk of suicide. The HPA axis is the hub of the body's stress mechanism. It is through the HPA axis that emotions exert their most direct effects on the immune system and on other organs. Higher level of stress causes higher cortisol output via the HPA axis, and cortisol inhibits growth and development, can inhibit wound healing (Maté, 1999, 2003), and can compromise the immune system, which may result in frequent illness, poor hair and skin condition, and an overall frail, waif-like appearance (Howe, 2005). "Psychological factors such as uncertainty, lack of control, and lack of information are considered the most stressful stimuli and strongly activates the HPA axis" according to Maté (2003, p. 90),[12] which results in chronic, or *toxic*, stress.

As noted earlier, for a child, stress can start before birth and continue after birth if the environment remains chaotic and/or unsafe, resulting in basic and emotional needs not being met. In short, infants raised without a loving touch and security have abnormally high levels of stress hormones. In the absence of the buffering protection of supportive relationships, this toxic stress can, over time, damage brain architecture and genetic expression, and become literally built into the baby. This is not easily healed (National Scientific Council on the Developing Child, 2005, 2008). Thus, the early environment, consisting of both pre-natal and post-natal periods, can have a profound life-long effect at all developmental stages, invariably impacting adolescent and adult patterns of behaviour (Maté, 2008).[13] In studies, high levels of the stress hormone cortisol have been found in the amniotic fluid bathing the baby in the womb when mothers are under stress (Maté, 2008). Researchers have found stress caused by verbal conflicts with, or violence by, a partner particularly damaging to the unborn (Maté, 2008),[14] though poverty, threatening neighbourhoods, and social upheaval can also be a source of toxic stress (Maté, 2012, video; National Scientific Council on the Developing Child, 2005, 2008). Kagan (2004) echoes this in that a pregnant woman stressed from her own traumas produces heightened levels of cortisol, increasing the likelihood of blocking neural connections in the foetus's developing brain or decreasing the number of brain cells. Parts of the brain needed for memory, learning, and the ability to sustain attention may particularly be impaired.

Norepinephrine, a critical hormone for self-protection, can also have an adverse effect on infants and foetuses. Norepinephrine brings a person to the 'flight-or-fight level' needed for survival. Too much, however, can lead to panic. The level of agitation can become a persistent state in which he or she is always on guard looking for threats and expecting harm. High levels of norepinephrine increase excitable neurons so even normal events can ignite the pre-programmed stress response, a process referred to as *kindling* (Kagan, 2004). In reference to the high-risk youth population, this persistent high level of agitation, or hypervigilance, brought on by toxic stress, has often been observed, particularly in those who have lived sad and disturbed lives from infancy and who have had to be on their guard, not knowing who to trust or who is safe.

Infants exposed to ongoing traumatic experiences such as physical, emotional, and sexual abuse, as well as neglect, are prone to acute stress responses that are not controlled by normal regulatory systems (Kagan, 2004). Trauma and toxic stress alter the early development of the right brain, thereby leading to serious vulnerability in this part of the brain and compromising the capacity to cope with emotional stress (Farmer, 2009). Farmer (2009) further writes:

> The right brain represents the centre for dissociation, withdrawal, and avoidance, but it is also the place where the internal working model of the attachment relationship is laid down. In other words, the blueprint for the child's original attachment relationship is located in the right hemisphere of the brain and becomes part of the child's memory system.
>
> (p. 96)

Dissociation and Post-Traumatic Stress Disorder (PTSD)

When the stress of life becomes too overwhelming and there is no escape, the mind may take over and do what the body is physically unable to do – detach from threatening and dangerous events. Children may learn this from a very early age. If they are dependent and physically leaving a traumatic situation is not an option, their mind will shut down to protect them from something too horrific to take in. They may be witnessing their mother being beaten and raped, witnessing a sibling being tortured, or being left alone to the point they do not believe anyone will come to their aid. The child may be living in a chaotic environment in which dissociation becomes a "psychological anesthetic" (Maté, 1999, p. 118) (see Box 3.4).

Box 3.4   Dissociation

"An altered state in which thoughts, emotions, perceptions, and/or memories are disrupted and split off from the reality of what is happening in the present."

Cheryl Regehr and Graham Glancy (2010, p. 246)

The dissociative process allows the brain to prepare the body for injury, thus maximizing the potential to survive (Farmer, 2009). The longer the traumatic experience lasts, the more likely the victim is to react with dissociation (van der Kolk, 2003). This can be a powerful and critically important coping mechanism when a child, but can become problematic when older if dissociating becomes generalized to situations that may only be mildly stressful to others. Over time, this state of mind can take on a life of its own and happen even when there is nothing of a distressing nature present (Heller & LaPierre, 2012; Maté, 1999). At this point dissociation can become a hindrance in that it slows psychological growth. The tuned-out individual has difficulty learning from experience and struggles to make contact with others. This "inner retreat from psychological reality means that he [or she] may never learn to cope with emotional setbacks in a creative and positive way" (Maté, 1999, p. 120).

Dissociation can take many forms and be unnoticeable much of the time (see Box 3.5). General dissociation is very common to all people and could range from simply tuning out of a lecture to think about plans for the evening to avoiding, having an absent facial expression, freezing, being uncommunicative or beyond reach, or having an out-of-body experience (for example, is also not uncommon for sexually exploited or rape victims to talk about leaving their bodies, thus making them numb to the abuse). Youth may also use cutting as a way to dissociate, as they attempt to reduce their anxiety, escape from reality, and benefit from the release of opioids (brain chemicals that produce pleasure and contentment) in the brain during this experience (Perry & Szalavitz, 2006; Szalavitz & Perry, 2010). At the extreme, dissociation can take the form of Dissociative Identity Disorder (formerly Multiple Personality Disorder) (Heller & LaPierre, 2012).

Box 3.5 Jeremy's story: reflection on dissociation

High-risk youth don't typically have the best attention spans when it comes to serious conversations. Perhaps they may come to visit the office when high on some drug or they may simply not be in the mood to talk. However, there are times when I go against my better judgement and insist on having such a conversation regardless.

I have a connection with 'Jeremy' and, satisfied I have established some level of credibility over the past year or so, I start talking with him about his lack of motivation and why he pushes people away when they show they care about him. I try to link his patterns of communication with others to his childhood experiences. Jeremy responds superficially initially, but I press on as I believe he needs to start thinking about his future and who will be his supports as he transitions out of the child welfare system. I keep rambling and Jeremy nods. Perhaps he agrees or perhaps he feels he needs to agree in order to keep getting bus tickets and groceries. I ask a pointed question about his relationship to his parents and Jeremy responds by apologizing and asking what we were talking about. I am frustrated so I challenge by him asking if he has been ignoring me for the past 20 minutes. I ask if he heard anything I said. I put it back on him and tell him he is clearly not in the right frame of mind to talk.

I have a different take on this now. While I know many of our high-risk youth have lived very sad and frightening lives, I don't always know all of the details. I don't always know the horrific memories they are carrying (implicitly or explicitly). I can tend to see situations through my own lens. In Jeremy's case, I was taking the lead and expecting him to follow. I felt the need to talk, so he should have followed my lead. I don't necessarily know which words I use, or which events I bring up, that may trigger traumatic memories for him. Looking back, a response like Jeremy's may have more to do with dissociation than being disrespectful. He may not have even been aware of what he was doing. I can't say he dissociated for sure, but we were talking about really tough stuff, so perhaps I should be giving him the benefit of the doubt. I can't really blame him after all.

In hopeless, helpless, stressful situations, when early trauma is experienced as "psychotic catastrophe," dissociation represents the "last resort defense strategy; the escape when there is no escape" (Schore, 2003, p. 126). This process of dissociation decreases blood pressure, metabolic activity, and heart rate, despite increases in circulating adrenaline. "This elevated parasympathetic[15] arousal, a basic survival strategy, allows the infant to maintain homeostasis in the face of the internal state of sympathetic hyperarousal" (Schore, 2003 p. 126). Schore (2003) further states that "the child's dissociation in the midst of terror involves numbing, avoidance, compliance, and restricted affect, the same symptom cluster found in PTSD" (p. 127). Kagan (2004) writes:

Beliefs about safety, and what they can do, how the world works, and what the future holds in store will be transformed by trauma. Life-threatening violence often leads to flashbacks nightmares, and anxiety shown by their high level of arousal, hypervigilance, and agitation. Violence leads to other physiological changes shown by their excitability, distractibility, impulsiveness, and attention-deficit problems. Researchers have also found a link between dissociation and depersonalization in delinquent youths with a history of neglect and abuse (Carrion & Steiner, 2000).[16] These are symptoms of Post-Traumatic Stress Disorder (PTSD) in children, a pattern of behaviours learned to cope with unresolved danger.

By definition (American Psychiatric Association, 1994)[17] children with PTSD have experienced events outside the realm of normal human experience that are often perceived by children as life threatening. These traumatic events include family violence and multiple out-of-home placements. Children can develop PTSD as victims, witnesses, perpetrators, or a combination of experiences. They show physiological reactivity such as headaches or stomach aches when faced with reminders of traumatic events. They experience intrusive thoughts or memories, and they may shut down their feelings and present with constricted or blunted affect.

(pp. 38–39)

Indeed, it can be confusing and frightening to disorganized/disoriented and dissociated children when they find it difficult to experience themselves as "mentally together" (Howe, 2005, p. 62). But, as is a familiar theme, it is making healthy reconnections or developing new positive relationships that can help relieve the distress, create a sense of safety, and reduce the reliance on 'tuning out.' Appropriate and nurturing touch can also act as an "antidote" to dissociation (Heller & LaPierre, 2012). The challenge, however, can be that "kids who dissociate don't tend to come to the attention of professionals because they may be odd" but "they don't piss us off" (Perry, 2010, lecture).

The ACE study

Physical and mental health issues and the related chronic stress are also tied into other harmful behaviours including smoking, drug and alcohol addiction, a proneness to end up in more violent relationships, and a greater chance of engaging in high-risk sexual behaviour (Howe, 2005). This was highlighted by Dr. Vincent Felitti, a physician who spearheaded one of the largest investigations of its kind assessing associations between childhood maltreatment and later-life health and wellbeing. Between 1995 and 1997, over 17,000 middle-class American adults of diverse ethnicity cooperated in a study to help answer the question of whether, and how, childhood experiences affect adult health decades later. The *Adverse Childhood Experiences (ACE) Study* "reveals a powerful relationship between our emotional experiences as children and our physical and mental health as adults. . . . The study makes it clear that time does *not* heal some of the adverse experiences" (Felitti, 2002, p. 1). He found the ACEs are surprisingly common, although typically supressed and unrecognized. He also found that ACEs have a profound effect 50 years later, although now transformed from psychosocial experiences into organic diseases, social malfunction, and mental illness. Felitti concludes that ACEs are the main determinant of the health and wellbeing in the United States.

Felitti had become interested in this area in the 1980s when it was observed that patients successfully losing weight in the Weight Program were dropping out. It was discovered that overeating and obesity were often being used unconsciously as protective solutions to unrecognized problems dating back to childhood (Felitti, 2003). Felitti defined eight categories of ACEs commonly observed in the Weight Program: 1) recurrent and severe physical abuse; 2) recurrent and severe emotional abuse; 3) contact sexual abuse; as well as growing up in a household with 4) an alcoholic or drug user; 5) a member being imprisoned; 6) a mentally ill, chronically depressed, or institutionalized member; 7) the mother being treated violently; and 8) both biological parents not being present. Study participants were assigned a score of '1' per category if any of these experiences applied to them. Felitti pointed out that a design flaw was not scoring 'subtle issues' such as low-level neglect and lack of interest in a child who is otherwise the recipient of adequate physical care, which, as we know from above, can also have a dramatic impact on children. The study showed that people with a score of '5' as opposed to '0' were 550% more likely to be alcoholics. Even understanding the long-term consequences, people will "sell their future to get instant relief from adverse childhood experiences" (Felitti, 2009, lecture).[18] This was also true for drug use. A male child with an ACE score of '6' was 4600% more likely to become an injection drug user than a male with an ACE score of '0.' Analysis shows that 78% of drug injection by women can be attributed to adverse childhood experiences. With respect to smoking, this was found to have a strong correlation to ACE. Other areas impacted by ACE include: Depression being prevalent in 60% of those with an ACE score of '4' and significantly higher incidents of suicide with a score over '4'; the prevalence of rape in 5% with a '0' score and 33% with a score of '4' or higher; and hallucinations (controlling for alcohol and drug use), amnesia, psychosis, and dissociation being more prevalent as ACE scores increase. The onset of teen sexuality and promiscuity are similarly impacted and this is also reflected in the high-risk youth population in Edmonton.[19] All of these reactions to the adverse childhood experiences are costing society an enormous amount financially, but there is, moreover, the bigger cost of people's lives being dramatically impacted or lost.

In addition, Felitti said the bottom line is that major health issues are related to adverse childhood experiences and the reason that people simply do not 'get over it' is because of the way neglect and abuse impacts the brain. He is clear that "abandonment is extra-ordinarily destructive" and people do not simply bounce back. Felitti continues to call for the ACE Study to be recognized in the medical community.

In my work with high-risk youth, all of these physical, mental health, and interpersonal and social relationship concerns, and the associated behaviours, have been noted repeatedly. It again reinforces the positive impact that nurturing and the feeling of being loved have on physical and mental health, while feeling unloved, rejected, and abandoned, and living with toxic stress, have such a negative impact.

There is hope

Obviously, there appears to be an endless amount of life-long struggles for those challenged by a lack of or broken attachments, trauma, and toxic stress due to the impact these have on the brain. However, there is hope in what otherwise appears to be a frightening, lonely, and dark world for these children and youth. While the long-term damage is monumental, sadly, this chronically activated stress system that comes from this dark world does serve a purpose, as it is exactly what is needed to survive in "an environment where life is nasty, brutish and short – being hypervigilant helps the child detect, evade and cope with threat" (Szalavitz & Perry, 2010, p. 114). A child's brain will adapt in a way that appears to be most adaptive to the world around him or her. So, if it is a brutal world, those adaptions will predispose him or her to behave that way as well. Not trusting others is appropriate when there is a chance of being exploited and having a quick temper can instil a sense of fear in others, reducing the chances of being challenged or harmed (Szalavitz & Perry, 2010). Unfortunately, the value of these behaviours for high-risk youth tends to be overlooked by professionals. These behaviours are not understood as the youth making sense of their chaotic world, but rather they are seen as defiant, uncooperative, and manipulative (Smyth & Eaton-Erickson, 2009; Ungar, 2004, 2005). It is no wonder why they resist help and fight engaging in relationships. This ability may have disappeared a long time ago. As Szalavitz and Perry (2010) point out in their book *Born to Love: Why Empathy is Essential – And Endangered*, "[R]epeated partial bonding and loss prevents secure bonds from developing. Over time, it becomes too painful . . . for a baby to even try to connect again" (p. 127).

To heal, the child and youth ultimately will have to let go of the fearful controlling behaviours that have actually served them well in environments of fear and danger (Howe, 2005). A requirement of healing, or becoming whole, is developing circuitry in the brain that can carry different messages and a different, non-helpless image of the self. There is strong evidence that such circuits can develop at any time in life, as can neural pathways to help the cortex do its job of inhibition and regulation (Maté, 2005), which is necessary to be able to make connections and build relationships. Indeed, the brain is remarkably malleable during development and, once organized, the brain is still capable of being influenced, modified, and changed (Maté, 2008; Perry, 2009). This ability of the brain to adapt and lay down new pathways is referred to as *neuroplasticity* or simply *brain plasticity*. It is the brain's equivalent to resilience, adapting to cope with challenge through interacting with the environment.

New understandings of the plasticity of the brain continue to emerge. The brain can regenerate and, with much consistency and repetition within a nurturing relationship, new neural pathways can be created throughout life (National Scientific Council on the Developing Child, 2007; Perry, 2006, 2009). Such positive connections can help children and youth recognize, experience, and regulate their emotions, potentially reducing their need to be watchful, vigilant, anxious, and frightened much of the time (i.e., being in survival mode). As the new neural pathways form, the expectations that adults will be rejecting and abusive can diminish and the youth can start taking risks and making connections with people who are emotionally stable and accepting (Howe, 2008).

Kagan (2004) further points out that brain centres most relevant for cognition and higher-order thinking operations such as problem-solving, reasoning, self-regulation, and strategic thinking develop well into adolescence. In fact, as noted earlier, the frontal lobes of the cortex, which regulate planning, self-control and abstract thought do not complete their development until late in adolescence, showing significant reorganization well into the early twenties (Perry & Szalavitz, 2006). But, it is "the power of relationships to nurture and heal the mind" (Howe, 2005, p. 261)[20] that is critical in helping the brain *reorganize*. Indeed, these vital neural connections are what so many of the high-risk youth continue to be missing throughout their adolescence and into young adulthood. Given the social environment typically continues to be chaotic for these youth, this high-order thinking is still at a very immature point and the ability to self-regulate is still, for the most part, impaired or absent. These youth have not had the opportunity to discover this type of regenerative power in a relationship, despite their "unconscious yearning for attachment, dating back to the first years of life" (Maté, 1999, p. 126). Perry (2009) also talks about the power of healthy relationships:

> [T]he presence of familiar people projecting the socio-emotional cues of acceptance, compassion, caring, and safety calms the stress response of the individual: *You are one of us, you are welcome, you are safe.* This powerful positive effect of healthy relational interactions on the individual – mediated by the relational and stress-response neural systems – is at the core of relationally based protective mechanisms that help us to survive and thrive following trauma and loss.
>
> (p. 246)

Building relationships with high-risk youth can be particularly challenging, as they are very well defended, they have learned they are on their own in the world, and they do not trust adults and authority figures. They experience a poverty of relationships and typically push away those who try to get close, whether consciously or subconsciously. As they come from traumatic backgrounds, they have had a lot of time and practice to develop this unfortunate, though understandable, pattern of behaviour (working through this resistance will be discussed in Chapter 7). However, it is persistence, patience, and understanding that are needed to develop healthy relationships, and healthy relationships are critical if there is to be any chance of working through the stress and trauma. Creating the opportunity for the youth to feel cared for and safe might, quite possibly, be a first-time life experience for them.

When the child or youth does not have to be concerned about seeking emotional contact, the prefrontal cortex is freed to allocate attention to other tasks. When not consumed with having to protect the self from further hurt, there is more energy for development and growth. Greater security means less anxiety and more focused attention (Maté, 1999). Those who can access and process the full range of their thoughts, feelings, and behaviour not only do not need to employ defences, but they also have the widest range of options in complex socio-emotional situations (Howe, 2005). Howe (2008) summarizes the power healthy relationships can have on the brain:

> Quality of care can help bring about changes at the neurological and neurochemical level. . . . [E]xposure to sensitive, emotionally intelligent care . . . not only helps these children feel emotionally managed and manageable, it also increases the density of neural connections between the brain's emotional centres. In turn, this leads to improved behaviour and social competence. . . . The brain can 're-structure' itself in the light of new experiences. . . . All of this has exciting implications for therapy, counselling and relationship-based social work.
>
> (p. 95)

If we, as service providers, understand this, it gives us a direction and the opportunity to be intentional and mindful about how we interact with high-risk youth so we can start helping create these new neural pathways. The alternative is to remain stuck in the punishment-consequence model, which can serve to reinforce the youths' negative view of the world while preventing them from taking the risk of making a connection. Early negative templates of being unsafe are easily reinforced. Creating a new positive neural pathway, or 'memory,' takes time, effort, patience, and much patterned repetition allowing the brain to become 'use dependent'[21] without the fear-based associations of the past. Over time, the youth may be able to be more optimistic about their future rather than relying on templates created as a result of aberrant early experiences (Perry & Szalavitz, 2006).

Therefore, consistency of relationships, creating safe environments (in the home – whether in or out of care – in school, in social activities, etc.) and reacting to the youth in consistent ways (i.e., in ways that are relationship based) are critical. The challenge is that everyone involved with the youth needs to be working from the same script and providing the same messages with consistent interaction. If one person is inconsistent, or is not invested in the service plan, the whole process can be undermined, the youth will remain hyperaroused and hypervigilant, and the new neural pathways will not become use dependent. This is why collaborative efforts and open communication become very important, as youth need to understand that they have a safety network under them all working *with* them toward common goals. Anything less is an injustice to the youth as they will continue to live with the consequences.

We can be hopeful for the youth, though we need to accept that, having experienced challenges, change is not going to come quickly. There can be positive outcomes for the high-risk youth, but it can take years just to establish a meaningful relationship. It takes even more time for the youth to feel safe enough to come to terms with their traumatic experiences and rejection and abandonment by the very people whose attention and nurturing they crave the most. If individuals and systems are patient, there is hope that a youth can experience positive relationships, see a future for themselves, and let go of their shame, guilt, and profound sense of failure. We are living in a fantasy if we believe that we can change 10, 12, or 15 years of "humiliation, degradation, rejection and trauma and abuse in 45 minutes once a week" (Perry, 2010, lecture).

A call to act

Richard Kagan (2004) challenges adults to 'answer the call' as the children and youth test our commitment of whether attachment is even possible. He writes that hurt children do not simply change their behaviours. They have to show us the worst parts of their lives to see if we, the adults, "can handle the pain, fear, and shame they carry inside" (p. 47). As we know in child welfare work, children and youth test us. While they crave building a safe relationship, they will often give up if we do not respond to them; if we do not understand them. We can often reinforce their lack of hope and their sense of helplessness because we are perceived as being more attached to 'the system' with its policies and rules than we are attached to the children and youth we are supposed to be serving. As Dr. John Seita, a former troubled youth who is now a resilience expert, said, "relationships change people, not programs." Indeed, programs are only of value if they strengthen human connections (Brendtro & du Toit, 2005). Perry (2010)[22] reminds us that it takes a long time to build a "relational experience," which is crucial for the future of traumatized children and youth. As Perry repeats often, what is needed for them is long-term, repetitive contact. If children do not receive consistent help they may never be able to overcome the pain of their losses (Kagan, 2004) and will remain disconnected and facing life-long relationship troubles, and quite possibly involvement with child welfare, justice, health, and mental health systems.

However, in child welfare systems with 'least intrusive' mandates, high caseload numbers, and a high level of staff turnover, building meaningful connections are all too rare. Also disturbing is hearing child protection workers who do not even perceive that building a relationship is part of their role, as involvement is supposed to be as short-term as possible. Again, such a mandate may benefit bureaucratic expectations but may not be consistent with the needs of children and youth. Bob Lonne et al. (2009), in the book *Reforming Child Protection*, argue that the "current narrow theoretical discourse on child protection is largely failing children and young people . . . as . . . [i]n essence, relationship-based social work has been supplanted by case-management-driven proceduralism which is devoid of meaningful and respectful engagement" (p. 8). The consequence is that children become identified as problems, rather than persons (Kagan, 2004).

Knowing what the future likely holds for children and youth with attachment, trauma, and brain development challenges, we cannot simply accept the status quo. We must look to how even bureaucratic and mandated services can change to better focus on how critical it is to build programs that meet the needs of our children and youth (and, indeed, families), rather than meeting the needs of 'the system.' This means putting the emphasis on building relationships before the discussion around any meaningful outcomes, especially given the difficulty of getting any program buy-in from the youth when there is there is no connection established. Lonne et al. (2009) call for a "return to relationship and respect as core components of our work with children and families" and moving away from a "blaming approach" which serves to undermine meaningful connection (p. 11).

Children and youth can always benefit from a safe, healthy, positive relationship with child protection workers, probation officers, teachers, counsellors, group home workers, or any other adults in a position of authority. Although it may take a long time, there is always the potential for a rare, respectful, and caring relationship to leave a little bit of light in their otherwise dark world. It can perhaps give the children and youth the permission within themselves to take the risk of forming relationships in the future – thus leaving a blueprint for later relationships based on a positive experience that forces them to question their long-held templates. Complementary to this, part of the role of various systems (child welfare, justice, education, and mental health) is to connect youth to healthy formal and informal resources in the community where there is potential for longer-term relationships whether these are outreach agencies, mentorship agencies, volunteer organizations, or relatives and family friends (relationship-based practice and strategies for working with high-risk youth will be explored in Chapters 7 and 9, respectively).

The need to be informed

While relationships are essential, if we hope to have a positive influence in understanding, engaging, and working with traumatized children and youth, and particularly high-risk youth, it is imperative we have an awareness of key principles of neuroscience and neurodevelopment. There is minimal expertise in child welfare with respect to early childhood development or infant mental health for seriously mal-treated children and, in general, the life-long impact of early trauma is underesti-mated by professionals (National Scientific Council on the Developing Child, 2004a). Perry (2006) highlights the need for a "more developmentally informed, biologically respectful approach to working with traumatized children in the child protection sys-tem" (p. 47). Only then can we begin to improve practice, programs, and policy in child maltreatment. Without an appreciation of how the brain is organized and how it changes, not only policy, but "therapeutic interventions are likely to be inefficient or, sadly, ineffective" (Perry, 2006, p. 30). For example, sending a youth to insight-based therapy may be counter-productive without first addressing and improving self-regulation, anxiety, and impulsivity (Perry, 2009). Dr. Daniel Siegel, a psychiatrist and associate professor at the UCLA Centre for Culture, Brain, and Development, argues that the basic goal of psychotherapy is self-regulation, given most mental health prob-lems derive from a lack of self-regulation (Farmer, 2009).

Perry (2009) further asserts that there is rarely any teaching of the core concepts of neurodevelopment to trainees in education, social work, medicine, law, paediat-rics, psychology, and psychiatry, despite the fact that neurodevelopmental principles impact all child-related disciplines. An understanding of the backgrounds of the chil-dren and youth, the trauma they may have experienced, and the impact on their brain development could help foster a re-examination of how staff (social workers, child and youth care workers, youth workers, etc.) could find more effective ways to com-municate and approach the children and youth whether they are at home, in foster homes, group homes, shelters, and supported independent living programs, or home-less (living on the streets, couching surfing, engaging in survival sex). There is certainly a need to move beyond the 'tough love,' 'zero tolerance,' 'three-strikes' mentality. For high-risk children and youth who are hypersensitive to rejection, these interventions simply reinforce what they have come to fear and expect – more rejection. For chil-dren who have a right to be angry at the world; who often have developmental chal lenges; who have difficulty emotionally self-regulating; who feel unworthy, unwanted, uncared for, and unloved; and who live with a profound sense of shame and sense of failure, it is difficult to understand how more rejection and abandonment will do anything to change their lives in a positive way. In fact, "being further victimized and punished makes these youth angrier, not kinder" (Szalavitz & Perry, 2010, p. 159). Yet, the punishment-consequence interventions stubbornly persist, prompting Perry and Szalavitz (2006) to assert that, "we need programs and resources that acknowl-edge that punishment, deprivation and force merely re-traumatize these children and exacerbate their problems" (p. 244). Coupled with the ongoing ignorance of how trauma and attachment breaks have an impact on the brains of these unfortunate victims of circumstance, one wonders how they have a chance.[23]

If we are going to help our high-risk youth we must avoid reinforcing their emotional dysregulation and maintaining their hyperaroused and fight-flight-freeze responses. This can only be accomplished through engaging and working in relationship, and encouraging interaction through a calm and caring presence. If we as workers are frustrated and impatient, we cannot hope to create a calming environment for the youth, especially because defiant, impulsive, hyperactive, and angry behaviours are based in fear (Farmer, 2009). And, two things are often in short supply when working with traumatized children and youth: time and patience. Change can only go at the pace of the child or youth. As Perry and Szalavitz (2006) write, "[T]here are no short-term miracle cures. This is as true for a child of three or four as it is for a teenager" (p. 244). Fortunately, more recently, there has been more of a focus on the effects of negative childhood experiences on children and youth, resulting in an increasing awareness of how therapeutic approaches fail to address psychological dysregulation, limiting the effectiveness of working with early trauma (Heller & LaPierre, 2012; Perry & Szalavitz, 2006).

Traditional approaches to child welfare are even less helpful when there are frequent changes in workers and placements, when there is a focus on systemic outcomes, and when there are power dynamics that foster a reliance on the punishment-consequence model. As stated, punishment increases fear and reinforces the sense of shame that is typically right on the surface of these wounded children and youth. Consequences become a way of controlling behaviour, but they do not address the underlying developmental problem that is causing the behaviour. To break away from this model, human services workers must look at their own practice when children or youth are 'resistant,' 'defiant,' and/or 'uncooperative,' rather than blaming the recipient of the service. This again reinforces that case workers must understand and appreciate that, before any treatment goals can be attained, the *first* task is to establish a relationship (Farmer, 2009).

Farmer (2009) calls neuroscience the missing link for all those who work with people. Neuroscientific insights can improve our understanding of human behaviour and practice, and help practitioners to better cope with the increasing complexity of human and societal problems and diagnoses. Klain and White (2013) echo this, stressing that individuals and organizations must understand trauma and the reactions of the child before attempts are made to address it. This reflects the need for a comprehensive shift to trauma-informed practice at all levels of child welfare practice reaching not only case workers, but caregivers (foster care and group care and residential care), services providers, therapists, law enforcement officers, addictions workers, and court workers, all the way up to the lawyers and judges. Without such insights, the understanding of human thinking, emotion, and behaviour is incomplete (Farmer, 2009). If this knowledge can help us serve children and youth more effectively, and allow us to have more success engaging them and building relationships, it becomes imperative that we make learning it a priority. The futures of the youth may depend on it. Policymakers and program designers can also benefit from understanding the science of the brain and the nervous system by promoting environments and experiences that prevent trauma and attachment problems and remediate early difficulties for children impacted by such challenges (National Scientific Council on the Developing Child, 2008).

Programs and interactions that can help children and youth emotionally self-regulate, create opportunities for connections to happen, and reduce the fear of further rejection can decrease the chances of experiencing ongoing difficulties throughout life. Having numerous placements, workers and therapists coming and going, infrequent and inconsistent face-to-face contact, and authoritarian rather than nurturing interaction simply exacerbates such difficulties. I have heard from youth who were confused knowing that social workers came to their home and left them in their abusive situations. Some have vivid memories of being forcibly removed from their mother's arms. Others remember being very young and too afraid to tell a case worker what was *really* happening in their bedroom at night. They do not forget wondering why they could not eat at the same table as the foster family or why they simply had a mattress on the floor in the cold basement of their 'new family' home. They remember every time they were moved – foster home to foster home, then group home to group home. These types of memories are also captured in a powerful video that was released in 1997: *Multiple Transitions: A Young Child's Point of View on Foster Care and Adoption* by Michael Trout/The Infant-Parent Institute:

> I can't forget. (Even when my brain does, my body won't). . . . I'm not saying I was some cherished treasure or anything in my family. But what were you thinking . . . when you sent me to a foster home without telling them about the special ways I needed to be handled because I had never stayed anywhere long enough to get attached to anybody? Or when you then took me from those people who were so disappointed in me after a few weeks that they said I would have to be "disrupted" (whatever that means). . . . And when that family got rid of me, and the next, and the next, did you think I was going to take it all lying down? Did you think I was supposed to just be sweet and adorable and ready to connect to yet another family who were going to throw me away?
>
> After a while, I had just lost too many people that I might have cared about. I had been with too many "parents" who really weren't, because they couldn't hold me tightly in their hearts at all. . . . None of you got how I was being changed by all these losses (in my heart and in my behavior). . . . After a while, I began to get some pretty bad ideas about how things work.
>
> I wasn't going to let anybody like me. Not even me. . . . And so, now, I won't let you imagine even for a minute that I like you. That I need you, desperately. That I might ever grow to trust you. I am not, after all, a complete moron.
>
> And when the orphanage didn't last, and the first half-dozen foster families didn't last, something started happening to me. . . . A little bit of my spirit started to die.
>
> I will make you sorry you ever thought about trying to get close to me. I will make you feel almost as helpless and small as I have usually felt.
>
> So are you wondering what I need? Are you wondering what I would do about all of this if I had the power? First of all, it would help a lot if you would start with one simple, clear commandment to yourself: Never forget that I am watching. Never forget that every single thing you do matters immensely to me (even when I work like crazy to make you think it does not). And I will remember. You may be able to get away with treating me as if I am invisible for a while (perhaps long enough to "disrupt" me or move yourself to a different casework job). I was there, watching, I was having deep feelings about what was happening to me and I needed someone to act as if it mattered, hugely.
>
> I know it is a burden for you to think so carefully about me, and I know you might get a little nervous to realize that I am watching, and affected by all that you do. But you won't be sorry if you take me seriously. Someday, see, I will be *Big People*.

Indeed, there must be a "recognition by society at large that there is no more important task in the world than the nurturing of the young during the earliest years" (Maté, 1999, p. 111). Efforts made to ensure this happens will not only help reduce the costs of a host of issues we currently face, but, by properly supporting parents, reducing poverty, and reducing stress levels, it will allow the opportunity for children to avoid trauma, attachment problems, and life-long hardship. If we keep telling ourselves that children are our most valuable resource, and that children are our future, then we can at least strive to maximize the potential that they can live emotionally healthy and fulfilling lives, surrounded by people they can genuinely trust.

Discussion questions to consider for Chapter 3

1 *Knowing the damage that abuse, neglect, rejection, and abandonment do to children, and knowing that the younger the child the better their brains can recover, does this justify removing children from their homes at an earlier age if it appears the parent(s) are struggling to bond with their child?*

2 *What is the best way to ensure every member of a support team for a youth is giving a patterned, repetitive, and consistent message to help foster the development of new neural pathways in children who have a negative internal working model?*

3 *Why do educated service providers cling to the punishment-consequence models of practice even though research tells us it is ineffective for high-risk youth, in particular?*

4 *How can supporting women during pregnancy impact the brain development of the child?*

5 *Are attachment and brain development concerns, and the early childhood histories, given enough weight when children and youth have behaviour issues and are being diagnosed by psychiatrists and/or psychologists?*

6 *If you experience a conflict between the practice model at your work and your own ethics and values, what would be the best way to navigate your own practice in this environment?*

7 *How would you attempt to educate colleagues on how youth are impacted by attachment, trauma, and brain development issues, and why punishment-consequence approaches exacerbate their negative view of adults and the way they view the world?*

8 *What is the most effective way to intervene with children and youth who have suffered adverse childhood experiences, and who have received no previous intervention? In what ways would you see hope in working with this population?*

9 *Are there times you can reflect upon in which children and youth you were talking to might have been dissociating?*

Notes

1 From the book, *In the Realm of Hungry Ghosts: Close Encounters with Addiction* (2008, p. 185).
2 David Howe is quoting: Erickson, M. & Egeland, B. (2002). Child neglect, In J. Myers, L. Berliner, J. Briere, C. T. Hendrix, J. C. Reid, & T. Reid (eds.), *The APSAC Handbook on Maltreatment*, 2nd edn. (pp. 3–20). Thousand Oaks: Sage.

3 Information on the development of the brain is taken from a number of works by Dr. Bruce Perry, senior fellow of the Child Trauma Academy and adjunct professor of psychiatry at Northwestern University of Medicine in Chicago. For two of these sources, he is co-author with Maia Szalavitz, an award-winning journalist who specializes in science and health: Child Trauma Academy (2002), Perry (2006, 2009), Perry and Szalavitz (2006), and Szalavitz and Perry (2010).

4 The right brain is involved with most communication; reading eye contact, facial appearance, posture, gestures, tone of voice, and touch. The left-brain has the capacity for language-based reasoning, questioning, understanding, coping, and self-regulating (Kagan, 2004, p. 22).

5 With respect to explaining *endorphins*, Maté (2008) writes: "It was in the 1970s that an innate opioid system was first identified in the mammalian brain. The protein molecules that serve as the chemical messengers in this system were named endorphins. . . . because they are endogenous – they originate within the organism – and because they bear a resemblance to morphine" (p. 150). Szalavitz and Perry (2010) write: Endorphins are the brain's private heroin producing pleasure, contentment, and relaxation that the mother and baby enjoy together. . . . The release of endogenous opioids [i.e., endorphins] and dopamine is an aspect of the stress response, a part of the cycle that helps restore the system to balance. Though the nature of this reward system can make people vulnerable to pathologies like addiction, most of the time craving affection is natural and healthy, as is the interdependence it creates. There has to be a biological way to ensure that we will connect with others: These chemicals and the pleasure they produce are the glue that bonds us" (pp. 29–30).

6 Gabor Maté is quoting: Schore, A. N. (1994). *Affect Regulation and the Origin of the Self: The Neurobiology of Emotional Development*. Hillsdale, NJ: Lawrence Erlbaum Associates, p. 195.

7 Gabor Maté is quoting: Dawson, K. W. & Fischer, G. (eds.) (1994). *Human Behaviour and the Human Brain*. New York: The Guilford Press, p. 9.

8 This information comes from a press release from the media relations departments at McGill University and the Douglas Mental Health University Institute, as well as an article written by Margaret Munro, Canwest News Service, appearing in the *Edmonton Journal*, Canwest News Service, February 22, 2009.

9 *Epigenetics:* A new and rapidly growing science that focuses on how life experiences influence the function of genes (Maté, 2008, p. 204).

10 David Howe is quoting from: Allen, J. (2001). *Traumatic Relationships and Serious Mental Disorders*. Cichester: Wiley.

11 Gabor Maté is referencing a two-part article published in the *Canadian Medical Association Journal* in 1996 (Anisman, H. et al. (15 October 1996). Anisman, H., Baines, M. G., Berczi, I., Bernstein, C. N., Blennerhassett, M. G., Gorczynski, R. M., . . . Warrington, R. J. (1996). Neuroimmune mechanisms in health and disease: 1. Health. *Canadian Medical Association Journal, 155*(7): 867–874; and Anisman, H., Baines, M. G., Berczi, I., Bernstein, C. N., Blennerhassett, M. G., Gorczynski, R. M., . . . Warrington, R. J. (1996). Neuroimmune mechanisms in health and disease: 2. Disease. *Canadian Medical Association Journal, 155*(8): 1075–1082.

12 Gabor Maté is quoting: De Kloet, E. R. (1992). Corticosteroids, stress, and ageing. *Annals of New York Academy of Sciences*, 663, p. 358.

13 Gabor Maté is quoting from: Colvis, C. M., Pollock, J. D., Goodman, R. H., Impey, S., Dunn, J., Mandel, G, . . . Nestler, E. J. (2005). Epigenetic mechanisms and gene networks in the nervous system. *The Journal of Neuroscience, 25*(45): 10379–10389.

14 For this information Gabor Maté cites http://news.bbc.co.uk/2/hi/health/6298909.stm.

15 The *parasympathetic* nervous system is responsible for keeping the body in its normal state and is active most of the time ("rest and digest"). It is responsible for slowing down the heartbeat, lowering blood pressure, and increasing blood flow to the skin. Its main purpose in doing all this is to reverse the effects caused to the body by the sympathetic nervous system. The *sympathetic* nervous system readies the body for action and is responsible for the 'fight or flight' response. (http://www.reference.com/motif/health/functions-of-the-parasympathetic-nervous-system)

16 Kagan references: Carrion, V. & Steiner, H. (2000). Trauma and dissociation in delinquent adolescents. *Journal of American Academy of Child and Adolescent Psychiatry*, 39(3): 353–359.

17 Kagan references: American Psychiatric Association. (1994). *Diagnostics and Statistics Manual of Mental Disorders*, 4th edn. Washington, DC: American Psychiatric Association.

18 This quote comes from a presentation by Dr. Vincent Felitti at the Radisson Hotel in Edmonton, Alberta, on May 4, 2009.

19 Ibid.

20 David Howe is quoting: Siegel (2003). An interpersonal neurobiology of psychotherapy: The developing mind and the resolution of trauma. In M. Solomon & D. Siegel (eds.), *Healing Trauma: Attachment, Mind, Body and Brain* (pp. 1–56). New York: W.W. Norton.

21 The 'use dependent' development, according to (Perry & Szalavitz, 2006, pp. 29–30), is one of the most important properties of neural tissue, as it can be used to replace negative templates youth have developed through early patterned and repetitive traumatic experiences. This concept also has implications for helping children to create new neural pathways through making new positive or healthy associations. Again this requires patterned and repetitive experiences, though it is pointed out that this is very difficult to accomplish in a traditional counselling setting seeing a child for an hour a week. Perry and Szalavtiz (2006) give an example of a young girl whose early experiences of men was being sexually abused. The association made was that all men want sex with girls. Patterned and repetitive activity would be required to change this association in a use-dependent way, meaning that the systems in the brain that get repeatedly activated will change and the systems in the brain that don't get activated will not.

22 Referenced from notes taken at a presentation by Dr. Bruce Perry in Edmonton, Alberta, on November 15, 2010.

23 The impact of such rejection and the punishment-consequence interventions are further discussed in later chapters.

Chapter 4

Why a harm reduction philosophy is essential for working with high-risk youth

> Harm reduction is as much an attitude and way of being as it is a set of policies and methods.
>
> Gabor Maté[1]

As mystifying as it may be, despite being a very good fit for the HRYI, harm reduction is a very misunderstood concept. Aside from the negative comments (explored below) that the philosophy allows youth to run amuck with no moral guidance, it typically comes with questions asked in a surprised tone of voice: "You use harm reduction in government?"; "Isn't harm reduction too risky?"; and "Doesn't harm reduction mean no accountability?" These are all actual questions I have been asked, though it has changed now to some degree. In the mid-2000s, we were told to use a different name, as 'harm reduction' was too controversial. We did not, and now the philosophy is talked about much more openly, is a viable approach, and fits with the shift to relationship-based practice. There is still push back and, as noted already, confusion. However, I believe that in the not-too-distant future we will look back and wonder what all of the fuss and controversy was about when it comes to the harm reduction philosophy and practice.

Harm reduction comes to us from the addictions field. This tends to conjure up images of needle exchange programs, or even safe injection sites, such as the Insite Clinic in Vancouver, which gained wide publicity as the first safe injection site in North America, remaining open despite attempts by the federal conservative government to close it down.[2] However, it is actually surprising how mainstream harm reduction approaches actually are already when one considers ideas such as safe graduations, designated driver programs, smoking aids, and safer sex campaigns (Taylor, 2010). While a vast majority of high-risk youth struggle with addictions, making harm reduction strategies relevant in this area, this approach and philosophy has been adapted and expanded to be relevant in all areas of the HRYI and is seen a strong fit to the field of human services/social work in general. The challenge, however, has been finding harm reduction research and literature that goes beyond the area of addictions, though Bigler, in his 2005 article, 'Harm Reduction as a Practice and Prevention Mode for Social Work,' states that, "In more recent years, the harm reduction model has gained a great deal of attention and support outside of the addictions arena and in other areas of health and human services" (p. 73). Bigler (2005) adds:

Although it originated in the field of chemical dependency, the philosophy and strategies of harm reduction are pertinent to a wide variety of complex social welfare and public health issues. The harm reduction approach seems ideally suited as a guide to practice in virtually all social work settings and reflects fundamental values and beliefs of the social work profession including the inherent worth and dignity of individuals, client self-determination, and the strengths perspective.

(p. 69)

Logan and Marlatt (2010) write that harm reduction now applies to any decisions that have negative consequences associated with them:

At its core, harm reduction supports any steps in the right direction . . . The practitioner's goals are secondary to what the client wants. . . . Our goal is to meet you where you are and hope that harm reduction can fit as one tool in your practice toolbox. . . . If, however, a client is ambivalent toward or, in fact, resistant to change, then harm reduction gives us an opportunity to build rapport and help our client make steps in the right direction. Ideally, the client will make the choice to stop the problematic behavior.

(pp. 202 & 208)

This passage particularly speaks to the strength of the harm reduction philosophy when working with high-risk youth. We anticipate they will be resistant given their challenges with trust and relationships, but we can open the door to building rapport and simply focus on opening communication lines and creating safety (see Box 4.1). Within the *Get Connected* practice framework (of the HRYI), harm reduction is defined as a set of strategies and principles that aims to provide or enhance the skills, knowledge, resources, and support people need to be safer and healthier. The aim is to work to the strengths of the youth. It is empowering, non-coercive, non-judgemental, builds rapport, sees people as experts in their own lives, and improves quality of life for individuals based on their own perceptions and values (Taylor, 2010). Bigler (2005) defines the overriding principle as "reducing the harm associated with specific high-risk behavior" (p. 73), while Maté (2008) tells us, "harm reduction means making the lives of afflicted human beings more bearable, more worth living" (p. 312).

Harm reduction defined

Harm reduction has been a key principal in working with high-risk youth, encouraged through consultation with community partners and youth since 1999.[3] As noted earlier, this was driven by the need to find a better way to build relationships with the youth and involve them in the decision-making process. Adopted from the work of Richard Elovich and Michael Cowing (1993)[4], this definition of harm reduction was incorporated into the practice framework: A set of strategies and tactics that encourage individuals to reduce the risk of harm to themselves and their communities by their various behaviours. The *goal* is to educate the person to become more conscious of the risks of their behaviour and provide them with the tools and resources with which they can reduce their risk. The *principles* include:

- A humanistic approach.
- Does not deal solely with behaviours, but with the whole person and their complex needs.
- Accepts that risk is a natural part of our lives.
- Places risky behaviour on a continuum within the context of a person's life.
- Looks at a person's relationship to the behaviour as defined by him/herself.
- Accepts that behavioural change is often incremental.
- *Any positive change* is seen as significant.
- Interventions are not rigid but require creativity and innovation reflective of a person's life situation.
- Builds on existing strengths and capacities.
- Is helpful for communities most affected to be involved in creating safe places to get help by organizing harm reduction interventions and programs.
- Though commonly associated with drug use, harm reduction is applicable to any social welfare and/or public health issue (Elovich & Cowing, 1993).

The benefits of a harm reduction approach include the fact that services and supports meet youth where they are at rather than expecting them to conform to codes of conduct in order to access services; youth input is essential as it increases the chances that they will buy in, rather than imposing a service plan on the youth; and it empowers the youth to have more control in the working relationship. As one youth stated, "By working *with* us and not *for* us, solutions that make sense for our lives will be possible." Working from a harm reduction approach is about being aware of what the young person sees as important and remaining focused on their individual definition of success. It is a philosophical shift to define success through the eyes of a youth, rather than continuing to rely on the medical model, which defines the practitioner as the 'expert' (Elovich & Cowing, 1993). Being in the role of expert can invite an authoritarian stance, losing the opportunity to adopt the role of accountable ally, which incorporates a shift from teaching the youth to learning from them (Madsen, 1999). However, this philosophical shift will be difficult as long as we continue to emphasize problems rather than emphasizing competence. As is stated throughout this book, high-risk youth typically feel like they have failed, so reinforcing this by focusing on problems is not helpful. To avoid resistance and demoralization, "recognizing strengths and resources invites hope and possibilities" (Madsen, 1999, p. 27). This is particularly relevant if using the *Stages of Change*[5] in that it will be difficult to help youth move from *pre-contemplative stage*, in which they do not recognize or refuse to acknowledge that they have high-risk behaviours that could jeopardize their safety, to the *contemplative stage*, in which they may start to recognize the concerns but are not sure how to deal with them, let alone progress to the *commitment to action* (or *determination stage*) in which to develop a plan to work through the issues. The youth will require positive help and support in the *action* or *implementation stage*, if they are to stay safe and move forward in to the *maintenance stage*, especially if they relapse, which is not uncommon. The difference in not losing what steps they have made can be having someone to pick them up at such critical times – and not judging them for the setback.

Understanding risk and learning to let go

Box 4.1   Bryan's story: what is real risk?

A community agency refers a youth, 'Bryan' (16), to Child and Family Services. The agency staff had been supporting the youth as the situation is tenuous at home. He appears depressed, wants to leave home as he feels he is not wanted, and is tired of cleaning up the house after his parents drink, yell, scream, and throws things at each other. He has been terrified to have 'the system' involved, as he does not want to go to a group home or a foster home. When he has left home or, moreover, when kicked out, he stays with friends. Many of them are homeless so they sometimes end up sleeping in tents in the river valley. While some of his friends use crystal meth, and crack when they can get it, Bryan makes excuses to his friends that he tried these before but it makes him violently ill to the point he has to be hospitalized. They accept this as they don't want to have to get Bryan to hospital if a trip goes wrong. He does use marijuana and alcohol a number of times a week, but he fears if he is not able to get help he will give in to peer pressure and start using harder drugs. He is also on probation for stealing cars with his friends, but he acknowledges this was not a smart choice. Bryan attends an alternative school program as he is trying to catch up from missing a significant amount of classes over the past couple of years. This school provides some emotional support. The worker from the community agency has known Bryan for about a year and feels he has great potential, though he appears on the verge of giving up.

Traditional intervention

An assessor/investigator through Child and Family Services is assigned the intake. The family has come to the attention of child welfare authorities on three previous occasions over the past five years for domestic violence and alcohol abuse. On the first two occasions Bryan and his parents denied any concerns, though during the second incident, it was noted on file that Bryan appeared 'coached' and was anxious. On the third occasion, the parents acknowledged there has been an argument after some drinking, but the family was accessing counselling through their employee benefits. Like the first two occasions, the file was closed. On this fourth occasion, it was clear that there was damage to the house and the mother required medical attention. When Bryan was interviewed, the community worker was present and Bryan confirmed that these incidents are a regular occurrence. He said his parents deny and minimize the family problems and have never gone to counselling. While Bryan said he knows he can't be at home, he discloses that he is scared to go into care. The worker tells Bryan that she knows what is best for him and that, as he cannot go home right now, he will have to go to a group home. The worker concludes that, given he is using drugs and alcohol, is on probation, and has slept in the river valley, he is not capable of making his own decisions and, without being safely in care, he would simply get into more trouble. Bryan and his community support worker protest, saying that Bryan talked to the assessor to get help and that Bryan was fearful of having to go to a group home. The worker said she could ask for a foster home, but it was not likely to happen due to his age. Bryan states he does not want this either. He tells the assessor that he could possibly stay with a friend and his family. The worker states this is not possible because the friend's home would have to be approved and that this is a long process. Further, the worker states that he must follow the rules at the group home, see an addictions counsellor, go to therapy with his parents, and maintain school. She also tells Bryan that she hopes his parents will consent to him being at the group home and sign a voluntary agreement. Otherwise, he will be apprehended. He is told he would be able to get a lawyer in such circumstances. The community worker reminds the assessor that Bryan is 16 and could sign his own agreement. The response is quick and short, as the assessor has concluded that Bryan is not mature enough and that if he signs his own agreement he will never want to go home. Bryan stands up and looks at the community worker and states that he knew this would happen and that was why he didn't want Child and Family Services involved. He adds that this is all "bullshit" and, before stomping off, yells, "there is no way I'm is staying in a fucking group home." The assessor looks at the community worker and tells him that it doesn't seem like Bryan wants help after all.

Harm reduction intervention

The assessor/investigator meets with Bryan and the community worker. She hears his story and states she is impressed that he has found a way to avoid harder drugs and that he has created plans to avoid being at home when it becomes unsafe. She hears the concerns and fears of being in group care and foster care. They all acknowledge home is not the best place to be right now so they discuss possible options. The assessor is concerned about Bryan sleeping in the river valley, but asks questions about the friend and his family. She tells Bryan that she cannot tell him he should stay there as she cannot approve the home, but she can support him with some money for food and basic necessities until there is a chance to see if this is a possible longer-term solution. The assessor is also impressed that, throughout all of this chaos, he has started attending school more regularly. She also commends him for taking a risk by talking to Child and Family Services, as there are occasions in which things do not always work out the way a youth hopes it will. Bryan is asked what he needs for the time being. He is surprised to be asked such a question but states he sometimes has to miss school because he can't get any bus tickets. He also has been wearing the few clothes he has over and over, as he does not want to go home by himself to get more of his belongings. The assessor says she will work on getting some of his clothes and possessions, but if there is a lot of resistance, she will provide some interim funding. Bryan is asked if he would be open to addressing his drugs and alcohol. He said he doesn't think he has a problem. The assessor leaves this open, but adds she works with outreach addictions workers who could meet him casually over coffee with no pressure to be in a program. He squirms a little and agrees to think about it. Bryan is adamant about not going to therapy, however. He is fearful and not ready to talk about his family, especially in front of his parents in a therapist's office. Given he has been making some good decisions, the assessor explains that he can sign his own agreement if he wants some help and support. He looks at his support worker who asks a few questions to clarify what taking on this responsibility means. An agreement is signed with a safety plan. Bryan agrees to check in with the assessor by phone to let her know he is safe and doing okay. The assessor states she will drop off a food voucher and a bus pass at his friend's family home the following day. The assessor said she is not too concerned about the services plan at present, as they can get to that once they get to know each other a bit better. Bryan agrees to meet the assessor for lunch next week. He acknowledges that the meeting was a lot different, and a lot better, than he anticipated.

Risk

In traditional approach, Bryan left the meeting frustrated and refusing services. The worker appears to make the assumption that he no longer wants services, rather than reflecting on how her approach created a certain dynamic. Now, Bryan is on his own and will avoid the worker for fear of being apprehended and placed in group care against his wishes. The assessor will not know whether he is safe, if he will be able to get his basic needs met, or whether he is able to resolve any issues with his parents. There is the risk he becomes more chronically homeless, that he will be more at risk for being a victim of crime and violence, and that his addictions and criminal activity may escalate. Bryan could also stay away from his supports at the community agency and school for fear he could be found by the authorities. One could argue that this intervention from child protection actually increases the risk for Bryan.

In the harm reduction approach, Bryan felt validated and supported, and was empowered through the compliments for the way he has tried to cope with his circumstances and by having a say in the decision-making process. The message is that Bryan has an understanding of what might work as far as a plan for his future. He has been given choices and basic material support. The assessor has now become part of the support team that is being built under Bryan and the credibility of the community worker who encouraged Bryan to come forward and talk to Child and Family Services has increased, further building trust in that relationship. The assessor has also opened up communication with Bryan in a non-threatening way, giving the message that people care about him and want to see him be safe. This has also created space for Bryan to be able to reach out again if his placement option at his friend's family home is no longer viable. This situation has now considerably reduced the risk to Bryan and opened the door to building positive connections within a system he feared.

Given Bryan's scenario, does it make sense to abandon him because he is not being compliant? Do we not accept that he has something to contribute in his own future because we think we know better? Gabor Maté (2008) asks this about the people who are struggling with addictions in Vancouver's downtown Eastside, Canada's most notorious district for human misery. Of course, an addict would be better off without their habit, Maté (2008) argues, but are we going to cut loose those who are unable to give it up? Also relevant to high-risk youth, he asks, "Are we willing to care for human beings who suffer for their persistent behaviours, mindful that these behaviours stem from early life misfortunes they had no hand in creating?" (p. 317). For many there is too much pain in their lives, and, like Bryan, too few internal and external resources available to them. Maté (2008) continues:

> In practicing harm reduction we do not give up on abstinence – on the contrary, we hope to encourage that possibility by helping people feel better, bringing them into therapeutic relationships with caregivers, offering them a sense of trust, removing judgment from our interactions with them and giving them a sense of acceptance.
>
> (pp. 317–318)

Yet, given the general attachment to the punishment model, and even though we are working with youth, it is not uncommon in the child welfare system to be very rigid when youth make mistakes. We may terminate them from supported independent living (SIL) programs when they have a party in their apartment or lose their day program (school or employment). We may close their file if they do not maintain their addictions program. We might deny them services if they use aggressive language. Schools may expel a youth for getting caught with a joint. These fit with 'tough love' and 'zero tolerance' thinking and blanket policies that do not show an understanding of the circumstances faced by many youth. The youth in SIL programs may have not learned how to cope with loneliness and so had some friends over, who in turn invited others over, creating a situation beyond their control. The youth may have missed classes due to depression or fear of failure at school. The youth in the addictions program may have become overwhelmed with having to cope with their trauma without the chance to self-medicate with drugs and/or alcohol. We may not appreciate that a youth is reacting aggressively because the worker is threatening to cut them off, escalating the anxiety of the youth and triggering feelings of personal failure that have been reinforced over and over by his or her parents. For the youth in school, staff may not have considered how the student had been able to stop using crystal methamphetamine and alcohol, getting down to the odd joint. Thus, they have missed the opportunity to work together to avoid similar incidents. Perhaps we are too busy, we are just following policy, we feel that we have to teach youth what it is like in the real world, or we fear losing control. Whatever the reason, the end result is that we lose the opportunity for building a relationship, problem-solving together, opening the window for trust, and giving the message of acceptance. Again, this is not to say that there are not workers who do follow the principles of harm reduction (whether aware of the fact or not), and certainly not to dismiss that practice is changing, but there are far too many situations in which the natural response is to be reactive and inflexible, refusing the youth any say into decisions that are being made about their lives.

Hartman, Little and Ungar (2008) discuss replacing 'zero tolerance' policies with harm reduction approaches to make practice congruent with models that are individualized and engage youth. Harm reduction in which youth are encouraged to manage their exposure to risk without necessarily demanding complete cessation of risk-taking behaviours fit with narrative practices[6] (incorporating a social justice perspective) which value young people's wisdom while respecting the meaning of their behaviours for them. The authors reinforce that "a harm reduction approach makes youth the central party in deciding the steps they will take to address the problems affecting their lives" (p. 55). Levy and Orlans (1998) further write that "Adolescents need to have input into decision making about their lives and future, consistent with their need to have increasing control over life events in general" (p. 227). This means allowing youth to take risks, make mistakes, and learn from these experiences (Perry & Szalavitz, 2006; Ungar, 2007a).

It is my overwhelming experience that youth want to engage and will cooperate with paperwork, appointments, waiting in court, attending programs, and meeting other service providers. By involving and engaging youth more, this process invites them to take responsibility (Hartman et al., 2008), though this is generally not the case if they are ignored in the decision-making process. To get to this point we need to let go of control and work in partnership with the youth; we must accept them for who they are. Maté (2008) writes that this is the "essence of harm reduction, but it is also the essence of any healing or nurturing relationship" (p. 87). And this is why harm reduction approaches indeed have an important place in working with high-risk youth, whether for a community outreach workers, an agency service provider, or a child protection case worker. The issue is not whether they will or will not make mistakes, but whether we have developed the relationship with our high-risk youth to help pick them up again and continue moving forward. Do they feel safe enough to reach out and ask us to help pick them up or do they try to hide their mistakes and feel like a failure?

Focusing on competence

The harm reduction model promotes non-punitive responses where mutual support and accountability exist (Bigler, 2005, p. 74). This means that working in this approach prompts intentional conversations around safety and goals. If a worker is not engaging in such dialogue, they are not practicing from a harm reduction perspective, as it does not mean leaving a youth to their own devices. A safety plan (see Chapter 11 for more detail) can be a start to talking, as it recognizes and accepts that the youth will struggle on occasion, make poor decisions at times, and will need support.

The case worker, service provider, or outreach worker may have plenty of suggestions, but the youth is prompted to think and identify what is important to them. Often the youth are quite aware and their perspective is not much different than their support team. At times, and typically early in the relationship-building phase, the youth may be embarrassed to answer these questions. Or, depending what is going on in their lives, they may not have given these issues much thought or they may have developmental challenges or a variety of diagnoses in which they cannot easily think about or write down how their behaviours could jeopardize their safety. Such youth can be guided through safety plan conversations, but it is important that their thoughts and perspectives are honoured in the process. This can help the youth to start making connections about the choices they make and perhaps recognize who might be safe and unsafe people in their lives.

Youth are more likely to identify friends as placement options and support initially, but as connections are established, the youth will add people from their professional support team, which can be particularly helpful for emergency services if workers can look on the computer database and be able to contact these people for background information and to work out a solution with the youth, who may be reluctant to talk to yet another professional who is a stranger.

Harm reduction and the doorway to healthy relationships

Within the philosophy of harm reduction, Taylor (2010) discusses the importance of a *healthy client-worker relationship*. This means respecting all service users, using a strengths-based perspective (see Chapter 5), taking the time to build rapport, being patient with yourself and the service user, and being non-judgemental by accepting people's decisions and lifestyle choices. This can be a struggle given that many youth are not yet 18, but are making decisions that stretch our comfort or tolerance levels, and even our values and ethics. On the harm reduction continuum, there may be situations in which severe harm is imminent and there is a responsibility to intervene, but generally, we need to check our judgements and work through our struggles, lest we drift back into power-and-control and punishment thinking.

Taylor (2010) continues advising that we must separate the drug/behaviour from the person, recognizing that this is a person who happens to use drugs or engage in risky behaviours. We must be tolerant and supportive despite relapses or backward steps, offering positive feedback and being generous with our time. This can be an ongoing challenge, especially working within a government bureaucracy where there can be a focus on administrative tasks, in which building relationships can be secondary to proceduralism, and in which high caseloads can result in the abdication of this direct work to other service providers (Altman & Gohagan, 2009; Herbert, 2007; Lonne et al., 2009).

Taylor (2010) further advises us to listen to the youth who have been there as the answers are not necessarily in a textbook – hear their stories. This is key in building relationships and helps us learn about the context of people's experience and how the youth got to the place they are currently in. It can prevent us from making assumptions and feeling we have the answers for them. This is consistent with acknowledging that people are experts in their own lives and that solutions to making changes in their lives may very well come from the stories they share. The final aspect of the healthy client-worker relationship is to expect the working boundaries to be tested by the service users. It is not the role of youth to set boundaries within the working relationship, but rather it is up to us to establish such boundaries, while still maintaining a positive relationship. Unhealthy client-worker relationships can diminish the potential of a harm reduction approach. In addition to not establishing proper boundaries this may include acting superior for having made different or 'healthy' choices; preaching or expecting abstinence – people will not quit until they are ready; talking down to people; not valuing the individual's right to self-determination; or trying to 'save' the individual. These can reinforce the 'power over' mentality rather than 'power with,' which is ultimately what the youth are seeking from us, if we are open to it (Herbert, 2007).

Harm reduction has its critics

The harm reduction paradigm does not come without its critics. Again, there is little evidence of any critical literature with respect to harm reduction and working with high-risk children and youth. However, the general philosophy is attacked for condoning, or even encouraging, risky behaviour and thus being a socially destabilizing force that implies that anti-social behaviour is acceptable. Harm reduction practice has been criticized for maintaining self-destructive behaviours, for not encouraging personal responsibility, for coddling people, and as a way of allowing service users to avoid dealing with their issues (Brocato & Wagner, 2003; Canadian Nursing Association, 2011; Maté, 2008; Taylor, 2010). In a neo-liberal society, harm reduction is also seen as squandering resources on those who are undeserving and who make poor choices, leaving others to pay the costs (Maté, 2008). However, though referring to addicts, Maté (2008) challenges such thinking:

> If the guiding principle is that a person who makes their own bed ought to lie in it, we should immediately dismantle our health care system. Many of our diseases and conditions arise from self-chosen habits or circumstances that could have been prevented. The issue is not whether the addict would be better off without his habit – of course he would – but whether we are going to abandon him if he is unable to give it up. . . . There is, for now, too much pain in their lives and too few internal and external resources available to them.
>
> (p. 316)

Likewise, without a harm reduction perspective, we risk abandoning youth due to their behaviours without considering that they come from a background of early trauma which has impacted their present functioning and feelings of self-worth. We have responded by denying services, kicking them out of school, or sending them to jail where they associate with many other youth with emotional and mental health problems. While youth need to take responsibility for their behaviour and the crimes they commit, and public safety needs to be taken into account, most high-risk youth are going to respond better through relationship than through repeated punishment. Without relationships they have little to lose by lashing out at society. As Maté (2008) tells us, "The immediate goal is to reduce harm and, beyond that, establish a relationship" (p. 313). It is not coddling. Many high-risk youth have told me that they do not care if they live or die, especially those who have no family connections, have few other supports in their lives, and are lost to how to build any connections in which they feel safe.

Another issue for detractors is the public tolerance for allowing risky situations to persist and giving youth too much say when they do not know what is good for themselves. The reality is that no matter how hard we try, and no matter how policy and procedures are implemented, risk will never be eliminated, ever. However, when something goes wrong or there is a tragedy, the finger tends to get pointed at harm reduction strategies. However, it is youth who are estranged from the child protection system and who lack the opportunities to develop relationships who are more at risk.

As Lonne et al. (2009) and Munro (1999) point out, child protection systems have been strongly reacting to public pressures and are preoccupied with managing and trying to eliminate risk through creating policies and adopting reactive approaches to the point that intervention may actually be doing more harm than good. A reduction in harm may or may not be sufficient for a client, but at least it's a starting point to building rapport, encouraging change, and supporting efficacy (Logan & Marlatt, 2010). After all, harm reduction is based on principles of "compassionate pragmatism rather than moralistic idealism" (Bigler, 2005, p. 79). In addition, Munro (1999) states, "[T]he simplistic view that children can be rescued from harm and live happily ever after needs to be replaced by an understanding that the work usually involves choosing between two undesirable options and hoping to pick the one that does the least damage" (p. 126). High-risk youth live high-risk lifestyles. That is why they are part of the HRYI. Risk cannot be eliminated, so workers partner *with* the youth to support them and open the door to helping them make healthier decisions, eventually increasing their safety to the point they see no need for such risk-taking.

A further concern was raised with respect to using harm reduction approaches with youth who struggle with Fetal Alcohol Spectrum Disorder (FASD). This is particularly significant as it is estimated that 30–40% of youth in the HRYI struggle with FASD.[7] It was argued that youth who struggle with this brain injury cannot manage such decision-making and that it is like putting an eight-year-old child in their own apartment and expecting them to manage. Not that low IQ always goes hand in hand for those living with FASD, given a wide range of IQs have been documented, but clearly the point is well accepted that there are deficits with cause-and-effect thinking, problem-solving, learning from experience, impulsivity, and possibly self-regulation (Lawryk, 2001). These are obviously key areas when involving youth in developing their safety plans and service plans and when referring them to supported independent living placements. I cannot argue that these youth, and indeed all high-risk youth, would benefit from a more structured setting in which there is less flexibility and more predictable routines. In fact, they often demonstrate the benefits of this when they are in young offender centres or secure environments getting treatment. Indeed, we do generally provide our eight-year olds with a lot of structure at home and give them responsibilities that match their development age.

The problem is that this comparison falls short for our youth. In some respects they are very young, but they have had more tragic life experiences in their early years than most people have in their whole lives. When they come to the HRYI they are already street-involved, have learned survival skills, and are used to running away from placements that, in their minds, are "like jail." We know they do not do well in foster care or traditional group homes, and that more rules and structure exacerbate the situation and inevitably result in the youth hiding from authorities, increasing their risk. It is as if the FASD means they could do well with structure and routine, but the trauma makes them resistant to structure and routine, as it may represent losing control, being vulnerable, and building relationships. Thus they are caught in this contradiction which may not even make sense to them and the latter typically wins out. In addition, we do not have facilities that can contain children and youth indefinitely to provide them with structure and routines. While some would argue that this would keep them safe in theory, there are always dangers within confined settings, including the chance to self-harm. There are also obvious challenges on an ethical and human rights level. It is frustrating to get reports from psychologists, psychiatrists, or clinical social workers recommending that a youth be placed in a long-term restrictive and structured setting because such facilities do not exist – nor should they.[8] If a facility is not restricted (i.e., locked), we know youth will run away. Both outcomes are unhelpful to youth, again demonstrating that traditional approaches and recommendations do not work well with this population.

Therefore, in an effort to keep youth safe and help them manage their high-risk behaviours, the HRYI adopts a harm reduction approach whether the youth are afflicted with FASD or not. My experience has shown repeatedly that shelter placements that have dropped ruled-based programming and adopted a harm reduction approach, and now focus on building relationships, are keeping high-risk youth longer and the youth are responding more positively to services that are offered. There are numerous examples in which youth have never stayed in any placement before but have stayed in such placements for many months, surprising everyone – even themselves!

On a more personal note, when I was starting the first high-risk youth caseload in 1999, the harm reduction approach was not taken seriously by other case workers with whom I worked. It would be an understatement to say there was an atmosphere of cynicism. Comments reflected that this thinking and practice was not real social work, that it allowed youth to take control ("soft-on-teens unit"; "you allow the youth to walk all over you"), and that the project was for bleeding hearts, reflecting the cynicism in society, the media, and by politicians on occasion in dismissing "the soft nature of relationships" as "gullible, namby-pamby and 'do-gooding' " (Howe, 2014, p. 127). It certainly caused me to doubt what I was doing and feel naïve. Not infrequently, I was told that harm reduction simply allows the youth to manipulate and gain control. In my experience, however, it never felt this way and I have never met a child or youth who did not manipulate. Emotionally healthy kids do this when they try to play mom and dad off of each other. Our high-risk youth are good at it, whatever their level of functioning, as it helps them survive on the streets, or in jail, or when with peers in various placements. This is a sign of resiliency, though being manipulative is one more negative label we attach to our youth.

In fact, I've never met a case worker who did not use manipulation, including myself, though I have seen workers get very worked up about being manipulated as if it represents losing power and control over a youth. We use manipulation as workers to try and make connections and help youth be safe. We do not have an ethical crisis about this because we do this in the service of helping our youth (Dennis & Lourie, 2006). We offer youth a lunch if they come to see us because we know they struggle to access sufficient food – and we want to know they are safe. "Yes, I can give you bus tickets, but can you come to the office and pick them up?"; "If you complete this assessment to help you access adult services, we can look at getting that iPod"; "Let's just visit this group home and you don't have to commit to staying, but just meet the staff and see what the place looks like – and then we will grab lunch." These are all examples of manipulation, but the worker is not gaining anything through such actions other than the satisfaction of the youth being safe and a chance to spend time getting to know each other better. This is benevolent manipulation and, if it is not done with a level of sincerity and genuineness, the youth will see through it – we know they can spot this a mile away – and it can do more damage to the youth. So, we cannot avoid manipulation, we all do it, so we need to get over the sensitivity to it and stop punishing youth, or even denying them services, because we can't handle youth being manipulative.

Lourie's Law of Manipulation recognizes the positive power in manipulating and being manipulated when it comes to working with youth. Lourie's Law states:

> It is alright to be manipulated as long as the following criteria are met: 1) you know you are being manipulated; 2) the person manipulating you knows you know; 3) you get to manipulate back, as long as that manipulation is in the service of helping the child. When one adheres to Lourie's Law, manipulation stops being a dangerous and destructive thing and begins to take its place as a potentially beneficial tool.
>
> (Dennis & Lourie, 2006, p. 50)

While there is still a lot of cynicism when it comes to harm reduction, it is getting less, and there is more of a level of curiosity. In turns out that harm reduction values are consistent with social work ethics and values (Bigler, 2005), and those of other professions as well. In fact, Bigler (2005) writes that "the marriage of social work as a professional discipline and harm reduction as a model to guide practice is a natural one, with the potential for a long and positive relationship" (p. 81). The author further states:

> Social workers understand that many of today's problems require new and innovative thinking. Unfortunately, these insights are often gained on the frontline level where workers seem to apply harm reduction principles and strategies in their work almost intuitively because this model is so consistent with their core personal and professional beliefs.
>
> (p. 80)

Conclusion

Accepting harm reduction as a preferable option to traditional approaches to intervention is overdue, and high-risk children and youth will remain disengaged, disconnected, and unsafe as long as we continue to debate rather than act. It is time that policies reflect the change in thinking and practice so that control-and-punishment thinking is replaced by caring and connecting, as well as appreciating that honouring what youth say and contribute does not mean setting no limits (Siegel, 2013). As one builds credibility with the youth through making a connection, youth can be gently pushed to reflect (having assessed their capacity) on their behaviours and choices. However, respect is maintained as the youth are not judged, youth continue to be met where they are at, and they remain experts in their own lives. It is not *doing to* or *doing for* the youth. It is not, "Come, I'll change things for you"; it is, "Come, I believe in you, you have something to offer, you can change things yourself" (Ungar, 2004, p. 270).

Once practicing within a harm reduction philosophy, it would be a significant challenge to return to traditional practices. There are so many positive aspects of the harm reduction approach, including that it is on a continuum, reflecting how all youth are unique and require individualized attention, support, and services. This improves practice, making workers more reflective and thoughtful. It challenges workers to be creative rather than relying on formula responses (problem 'A' identified, so routinely implementing solution 'A' regardless of the unique circumstances and characteristics of individual). This approach also invites feedback and discussion with the youth and the support team, as everyone has a stake in the life of the youth, meaning harm reduction strategies are anti-oppressive.

To end on a 'corny' note, Maté (2008) quotes Dr. Bruce Perry:

> We really need . . . and I know it sounds kind of corny . . . we need be very loving, very accepting, and very patient with people who have these problems. And if we are, they will have a much higher probability of getting better.
>
> (p. 309)

A harm reduction approach to working with high-risk youth allows this to happen.

Discussion scenarios to consider for Chapter 4

There are no right or wrong answers to these four scenarios, but readers are encouraged to view these through a harm reduction lens.

Scenario #1

A youth, age 15, is absent from her group home but agrees to meet you at a coffee shop. She tells you she is staying with her boyfriend and his family. There is no child welfare involvement with his family, but you have concerns that he is verbally, if not physically, abusive. She agrees to return to the group home but not until after the weekend, as she is turning 16 on Saturday. You ask if she will be drinking and she responds by saying, "It's my birthday, what do you think?"

- What is your next step?

Scenario #2

A 15-year-old male youth drops by your outreach agency. You are glad to see him because for the last two weeks it seemed like he had fallen of the face of the earth. You comment that he looks tired and rough, though he is well dressed – overly so from his usual appearance. As you probe a bit more he becomes agitated. You have established some credibility in the eyes of this youth over the past year or so; you push a little harder as you sense something is wrong. Finally, he tells you he wants to change as his life is going to shit. He states that the cops are looking for him as he has a number of warrants and they want to question him about an assault he witnessed. He has thought about turning himself in but he does not want to go back to the young offenders centre. He is shaking at this point and shares that he has a drug debt to a guy who has gang friends. He also discloses he has been stealing cough and cold medicine to sell so he can pay back his debt. His problems are complicated further by the fact he has started using crystal meth again. You suspect his backpack is stuffed with cough and cold, and he doesn't deny it. He feels like he is fucked now, having to choose between jail (where he may be threatened), being beaten up or stabbed on the street, or risking more charges selling stolen medicine. He asks if you can get him back into a shelter bed.

- You decide to . . .

Scenario #3

A 17-year-old female calls you requesting a meeting, as she hasn't eaten all day and she has no place to stay. You meet close to 8:00 p.m. and you call emergency child protections services, but you are told there are no beds available. The after-hours worker sounds frustrated, as beds have been found for this youth before, though she rarely uses them. There has been a lot of suspicion that this youth has been sexually exploited and that her boyfriend is her pimp. After you both have had some supper, she becomes angry that she has no place to go. She is resigned to going back to her boyfriend's apartment. She starts crying and tells you her boyfriend will be pissed at her if she doesn't return with some money. She reveals that she does not want to be around him as he is an asshole, but then she sounds resigned, adding that at least she can sleep, shower, and eat when at his place. She asks to be dropped off at a run-down motel before she returns to her boyfriend's place, but will not disclose who she is meeting there.

- What do you do next?

Scenario #4

You have your work cell phone on as you have an arrangement with a pregnant youth on your caseload that she can call if she goes into labour. The phone rings at 3:30 a.m. and you quickly answer it. However, instead of this being the pregnant youth, it is a 14-year-old girl who is on your caseload. She is calling from a pay phone and is crying and lost. She left a party because a boy was trying to get her to have sex. You are able to identify what part of the city she is calling from. She wants you to pick her up as she is scared. You establish that she has been smoking weed and drinking. While she is a little inebriated she tells you she is feeling extremely tired. She starts to escalate and goes between pleading for help and demanding help. You suggest you could get her help through emergency child protection services and/or the police. Emphatically, she tells you she will run from the pay phone and hide. She again says she wants you to pick her up, as you are the only person she can trust.

- The next thing you say is . . .

Notes

1 From the book, *In the Realm of Hungry Ghosts: Close Encounters with Addiction* (2008, p. 318).
2 Insite, open since 2003, is part of Vancouver's notorious downtown eastside. The safe drug injection clinic became known across Canada for resisting the efforts of the federal conservative government to close access to people struggling with addictions to shoot up (use needles)

in a safe, controlled, and monitored environment. As anticipated, the service did reduce the number of deaths from overdosing and poor hygiene. Despite the research evidence the case went to the Supreme Court of Canada and, on September 29, 2011, North America's lone supervised needle injection site won a constitutional reprieve and was allowed to stay open with an exemption under federal drug law. The country's top court blasted the Conservative government for its 'arbitrary' and moralistic approach. In a decision that sharply pitted the court's view of a coherent drug strategy against that of the Conservative government, the Supreme Court of Canada ruled 9–0 that the health minister cannot deny a legal protection to addicts and clinical health workers who would otherwise be penalized by federal drug laws. The court acknowledged the overwhelming evidence that medical supervision of injections curbs infections and saves lives. (Tonda McCharles, the star.com, October 1, 2011).

3 In the early days, the High Risk Youth Initiative adopted a harm reduction approach for youth over age 14, believing we faced ethical challenges working within this philosophy if the youth were not developmentally at a point of understanding harm reduction concepts. As time went on, however, we learned it is all about the relationship rather than the underlying theoretical construct of what harm reduction means. While many people were alarmed enough that we were practicing a harm reduction philosophy with teenagers, we ended up getting rid of the age range because our agency partners were seeing more and more 11–13-year olds on the street and they were very difficult to engage in traditional ways. The harm reduction approach made sense given the needs of the youth, forcing us to further discuss the ethical implications and shift our thinking.

4 This definition and the principles of 'harm reduction' are adopted by the High Risk Youth Initiative in relation to discussing different intervention strategies in working with high-risk youth. This definition is adapted from: Elovich, R. and Cowing, M. (1993). *Recovery Readiness: Strategies That Bring Treatment to Addicts Where They Are*. National Harm Reduction Working Group Report from the October 21–23, 1993, Meeting.

5 While the *Stages of Change* was developed to help professionals better understand people with alcohol and drug addictions and to help motivate them to change, it has been used in many other areas, including smoking cessation, weight loss, and, in this case, a variety of high-risk behaviours. The following is adapted from Mark Gold from psychcentral.com (2006): About 25 years ago, two well-known alcoholism researchers, Carlo C. DiClemente and J. O. Prochaska, introduced a five-stage model of change. Their model is based not on abstract theories but on their personal observations of how people went about modifying problem behaviours. *Precontemplation:* Individuals in the precontemplation stage of change are not even thinking about changing their behaviour. They may not see it as a problem, or they think that others who point out the problem are exaggerating. *Contemplation:* Individuals in this stage of change are willing to consider the possibility that they have a problem and the possibility offers hope for change. However, people who are contemplating change are often highly ambivalent. They are on the fence. Contemplation is not a commitment, not a decision to change. But even with all these negatives, they still cannot make a decision to change. In the contemplation stage, often with the help of a treatment professional, people make a risk-reward analysis. They consider the pros and cons of their behaviour and the pros and cons of change. They think about the previous attempts they have made to stop their challenging behaviours and what has caused failure in the past. *Determination – Commitment to Action:* Deciding to stop the negative behaviour is the hallmark of this stage of change. All the weighing of pros and cons, all the risk-reward analysis, finally tips the balance in favour of change. Not all ambivalence has been resolved, but ambivalence no longer represents an insurmountable barrier to change. Most individuals in this stage will make a serious attempt to change their behaviour in the near future. Individuals in this stage appear to be ready and committed to action. *Action – Implementing the Plan:* Individuals in this stage of change put their plan into action. This stage typically involves making some form of public commitment to change in order to get external confirmation of the plan. If they have not done so already, individuals in this stage may enter counselling or some form of outpatient treatment. Making such public commitments not only helps people obtain the supports they need to recover, but it creates external monitors. People often find it very helpful to know that others are watching and cheering them on. *Maintenance, Relapse and Recycling:*

The action stage normally takes three to six months to complete. Change requires building a new pattern of behaviour over time. The real test of change is long-term sustained change over many years. This stage of successful change is called 'maintenance.'

6 Narrative therapy is the "pioneering and seminal" work of Michael White and David Epson (*Narrative Means to a Therapeutic End (1990)*). It offers important contributions to the person's understanding of how the problems they face relates to forces in society, as well as their own heritage. It helps the person(s) link their lives to the past and to their desired futures. It neither promotes nor emphasizes work with any particular unit, but uses support available to provide the person with room to re-author their lives (Abels & Abels, 2001). Hartman, Little and Ungar (2008) moved away from youth care practices that were not in line with social justice aims or with its goal of helping youth move closer toward their goals. They used narrative approaches partly because they came to understand, through traditional practices, that the more youth come to accept negative descriptions of themselves, the more likely they are to act in ways that affirm the negative stories others tell about them. They found that staff could contribute to the creation of alternative (less problem-saturated) stories of identity for youth, that staff can balance the need for safety and routine with the nurturing of healthy identity stories (narratives that define how youth see themselves), and that aspects of day-to-day practice can integrate much of the theory of narrative practice in a variety of youth care settings, other than office-based counselling. . . . "Narrative practices focus on centering the client in the process of their healing, something that requires significant respect for a client's perspective and appears to result in effective relationship building" (Hartman, Little & Ungar, 2008, pp. 45–47). Little, Hartman and Ungar (2007) outline the following narrative-based ideas: truth is negotiable; people are not their problems (Michael White points out that "the person is not the problem, the problem is the problem"); from unique outcomes come new stories; and we need a powerful audience to help turn the volume up on the new stories we want to tell about ourselves. "Those labels we assign youth are nothing but stories we tell. Like all stories they can be changed when people start to tell different stories. With the right supports and opportunities, a youth can re-author a problem story, replacing it with a story that details strength and resilience" (p. 38). Ungar (2004, p. 30) writes that "when treatment is effective, it can nurture for high-risk youth what Michael White called an 'emancipatory narrative.' White's work is overtly political, in that it seeks to add power to the silenced voices of those who are marginalized by allowing them to interpret their experiences in ways that give their stories power" (p. 30).

7 This percentage range is an estimate. While a number of youth involved with the HRYI are diagnosed with Fetal Alcohol Spectrum Disorder (FASD), others are suspected given their histories and behaviours. Medical personnel have been reluctant to give such a diagnosis as the mother could not be located or denies drinking at the time of pregnancy despite accounts of others. However, requiring the mother to definitely confirm drinking when pregnant (which understandably would be hard given the shame, guilt, and embarrassment) is becoming less and less required for a diagnosis of FASD and testing becomes more sophisticated. FASD is a term that describes a range of disabilities that may affect people whose mothers drank alcohol while they were pregnant. The diagnoses of FASD are: Fetal Alcohol Syndrome (FAS), partial Fetal Alcohol Syndrome (pFAS), alcohol-related neurodevelopmental disorder (ARND), and alcohol-related birth defects (ARBD). FASD affects approximately 1% of people living in Canada (Public Health Agency of Canada, 2005).

8 Short-term restricted placements exist, such as child and youth psychiatric wards, with the rare child or youth who may be court-ordered to stay on a long-term basis due to a severe mental health problem that they cannot be safe in public. However, in Alberta, at least, outside of the criminal system, there are no placements that youth can be locked in simply for behaviour challenges.

Chapter 5

Building from strengths and promoting resiliency

It is easier to build strong children than to repair broken men.

Frederick Douglass[1]

Clifford Lammeren is a 63-year-old man who continues to wrestle demons from his childhood. Featured on the front page of the *Edmonton Journal* (2009),[2] he is healing by dedicating his life to helping others as a volunteer artist with special needs students. When Clifford was a child his mother took him away from his father and siblings and put him in a foster home, where he was abused and bullied. When re-united with his mother, he watched her get savagely beaten by his step-father, who also turned on him when he intervened. Clifford described his living conditions as "third world," with his home being a cellar with rats. There was no running water; he had no clothes and no food. When later placed in a group home, he was further abused but felt he had no one to tell. At age 11, he could not read or write. By the time he reached his teens, Clifford was seeking refuge in alcohol, was angry, and was "pretty messed up." He was homeless at times. Clifford said he eventually cried out for help by repeatedly attempting suicide through drug overdoses and slashing his wrists. He did receive help, allowing him to start coping with his pain. He has been 'paying it forward' since then and has received awards for his dedication to his career as a truck driver and as a community volunteer.

Why did Clifford not give up and lose his sense of compassion and his ability to empathize? After being let down and abused by so many people, how was he able to see good in others? Given the way he started out, he would have the right to be angry at the world. He could have given up – as he almost did – on believing anybody would care enough about him to help. Clifford calls his suicide attempts a cry for help, so a part of him must have had hope that someone would come and help him. He must have received enough help that he felt a need to dedicate his life to giving back. Perhaps just as easily he could have died from an overdose, be living on the street, or ended up in jail. Rather he is recognized for his volunteer work and states that: "I love people and I love giving back. The accolades are nice, but what I do is not about accolades. It's part of my own healing." He must be very resilient.

Creating resilience through strengths-based approaches

The traditional definition of 'resilience' speaks of someone who has overcome adversity in their life (see Box 5.1). It is a person who, despite great odds, has risen above their challenges and persevered.

Box 5.1 Definition of *resilience*

The individual's capacity for adapting successfully and continuing to function competently under stress and adversity.
David Howe from his book, *Child Abuse and Neglect* (2005)

An individual's competence and successful adaption following exposure to significant adversity and stressful life events.
Psychologist Terry Levy and therapist Michael Orlans from their book, *Attachment Trauma and Healing* (1998)

Sybil and Stephen Wolin, co-authors of *The Resilient Self: How Survivors of Troubled Families Rise Above Adversity* (1993), tell us on their 'Project Resilience' website that attempts to describe the qualities of resilient individuals have pointed to specific skills, behaviours, or competencies that are internal to them as well as to factors such as caring adults, high expectations, and opportunities that are external. Resiliency develops as both the internal and external interact. Caring relationships, for instance, can trigger a positive cycle in which youth gain a sense of connection and confidence, which increases their motivation to try, which attracts more positive attention from adults, and so on. Despite the interaction of internal and external factors, Wolin and Wolin focus on specific behaviours or resiliencies that youth use to help themselves in times of trouble. Since behaviours can be taught, modelled, and learned, by defining them, they aim to take the mystery out of resilience and provide concrete guidelines that youth can use as they struggle with the hardships in their lives. As Wolin and Wolin (1999) advise:

> The most important part of a strength-based approach is believing that youth in trouble actually have strengths and can act on them. Sometimes holding on to this belief is difficult. If you are a clinician, teacher, or prevention specialist you can help yourself by learning about the behaviours that youth use to pull themselves through trouble. You can acknowledge those behaviours when you see them, and you can try to instil them when you don't.

('Project Resilience' website)

Wolin and Wolin (1999) have used the word 'resiliencies' to describe clusters of strengths that are mobilized in the struggle with hardship. Their *vocabulary of strengths* includes seven resiliencies: *Insight*, asking tough questions and giving honest answers; *Independence*, distancing emotionally and physically from the sources of trouble in one's life; *Relationships*, making fulfilling connections to other people; *Initiative*, taking charge of problems; *Creativity*, using imagination and expressing oneself in art forms; *Humour*, finding the comic in the tragic; and *Morality*, acting on the basis of an informed conscience. These may be easier said than done for our population of high-risk youth. Much patience is required to get to the point of building these strengths and determining the youth's capacity to negotiate some of these resiliencies.

However, using humour and allowing youth to express themselves in art forms have shown to be particularly popular and helpful in engaging high-risk youth and prompting them to tell stories about themselves. Many outreach agencies in Edmonton, Alberta use various art forms and typically have art supplies on hand. There are also recording studios, instruments, painting studios, materials for various crafts, and more. The aim is not only to help youth keep busy and make connections to help keep them safe, but such activities allow the youth to demonstrate their talents, feel empowered, express themselves in a healthy and therapeutic way, build relationships, expand their resources, and demonstrate how resilient they can be. One group used arts and crafts and forum theatre to not only have high-risk youth create skits dramatizing challenges they have had in their lives as a therapeutic tool, but also to teach people who work with youth, or have contact with youth, how to be more effective and better able to relate to all youth.

Dr. Wayne Hammond from Resiliency Canada and Dr. Simon Nuttgens from Athabasca University (2007) discuss the need for a paradigm shift from *risk* to *resiliency*; from a deficit-focused or problem-saturated model to a strength-based approach. In short, strength-based practices promote resiliency in youth. Dr. Michael Ungar, who studies resiliency in cultures from around the globe (2006), notes that many of the strength-based interventions now being used around the world demonstrate that we can help youth in ways that they will embrace. He adds that if we make judgements, override their choices by stepping in with the message that we know best, or try to save them, we risk undermining their belief that they can make decisions and damaging their self-esteem. And in all likelihood they will do what they want anyway. In his earlier experiences, Ungar (2002) writes, "I know of nobody who listens really well to people who are critical of their every move" (p. 66). Indeed, we know high-risk youth tune out when they are not heard or are feeling controlled, often resulting in them pushing away. They miss the point that deficit approaches are a misguided attempt to help and instead interpret them as rejecting, reminding them of previous interventions that did not help or made things worse. Our youth frequently tell us their stories of how therapists, case workers, or service providers "just told me what to do," "didn't listen to what I had to say," "were on my parents' side," and "didn't know what they were talking about." The bottom line is that without the use of strength-based practices, such as harm reduction approaches, high-risk youth are not likely to engage, nor will it help them become more resilient.

Hammond and Nuttgens (2007) and Saleebey (1996) state that the helping community has been preoccupied with the deficit, or at-risk, paradigm for understanding and serving children and youth who are in trouble. This is reflected in the medical model or deficit language embedded in policies and programs, leaving the perception that bureaucracies and other organizations are "often diametrically opposed to a strengths-orientation. . . . Pursuing a practice based on the ideas of resilience, rebound, possibility, and transformation is difficult, because, oddly enough, it is not natural to the world of helping and service" (Saleebey, 1996, p. 297). In education youth are often labelled *disruptive*, resulting in punishment (reprimanded, suspended, expelled), while in social work or child protection they may be called *dysfunctional* and in corrections youth are *delinquent*. Behaviourists may describe youth as *disordered* (requiring assessment, behaviour modification, and time out), while in medicine they are *diseased* (diagnosed, drugged, or hospitalized). Psychopathologists may say they are *disturbed*, requiring testing, treatment, and restraint, especially when uncooperative (Hammond & Nuttgens, 2007). Ungar (2004, 2006) tells us that helping professionals, lay service providers, families, caregivers, and communities can impede healthy development in children and youth when participating in the construction of problem-saturated identities. Youth who receive the most attention are labelled by those who have the power to do so as *dangerous, delinquent, deviant*, and/or *disordered* (4Ds). These labels stick to the youth, limiting their options on the one hand, but providing a perfect script for how to act out his or her vulnerability on the other. Ungar (2006) adds that youth all over the world who are convinced they are one or more of these '4Ds' will "play each role for all its worth" (p. 11). When options are few, adolescents make do with what they have. Whether being called the '4Ds' or being labelled as 'manipulative,' 'defiant,' 'conduct disordered,' 'oppositional,' 'depressed,' 'FASD,' 'promiscuous,' or 'high risk,' through these labels and problem-saturated language, youth create their identities and these become challenging to shift over time. Ungar (2004) explains:

> High-risk youth challenge these identities by arguing, ironically, for recognition of the health-enhancing aspects of deviant behaviours such as drug and alcohol use, early sexual activity, time spent living on the street, negative peer associations, truancy, and custodial dispositions. These potentially self-destructive pathways to tenuous but healthy identities can bring with them, youth tell us, a sense of meaning, purpose, opportunities for participation in social action, a sense of belonging and attachment, recreation, financial stability, personal and social power, social support, and even basic necessities like food and shelter. Mental health outcomes are closely linked to the control high-risk youth exert of labels that define their health status, a control largely denied them in mental health discourse of institutional and outpatient settings, their communities, and their families. . . . For many children, patterns of deviance are healthy adaptions that permit them to survive unhealthy circumstances. The implications of this understanding of resilience among dangerous, deviant, delinquent, and disordered youth has the potential to dramatically change how caregivers and service providers respond to them.
>
> (p. 6)

We can start to bring about change by being more thoughtful and intentional about our language, as the words we use create or construct our reality and that of our youth. If we use the language of problems, weakness, failure, and shame, it shapes how we may see our youth, how others see the youth, and how youth see themselves, having internalized these labels that then become part of their identity (Gaughan & Kalyniak, 2012; Saleebey, 1997; Ungar, 2004). If, in addition, we deny youth resources and opportunities to allow them to express themselves in positive ways, we should not be surprised when they use these negative labels to express themselves in ways we, and society, see as destructive to themselves, their families, and their communities. This is still a search for health and identity but only through the narrow parameters that we allow. Further, as bureaucratic professionals we have a tendency to see youth as cases, fitting them into predetermined categories and formulaic solutions. We see youth *as* the problem rather than separating them from their problems, thereby allowing them to gain some power and control over their life experiences. Not surprisingly, the lack of warmth and connection is not lost on the youth and their resistance brings further labels. By not seeing the youth as a unique individual, thus objectifying them, we miss important elements of the youth's life, including their cultural, social, political, ethnic, and spiritual aspects (Graybeal, 2001; Saleebey, 1997). As a result, we then act as an oppressor toward the youth, acting as an authority and demanding change, typically resulting in the youth seeing their support team as irrelevant.

Having people around who identify strengths in youth, who use appropriate and health-enhancing language, and who develop relationships contribute to building protective factors for youth that help to them become resilient and stay resilient. There are *internal protective factors* that come from within each of us to help promote resilience, including giving of oneself to others (showing empathy); using life skills such as making good decisions, assertiveness, impulse control, and problem-solving; sociability and the ability to form positive relationships; a sense of humour; self-motivation; flexibility; internal locus of control; autonomy; a good sense of self-worth; a positive view of the future; a capacity for and connection to learning; and a sense of personal competence. There are also *external protective factors* that can come from families, schools, churches, and the community that allow for the development of healthy and supportive relationships that are warm and positive. Such supports contribute to setting and enforcing clear boundaries, sharing responsibilities and promoting service to others, having high but realistic expectations, appreciating and affirming the unique talents of the person, expanding networks of support, providing access to resources to meet basic and emotional needs, and encouraging pro-social development (Hammond & Nuttgens, 2007).

The literature suggests that these internal and external factors are both required to overcome adversity, as resiliency doesn't simply come from within. However, I know from our high-risk youth that if they experience early adversity and broken relationships and do not have external protective factors, they typically do not develop the internal protective factors. They may develop coping mechanisms such as avoiding attachments, dissociation, or being aggressive to avoid further physical and emotional pain, but these, while serving a purpose at the time, become harmful over time and shut out potentially helpful future external protective factors. In short, it is the resources a person has within their environment that help build the internal resources that is key to being resilient (Ungar, 2004, 2013a, 2013b). Secure children have a growing ability to make sense of themselves and others as psychological beings, which gives them a high level of resilience. The child begins to appreciate that other people have minds, like that of the child, that are full of thoughts, feelings, beliefs, and intentions. Affect regulation, empathy, and relationship competence become increasingly difficult when the child does not have the ability to understand their own and other people's mental states (Howe, 2005). These children and youth, therefore, tend to have fewer protective factors to rely on and fewer resources to help their life circumstances change in a meaningful way.

Even when we can identify strengths within our high-risk youth, they themselves may have great difficulty identifying them given they typically carry with them a profound sense of failure and shame. We can tell our youth that they possess certain strengths but they are not likely to believe it unless we have established some level of credibility in their eyes. Therefore, we can build up their external protective factors by being a significant person in their life and by connecting them with other healthy adults and resources. Over time, when relationships have been established, they can perhaps come to see that they do indeed have some strengths or "hidden resilience" in that their behaviours that are misunderstood as maladaptive coping strategies are actually "sensible solutions in dangerous, emotionally toxic social ecologies" (Ungar, 2015, p. 5).

Studies of resiliency have consistently found that the most basic and important protective factor is the history of caregiver-child attachment. However, in absence of this, a secure attachment to secondary caregivers – including mentors, case workers, service providers, and outreach workers – can help a child overcome adversity (Levy & Orlans, 1998). Levy and Orlans (1998) also cite a 40-year longitudinal resiliency study of vulnerable children by Emmy Werner.[3] One third of children who experienced perinatal stress, poverty, parental alcoholism and emotional problems, and family disruption developed into caring and competent adults. Three types of protective factors were identified: 1) disposition attributes, such as sociability, intelligence, communication skills, and confidence; 2) affectional ties within the family that provided emotional support in times of stress; and 3) external support systems (school, church, community) that provided validation support and a positive belief system by which to live. Again, I would argue, given research in the area of attachment and brain development, that the first protective factor would be dependent on the following two, which points to environmental factors being crucial.

In the resilience and mentorship literature, over and above anything else, an attachment, or connection, with at least one key person in the life of a child and youth can be transformational, especially if the child or youth does not have that critical bond with a parent or caregiver. This could be a teacher, a coach, a distant relative, a neighbour, or someone just to show that child or youth they are worth something. As important as it is to have such informal supports who are not paid to spend time with child or youth, and who can be there for an indefinite period of time, some do not get this experience, possibly because their behaviours and interactions may be too challenging and they do a good job of keeping people at a distance. We as case workers and service providers need to get past thinking that, at least while helping them learn to make connections with healthy adults, we are not that person; that this is not our role, as I have heard case workers state. Many case workers and service providers got into the field to work with and help others, so it is always disturbing to hear of workers abdicating this part of their role. We *can* be that key connection that opens doors to youth to make further connections. We *can* model these behaviours and give youth a good experience with a healthy adult, as this *is* our job.

Howe (2005) tells us that experiences of sensitive, mind-engaging, and secure attachments promote resilience. Fosha (2003) goes further, stating, "a caregiver who possesses a high reflective self-function, can enhance the resilience of an individual.

Through just one relationship with an understanding other, trauma can be transformed and its effects neutralized or counteracted" (p. 223). Likewise, Maté (2008) reinforces that a child or youth needs to be in an attachment relationship with at least one reliably available, protective, psychologically present, and reasonably non-stressed adult, while Perry and Szalavitz (2006) report that traumatized children who have made progress have had contact with at least one supportive adult. Optimistically Boyd Webb (2006) writes that, "a single positive relationship can deter a life trajectory that appeared to be headed for tragedy" (p. 20). Anderson and Seita (2006) expand on the theme, adding that other factors that may contribute to a youth's resilience include a safe haven in the community. In short, our youth need someone who will connect to them, believe in them, not give up on them, provide them with fair and high expectations, and support them as they seek to find a purpose in life. As we have been able to demonstrate in the HRYI, this can be a case worker, or it can be a community service provider, and it needs to be at least until the work of incorporating informal supports into the network of the youth is done in collaboration with the youth.

Not without its critics

A criticism of strengths-based practice is that it simply reframes deficit and misery, suggesting that clients are not really expected "to do the work of transformation and risk action. Rather they are required to reconceptualise their difficulties so that they are sanitized and less threatening to themselves and others" (p. 302). However, Hammond (2010) and Saleebey (1996) argue that there is never an intent to deny reality. While is does require some reframing to create an attitude of possibility and opportunity, and to help the person to emerge from their labels, strengths-based work involves creating access to resources, allowing clients choices, and assisting with change. The strengths approach has also been called 'Pollyannaish' and therefore ignores the dangers of how manipulative, destructive, and dangerous certain clients can be. It also ignores that some people are simply beyond redemption. However, these issues are addressed in assessing the situation. Determining the motivation and aspirations of clients is an ongoing process, as there are always ups and downs, and feelings of hope and hopelessness. Service providers must avoid making assumptions and cannot ethically write people off as being beyond hope, as this may deter them from collaborating with clients and finding ways to best meet their needs. If one believes a person is beyond redemption it probably will not be hard to find evidence to support this, particularly when coming from a problem-focused perspective.

Graybeal (2001) and Hammond (2010) refute the serious criticism that the strengths perspective ignores or downplays serious problems. Again, it is the role of the helpers to assess the troubles, difficulties, pains, and disorders, but the diagnosis should not become a "cornerstone of identity" (p. 303), as we often see in our high-risk youth through the child welfare system, schools, justice, addictions, and mental health system. Assisted by narrative approaches, helpers can assist in drawing out how clients have managed to survive up to this point in their lives and what they have drawn on in the face of their adversity. These times, or exceptions, when they have risen beyond their pain and hopelessness can be used to generate new stories about the person they are, so they are not defined by their problem (Hammond, 2010; Madsen, 2007; Ungar, 2004; White, 2007). In short, strength-based practice is not about denying that people do experience problems and challenges but rather it is about seeking future possibilities. It is about avoiding attaching these problems to the individual at the expense of tapping into their wisdom and self-knowledge to discover what Ungar (2002, 2004) refers to as the *hidden resilience* in youth. It is about helping youth interact with their environment in order to help them build their formal and informal support networks (Ungar, 2013a).

Further, Canavan (2008) cautions that overemphasizing resilience can cause us to overlook the consequences structural inequalities (socio-economic, gender, ethnicity, disability, and location-based), that we know our marginalized, street-involved, and high-risk youth face frequently. Within the HRYI we see how our youth are denied access to resources, whether medical care, education, shelter, or other basic needs. We have also seen the 'criminalization of homelessness' in which youth frequently are fined and banned by police even though no crimes are committed (Gaetz, 2004; Gaetz et al., 2013). Canavan (2008) points out that a possible response is to be more aware of the structural inequities in society and being more reflective in one's practice. This can help to ensure that "collective social responses stay on the practice agenda" (p. 5) and that that we do not only stay focused on individual interventions when there are wider implications of social inequalities and discrimination at play. According to Ungar (2004), these social structures represent most of the problems confronting youth, especially given their ever-increasing length of dependency and prolonged engagement in a process of becoming capably functioning adults, as well as being part of a society preoccupied with the notion that youth today have something wrong with them.

The Michael Ungar perspective of resilience and the High Risk Youth Initiative

> That our bias against youth persists says more about adult fears and vulnerabilities than about the experiences of youth themselves.
>
> Michael Ungar[4]

Helping the High Risk Youth Initiative practice framework and philosophy evolve over the years has been the resilience perspective of Dr. Michael Ungar, a professor at the School of Social Work and co-director of the Resilience Research Centre at Dalhousie University in Halifax, Nova Scotia, Canada. His discussion of the resiliency of high-risk youth (or his preferred wording of *young people with complex needs*) helps make sense of how our youth, despite their many challenges and barriers in life, "are all waking up every morning committed to surviving" (Ungar, 2005, p. 2). We see on a daily basis how resilient our high-risk youth are, despite the fact they are in trouble with the law, they are homeless, they have dropped out of school, and they are using drugs and alcohol. We see how they cope the best they can with the little they have. Though mainstream society may not see how using drugs is a sign of resilience, it might be that this is their way of coping with traumatic memories, blunting the potential to lash out against others or themselves. Not ideal, but in a world in which they are often marginalized and judged, and in a world in which they have so few resources, this may be their way of coping and surviving. The average youth has an abundance of resources to draw on from those who provide material and emotional support, including family, extended family, friends, teachers, coaches, and mentors. Despite such a lack of positive and healthy resources, resilience is equally present in young people labelled as dangerous, delinquent, deviant, and/or disordered. Ungar (2005) continues:

> Resilient youth take advantage of whatever opportunities and resources that are available – even those we consider negative and destructive. That negative behaviour shown in troubled young people can actually signal a pathway to hidden resilience that is, just like the one chosen by their well-behaved peers, simply focused on the need to create powerful and influential identities for themselves.
>
> (p. 1)

Ungar argues that for many youth the ability to demonstrate resilience in positive ways is a reflection of the capacity of their homes, schools, and communities to provide them with the resources they need to be healthy adults (Ungar, 2005). Yet we know that high-risk youth in the traditional child welfare system continue to be estranged from the very system that should be helping them, quite possibly because programs are designed without input from the youth, given programs tend to be set up to meet the needs of the system rather than the youth being served, and because the punishment-consequence model is still so prevalent. In his work with youth, Ungar shares that it can become clear that the youth may have a better plan than any he can offer them. This poses a challenge in that we "have to stop looking at the individual child and think about what needs changing structurally in our society so that kids don't need to become delinquents or deviants to find ways to express themselves as non-conformists" (Ungar, 2002, p. 220). Problem behaviours are still a search for health; we just need to recognize this as such and build off these strengths – build on their *hidden resilience*. While a youth's pattern of coping is thought by others to be unacceptable, he/she may see their coping as effective, given their limited access to resources and the environment in which they find themselves situated. One's person view of coping may be seen as harmful, while to another it is a protective factor (see Box 5.2).

Box 5.2 Monica's story: looking past the crime

'Monica' came to Edmonton from a northern city in Alberta, Canada, at the age of 14. While I'm not quite sure how a youth can be banned from a city, this is certainly her understanding of why she was sent south to live. Monica had been arrested for dealing drugs, though she was quite pleased with herself that she got away with it for so long. At such a young age, Monica was able to get drugs to sell, compete with other dealers for customers, pay rent, pay her bills, and get groceries. Thankfully, she was arrested before she got harmed. She had no parent who could take her and no extended family who were able to look after her. Monica was sent out of her city, although she avoided having to spend time in custody. I was the courtesy worker while her case worker was from her home community.

The first time I meet Monica, she is with me and another youth who has an open file with the High Risk Youth Initiative and is now Monica's friend. We are going to a medical appointment for the other youth. They stay at the same place, though Monica is not there by choice but due to a probation order. Monica tells me she thinks social workers are a "fucking waste of time and they have never helped me anyway." She states that she liked one worker in the past but, as usual, this person didn't stick around. She wants her independence and doesn't need a "loser social worker" telling her what to do. I tell her I have heard stories of workers coming and going before and that it is unfortunate that she can't get the help she needs. I see her a few days later and ask how she is doing. She tells me her case worker up north is a "bitch" and doesn't want to talk to her. Staff at the shelter say Monica is cranky at times but has been doing well keeping curfew, not using drugs, and helping around the home. I focus on these positive aspects, suggesting she could be getting closer to a supported independent living placement. She doubts this would happen and again generalizes about case workers being quite useless and not following through on what they say. She tells me that once she turns 18 she is "out of here," so I congratulate her on her goal and ask how I can help her achieve it. Later she tells me she needs some clothes so I tell her I can call her worker and discuss it. Having been able to facilitate this, she is curious as to why I would help her when I'm not her case worker. Monica agrees to meet for coffee so I can learn more about her situation and we can look at options around her moving into an independent living program. She acts tough and swears a lot. She is honest, tries to get a reaction from some of her stories, and agrees she has a very difficult time trusting anybody, adding, "Why should I?" I agree and tell her people need to earn trust from her, but there is no rush. I ask for time so we can get to know each other better. I encourage her to try and work with 'the system,' as she is under permanent status with the government and won't be going anywhere for a while. Surprisingly, she starts thanking me for the opportunity to share what was on her mind.

Monica starts initiating calls with ideas about how she can get support. I think about how resilient she has been in her life, without a consistent caregiver, and about the amazing skills she has to negotiate her way around her community and survive. She has many skills that can be put to very good use, though in a legal, non-destructive way. I trust her ability to know what she can manage in being independent, although her having to be independent at her age makes me sad. From her earlier experiences, I appreciate that Monica can read people, will not be taken advantage of so easily, and can stay safer than most youth her age. She also understands and appreciates that I can give her access to resources that she cannot access alone. However, Monica does not want the system to control her, which makes sense. Fortunately, she has proven she can survive on her own.

Given that Ungar (2006) sees problem behaviours as a search for health, he believes we must "substitute rather than suppress" (p. 7). Youth need alternate choices to their dangerous, delinquent, deviant, and/or disordered behaviours, but these alternatives must offer the same or a better quality of experience than the young person achieved through the problem behaviour. Bullying, substance abuse, promiscuity, non-compliance with court orders, or refusing to attend school can be attractive to our high-risk youth because it can satisfy the need for power, recreation, acceptance, or a sense of meaningful participation in the community. We need to understand the good things that youth derive from 'being bad' because otherwise we will inevitably fall short of offering alternatives that draw youth to take advantage of new opportunities (Ungar, 2006). By helping teens substitute one identity for another, we can help youth be drawn into new positive behaviours. By offering them practical ways to experience themselves in different but powerful identities, creating opportunities for those who know the youth (in a negative way perhaps) to experience them through a new identity that demonstrates their attributes, and by becoming the ally rather than the enemy, we can be the people who the youth are drawn towards as able to offer powerful and socially acceptable identity substitutes (Ungar, 2006).

Our challenge working with high-risk youth can be finding socially acceptable substitutes that can also give them an identity at least equal to that which they derive from their "unconventional and destructive sources of strength" (Ungar, 2006, p. 8). How do we substitute for the acceptance and sense of belonging that a youth finds in his or her street family? How do we convince a youth that working at a fast-food place for $40 a shift is better than selling his or her body and making $500? How do we help a youth to see a counsellor to discuss their trauma rather than using alcohol or drugs to numb out and escape with almost immediate effect? Again, knowing the youth well through relationship helps, as it is key to find what might work for that unique youth.

I have worked with youth who have demonstrated leadership skills on the street but were using it to engage others in criminal activity for their own benefit. Over time, with much patience and the help of an outreach agency, I have seen some youth adopt a substitution for their negative behaviour and use their leadership skills to mentor youth and help get them off the streets. Others have been able to get positive feedback on their artistic talents and have earned money through selling their art. I have seen youth substitute their street smarts for academic smarts, once they have experienced some success and no longer assume they are going to fail. More than anything, I believe that relationship can be a substitute for many negative behaviours and can facilitate a shift to a more socially appropriate identity. A youth seen as the "psycho drunk" among friends also experiencing addictions, eventually became "the good mom" and "the smart student." The "brawler" shifted to become "the rapper," recording his own CDs. There was the "quiet meth head" who is now "the social worker." However, if we miss the hidden resilience of these youth, we are more likely to contribute to the negative labelling and we will not provide the opportunity to even see that their lives can be different.

Indeed, youth are searching for healthy identities. I have heard from youth frequently that they do not like negative, or perceived anti-social, identities, but this is what they know; it has become their comfort zone. If we continue to block any hope of trading them conventional but powerful opportunities to show themselves as healthy and in control of their lives (Ungar, 2006), we are only left with punishing them in an effort to have them conform. Yet, we know that does not work for this population (or arguably any population). As long as we continue to kick them out of school, marginalize them from mainstream society, and reinforce their sense of failure and shame, we can expect them to be shut out of opportunities to form healthy identities and make connections with healthy adults.

Box 5.3   An ecological definition of resilience

In the context of exposure to significant adversity, resilience is both the capacity of individuals to navigate *their way to the psychological, social, cultural, and physical resources that sustain their wellbeing, and the capacity individually and collectively to* negotiate *for these resources to be provided and experienced in culturally meaningful ways.*

Michael Ungar (2011, p. 10)

In more recent writings, Dr. Michael Ungar describes in depth his ecological perspective on resilience (see Box 5.3), helping further to better understand our high-risk youth and to be better able to understand their perspective of their own situation, interact with them more effectively, and appreciate how building relationships with them can enhance their opportunities for the future. Rather than defining resilience as the individual's capacity to succeed under stress, Ungar (2013a) defines resilience as the capacity of *both* individuals and their environments to interact in ways that optimize developmental processes. In situations of adversity, resilience is observed when individuals engage in behaviours that help them to navigate their way to resources they need to flourish. It is the quality of the environment that is dependent on whether resilience can manifest as either pro-social behaviours or pathological adaption. Therefore, it is less than a reflection of the individual's capacity to overcome life challenges as it is the capacity of the child's social ecology (informal and formal social networks) to facilitate positive development under stress. The ecological perspective "purposefully decenters individuals to avoid blaming them for not flourishing when there are few opportunities to access resources" (Ungar, 2013a, p. 256). Ungar (2013a) adds:

> This social ecological understanding of resilience implicates those who control the resources that facilitate psychological well-being in the proximal process (e.g., making education accessible; promoting a sense of belonging in one's community; facilitating attachment to a caregiver; affirmation of self-worth) associated with positive development in the contexts of adversity.
>
> (p. 255)

And indeed, these are thoughts I have heard from high-risk youth – they feel estranged from the school system; they feel marginalized in their communities (both in the city, in their home communities if they have drifted into the city, and at times from their Bands or Settlements if First Nations or Metis); and that they do not fit into foster care or group care placements. Many youth see little value in being in the system, commenting that "I only hear from my worker if I fuck up." This speaks to how they are not benefiting from any relationship or from any services being offered. Such sentiments do not represent all high-risk youth, but certainly far too many youth, including those who are in the child welfare system but not identified as 'high risk,' and those who are struggling but do not have status with the government, for a variety of reasons.[5]

Within this system we are part of 'the environment' on which youth depend – or should be able to depend – to enable them to be resilient. In collaboration with community agencies, we can provide the needed resources that can help them overcome adversity, despite the fact this comes with challenges and we are dealing with negative forces that have damaged these high-risk youth, most often very early in life. Done in relationship, youth can change their life trajectory, as they will be more willing to engage with the resources they require. As Ungar (2013b) writes, "[E]ngaging and transformative youth-adult relationships exert the greatest impact on youth who are the most marginalized" (p. 328). It is the high-risk youth population who are the most marginalized! It is for this population that we must have the greatest impact.

Much of the literature focuses on 'at-risk' youth; those who are at risk of dropping out of school, those youth who have parents who are trying to get their children help, or those youth who are experimenting with drugs. I would argue that these youth, who may still be struggling and experiencing genuine emotional difficulties, have some level of access to resources whether through family, school, coaches, and/or a religious community. Outside resources are less likely to have as big an impact, as they will not be seen as a significant part of their lives as they create their identities and make decisions about their futures. High-risk youth often have nobody, as their parents may or may not be involved, and if so perhaps struggle to be emotionally available or be a resource for their son or daughter. They are often in conflict with their outside 'supports,' as they know their teacher is waiting to suspend them, their probation officer is waiting to breach them, or their case worker is waiting to take them to a placement where they do not want to be. These are the youth desperate for relationship. Therefore, by building relationships we can help our high-risk youth to better interact – better navigate and negotiate – with their environment and help create the opportunity to build their informal and formal social networks (Ungar, 2013a, 2015).

In addition, literature shows, according to Ungar (2013a), that changing the environment, rather than changing the individual, will better mitigate the effects of trauma.[6] The more the environment is able to make available and accessible the resources that promote wellbeing, the more likely youth are to engage in processes associated with positive development such as forming healthy attachments, improving self-esteem, engaging in expressions of personal agency, and finding or keeping meaningful employment (Ungar, 2013a).

Seven factors related to resilience

In a 2014 keynote presentation at a conference in Edmonton, Alberta,[7] Dr. Michael Ungar shared the *seven factors related to resilience:*[8] 1) Access to supportive relationships, including peers and adults within the family and the community; 2) Development of a desirable personal identity, which involves a personal and collective sense of purpose, self-awareness, aspirations, beliefs, and values, including spiritual and religious identification; 3) Experiences of power and control, involving experiences of caring for one's self and others and the ability to affect change in one's social and physical environment in order to access resources; 4) Experiences of social justice, related to finding a meaningful role in one's community that brings acceptance and equality; 5) Access to material resources (as discussed above); 6) Experiences of a sense of cohesion with others, including balancing one's personal interests with a sense of responsibility to the greater good and feeling part of something larger than one's self socially and spiritually; and 7) Adherence to cultural traditions.

Research findings across cultures showed that youth who experienced themselves as resilient, and are seen by their communities as resilient, are those who successfully navigated their way through these seven areas. Resilient youth find a way to resolve all seven factors simultaneously according to the strengths and resources available to youth individually, and within their family, community, and culture (Ungar, 2007a). In the absence of healthy families, communities, cultural knowledge, and access to resources among high-risk youth, it becomes important that case workers and community workers together help youth become aware of these factors as they build their resilience.

Twenty skills for a social ecological practice

At the same 2014 conference, Ungar also highlighted the importance of helping people navigate and negotiate through the counsellor-client (or worker-client) process in order to access resources and create resiliency within themselves.[9] By supporting our youth to navigate to resources, our youth can better identify the internal and external resources that are *available*, how *accessible* the resources are to the youth, and the *barriers* to changing the client experiences, as well as which resources are most likely to address which barriers; learn which resources their support team is familiar with and how they can benefit from *building bridges* to make new resources accessible and available; explore which resources are the most *meaningful* given the youth's context and culture; explore solutions that are as *complex* (multisystemic) as the problems they address; identify possible *allies* who can help access resources and put new ways of coping into practice; explore whether the solutions they are using to cope in challenging contexts are *adaptive or maladaptive*, and the consequences of the choices he or she makes; discuss the level of *motivation* to implement the new solution the youth prefers; and learn how to *advocate* for themselves to make resources available and accessible (Ungar, 2014, 2015).

The youth must also be empowered to negotiate, as otherwise the resources that are provided may go unused. Youth can be helped by ensuring they are heard and are involved in designing their own service plans (Ungar, 2013b). Helping youth negotiate allows them to explore their *thoughts and feelings* about the problem that resulted in intervention; look at the *context* in which problems occur, and the conditions that sustain them; discuss who has *responsibility* to change patterns of coping that are causing problems for the youth and/or others in the youth's life; have their *voice* be heard when he or she names the people and resources necessary to make a better life; when appropriate, learn about *new names* for a problem and explore what these new descriptions mean for approaching a solution to a problem; choose one or more of the new descriptions that *fit* with how the youth sees the world; work together with the support team to find internal and external *resources* needed to put new solutions into practice; experience *possibilities* for change that are more numerous than expected; explore new ways he or she is *performing* his or her new identity, leading to discussion on who will notice the changes; and discover ways to change the *perception* of others and convince people that he or she has changed or is doing better than expected (Ungar, 2014, 2015). These processes can help create opportunities for youth to become leaders, which benefits the disadvantaged child the most (Ungar, 2013b). This can go a long way to changing potentially pathological adaption to pro-social behaviours by improving their access to resources, and consequently the quality of their environment (Ungar, 2013a). As Ungar (2013a) writes:

> A facilitative environment can change developmental pathways regardless of individual differences. Personal motivation, sense of agency, temperament, personality variables, and genetic predispositions toward particular behaviours (anxiety, impulsivity, etc) are triggered or suppressed by the environment. . . . In this regard, nurture trumps nature when it comes to predicting resilience.
>
> (p. 258)

Conclusion

> The strengths-based perspective honours two things: the power of the self to heal and right itself with the help of the environment, and the need for an alliance with the hope that life might really be otherwise.
>
> Dennis Saleebey[10]

A significant reason that Dr. Michael Ungar's work resonates with the High Risk Youth Initiative is that he doesn't see the struggles of youth as displays of weakness, but instead as part of a "celebration of spirit" (Ungar, 2002, p. 253) (see Box 5.4). Despite the struggles the youth face these words give a sense of optimism, demonstrates the potential of the youth, and helps us all stay positive, be strengths-based practitioners, and actually look for and see the value and talents present in all youth. Ungar's work has helped me to not take negative behaviours – or rather the a search for health and identity – personally, to be more patient, and to better appreciate the difficult life journey the youth have had to navigate. As Saleebey (1997) writes:

> In the end, clients want to know that you care about them, that how they fare makes a difference to you, that you will listen to them, that you will respect them no matter what their history, and that you believe that they can build something of value with the resources within and around them. But most of all, clients want to know that you believe they can surmount adversity and begin the climb toward transformation and growth.
>
> (p. 12)

However, there is much work to be done to truly adopt a strengths-based approach with the youth and to appreciate their 'hidden resilience.' Human service professionals need to move beyond a rhetoric with no substance. Many profess to work from a strength-based perspective as if it is obvious. It is not so obvious once reading report after report of problem-saturated language that would leave youth and parents devastated if they really saw what the case worker thought of them. Again, this is changing, but the deficit or medical model thinking certainly tends to get reflected on paper and, as Hammond (2010) points out, those receiving services through a strength-based approach is a rare experience, which is further evidence that workers may think their practice is strength-based, but it is not being felt by those who count. High-risk youth pick up on this disconnect when workers are pleasant to their face, but negative behind their backs. They value genuineness and workers who are non-judgemental. If we are not consistent this can deny youth the chance to engage in a relationship. Without relationship they are unlikely to accept the resources they need to build resilience.

On a systemic level there is also a challenge to put action behind the words. Bernard (2004) cautions that while it has become clear that all young people have the capacity for positive development, resilience research should never be used to justify social and political inaction on the grounds that, somehow, most kids make it. In the face of growing global poverty, abuse, violence, and other threats to children's development, they *somehow* can no longer depend on the luck of the draw. Increasingly, healthy youth development must depend on deliberate policies, practices, and interventions designed to provide young people with developmental supports and opportunities. Young people are resilient, but they are not invincible. There is still a responsibility for governments and the community to provide youth with the resources they need and to not assume they will navigate and negotiate their way to adulthood on their own. Rather than continuing to marginalize and disenfranchise the youth, by making resources that promote wellbeing available and accessible, there is an increased chance that youth will find their identities through pro-social and adaptive decisions and actions, and that an environment that supports a youth's process of growth will be created.

Box 5.4 Melissa Bigstone (21)

Closing speech at the High Risk Youth Conference 2014: Moving forward . . .
(May 13, 2014)

Hi, my name is Melissa. I was asked to share some of my story with you all. Community is about growth and resilience and the people I have met in my life who have helped show me what community is truly about. I come from an unstable home, environment, and community. I was in and out of care from a young age and by some unfortunate events I continued that cycle for my kids. All I ever wanted was to be better than the role models I had growing up; and to beat the cycle of addiction that plagued my family. However, when one is not taught the tools to care for themselves let alone survive the world, it can feel like an unsafe place. So while I was falling through the cracks of the system I found people who finally saw me for who I truly was. This was when I was 16. By this time I had already spent a majority of my life living and fighting drugs, and alcohol abuse and family dysfunction. I was trying to find a way out and didn't know where to start. I lacked trust, self-control, and didn't understand the meaning of unconditional love and support because no one ever taught me that. Then I met Wallis Kendal and Peter Smyth. Both of these individuals began to work with me and helped me see the strengths I had not been able to see in myself. They opened up the doors for me to create my own life and identity. They never said I was a youth with a past that defined me. They said "who do I want to be" and "what do I see for myself in life." Then they helped me create that for myself. I'm forever grateful for these people. For once in my life they showed me what unconditional trust and support meant. But not by their words; it was their actions that really truly meant more to me than anything. They never gave up on me no matter how much I wanted to give up on myself at times. They were there for many milestones on my journey, as well, like when I needed to cry, and they were there to praise me for doing good and also to thank me for also teaching them what fighting and resilience really means and helping them realize that we need unconditional support and love in our community. Not to give up when times get tough but to be tough when times get rough and always follow your dreams. They use to come with me to court, advocate for me whenever I needed it, and even in positive times like when I got my kids back, started post-secondary school, graduated high school, got years sober, got my driver's licence, moved into new places, climbed my first mountain. . . . They helped me fight a four year battle to get my son back when he was PGO [Permanent Guardianship Order] and because they helped me realize I can do anything I set my mind to. I got him back last November [2013]. I am currently going into my third year of a psychology degree program at Concordia [University-College in Edmonton, Alberta] and I live a sober life with my children. I don't believe I would be where I am at today if it wasn't for people like Peter and Wallis and everyone else who has helped me on my journey. For all the people that said to me they believed in me and never put barriers in my way but instead helped me find a way around the barriers being put in my path, they helped me break the cycles I was in and today I aim towards helping others do the same. As I think we all should!!!

Discussion questions to consider for Chapter 5

1   *What are your thoughts with respect to the nurture versus nature debate and its connection to resiliency?*

2   *How can we see resilience in youth when they are engaging in negative behaviours or what would appear to be self-destructive behaviours?*

3   *What are some negative labels we place on youth that might prohibit youth seeing strengths in themselves?*

4   *Can you illustrate how a youth might be denied access to needed resources and how program and policies may help or hinder?*

5   *Can you give examples of what might be pro-social substitutes for an otherwise anti-social search for health and identity?*

6   *Given the criticisms of strength-based practice, can you think of a situation in which it might not be helpful?*

7   *Can a youth be resilient without the benefit of a healthy adult relationship?*

Notes

1 Frederick Douglass (1818–1895), in fitting with a number of themes in this book, struggled with much abandonment and loss in his life but demonstrated incredible resilience. While not having his own family present, there were some people who helped him in different ways, no doubt helping him be resilient during the dark days of slavery in America. The African American later became a statesman and well-known leader in the abolitionist movement and campaigner for equal rights (Fenton, 2014).

2 The article was written by Darcy Henton and appeared in the *Edmonton Journal* on November, 23, 2009.

3 Levy and Orlans (1998) reference two works relating to the research of Emmy Werner: 1) Werner, E. (1989). High-risk children in young adulthood: A longitudinal study from birth to 32 years. *American Journal of Orthopsychiatry*, 59(1): 72–81; 2) Werner, E. & Smith, R. (1992). *Overcoming the Odds: High-risk Children from Birth to Adulthood*. Ithaca, NY: Cornell.

4 From the book, *Nurturing Hidden Resilience in Troubled Youth* by Dr. Michael Ungar (2004, p. 95).

5 Even though they may fit the definition of 'high-risk youth,' many youth have no status with the government. A few youth have stated (and is confirmed on the Alberta provincial database) that they have never had a case worker even though they were kicked out of their homes. Others have had government workers in and out of their homes all of their lives but only for a short time. Many have added that there was a lot of bad things going on but their parents knew what to say to child welfare investigators and nobody ever asked the child or youth what was going on. Further, youth would say that they had had bad experiences and did not want to be involved with the child welfare system, and others were led to believe that if they said anything they would be taken away and never see their parents again. Other youth did not know if they had a file open, or whether their file was still open, as they never saw their worker. It is not shocking to see files closed because the youth was noncompliant, manipulative, defiant, and/or uncooperative. Based on this, some workers would even write on the closure summaries that if a particular youth came to the attention of the system in the future, there was no point in opening a file, even if the youth had a history of problems and was living on the streets!

6 Dr. Michael Ungar is referencing the following literature: 1) Dumont, K. A., Wisdon, C. S., & Czaja, S. J. (2007). Predictors of resilience in abused and neglected children grown-up: The role of individual and neighbourhood characteristics. *Child Abuse & Neglect*, 31: 255–274; 2) Landeau, J., Mittal, M., & Wieling, E. (2008). Linking human systems: Strengthening individuals, families, and communities in the wake of mass trauma. *Journal of Marital and Family Therapy*, 34: 193–209; 3) Obrist, B., Pfeiffer, C., & Henley, R. (2010). Multi-layered social resilience: A new approach in mitigation research. *Progress in Development Studies*, 10: 283–293.

7 Dr. Michael Ungar was a keynote speaker at the inaugural High Risk Youth Conference in Edmonton, Alberta, May 12–13, 2014.

8 See also: Ungar (2015) and Ungar et al. (2007).

9 These steps of helping clients navigate and negotiate resources are adapted from Dr. Michael Ungar's keynote presentation at the High Risk Youth Conference in Alberta on May 12–13, 2014, in Edmonton, Alberta. The words in italics are the headings of the 10 categories for each section outlined by Ungar during his presentation and more recently released book, *Working with Children and Youth with Complex Needs: 20 Skills to Build Resilience* (2015).

10 From the article: 'The Strengths Perspective in Social Work Practice: Extensions and Cautions' by Dennis Saleebey (1996, p. 303).

Chapter 6

Engaging community, engaging youth

> The mark of a caring society is to ensure that children who might otherwise become lost along the tortured pathways of increasing developmental despair encounter others who can understand, value and contain them. . . . Encounters with minds that are stronger and wiser often act as a turning point for maltreated children.
>
> David Howe[1]

In the mid-1990s I was given the opportunity to be the child protection worker working out of a junior high school (ages 12–15) as part of a multi-disciplinary team. Not only was being involved in the Partners for Youth (PFY) program in a service-deprived area of Edmonton, Alberta, two of the best years of my social work career even to this day, but the experience changed my practice in two particularly significant ways. The first revelation was how deeper and richer connections could be made with the youth and their families, allowing the child welfare system to be seen as a resource rather than a threat. The second was how much more effective and efficient it was working with a team of professionals who were all invested in a common cause and who were, for the most part, open to learning from each other. This provided the flexibility and creativity to find new ways to provide services at a community level. As this program was intended to be a resource for the community rather than for one school who happened to have the space available, PFY eventually moved into a community-accessible site in the community. A community board was established and the agency operated for many years.

What became crystal clear through PFY was that child welfare work cannot, and should not, be done in isolation (Herbert, 2007; Smyth & Eaton-Erickson, 2009), especially as evidence suggests than solving social problems and significant social change comes from better cross-sector co-ordination rather than the intervention of individual organizations (Kania & Kramer, 2011). The same applies to working with high-risk youth. However, as much as *collaboration, partnership,* and *integration* are talked about, and while working together with community and outreach agencies is evolving, action does not match the amount of words we use to describe such practice. In child welfare we talk like we are heavily engaged in the community, but the voices in the community tell me they are still waiting for the day in which there are more than just a few examples of true partnership.

Unfortunately, while effective collaboration between government services and agencies is slowly being recognized as an important way forward, such community development work is hard to get to. When caseloads are stretched to the limit, there is ongoing crisis work, resources are minimal, and communication between the organizations is increasingly difficult to maintain (Hudson, 1999; Kreitzer & Lafrance, 2009). Collaboration can help change the negative perception of child welfare in society, but community development is not a natural part of the work we do. At present it is an 'add on,' meaning that workloads are not adjusted to accommodate the time it takes to do the community work and genuinely get to know community workers and their formal and informal service organizations (Herbert, 2007; Hudson, 1999). Largely it remains something workers will 'get around to' but never do because the workload never goes down and the main goal is keeping children and youth safe (Lonne et al., 2009; Wharf, 2002a).

As bureaucracies have grown the focus has been on internal issues rather than linking with local community stakeholders. Workers have been constrained by a need for the bureaucratic organization to have control, meaning there is little room for finding creative solutions. This leaves workers to only question what the rules and regulations are rather than questioning what *could* be done (Ricks, Charlesworth, Bellefeuille & Field, 1999). For too long this has left child protection systems "detached and remote from local neighbourhoods and communities, practicing on them rather than within them" (Lonne et al., 2009, p. 162). There is no time left to have coffee with the outreach workers at the local youth resource centre and thus "an opportunity is lost for the two functions [of protection and community work] to compliment, reinforce and support one another" (Hudson, 1999, p. 352).

Wharf (2002a) argues that there are ways in which the system needs to be changed, as "community social work and community organizing are neglected but potentially powerful strategies for improving child welfare" (p. 9). Rather than being based in large, rule-based organizations, effective practice must be based in the community. Stepping outside of corporate offices and being visible in the community sends a message that things are changing in the sense of being more available and more supportive. Workers need to make this part of their day-to-day practice so that rather than narrowly focusing on the child welfare mandate to protect by assessing the capacity of the parents to care for their children, the focus can be expanded to include the environment of families and issues such as poverty, substandard housing, and unsafe neighbourhoods. While community approaches are starting to get recognition, there is still fear and doubt, as well as clinging onto what is known and comfortable. The problem is that traditional approaches are not the best we can offer children, youth, and families (Herbert, 2007; Lonne et al., 2009; Wharf, 2002a). We need to reach a tipping point in which community initiatives represent a fundamental challenge to the status quo, both at practice and policy levels (Wharf, 2002c).

Interestingly, in the 1960s, there were positions in Canada called 'community protection workers' in which three-fifths of the job was a child protection caseload and two-fifths was community work activities. The provincial legislation included not only protection of children but preventing the circumstances that cause a child to need protection (Lee & Richards, 2002). This was in the radical 1960s, before neo-liberal thinking ushered in the dismantling of social programs starting in the 1970s (Mullaly, 2007; Silver, 2014; Wharf, 2002a). The 1970s also prompted a shift to social work education and child welfare being dominated by clinical approaches, resulting in community work becoming "virtually a foreign concept" (Wharf, 2002b, p. 60).

An alternative focus on managing administrative tasks stifled creativity and the tightening of regulations meant having less time to build relationships, not only with service users but also in the community (Kreitzer & Lafrance, 2009).

Community engagement and the High Risk Youth Initiative (HRYI)

With the shift in practice currently taking place, there is some understanding that finding common ground and working together with community partners is a better way to serve children, youth, and families. While barriers remain, certainly the HRYI sees community-based practice as not simply a nice thing to do if one has the time, but as essential part of the *Get Connected* practice framework and philosophy. In my previous role as team leader, and my current position in expanding the HRYI in Edmonton, Alberta, a significant amount of my time is spent building relationships with community agencies, workers, and stakeholders; developing programs that meet the needs of high-risk youth; trying to convince people we are a resource and not a threat; consulting; and doing joint training for government and community workers. This has helped develop a HRYI community of like-minded people with common values, similar perspectives, and the same passion for changing practice to better serve our youth. Ideally, we learn from each other, see each other as equals, feel comfortable airing our differences, and have constructive ways to resolve conflict. It is not perfect and we are still learning to trust each other and create safety, but there is more open communication and a focus on the needs of the youth rather than protecting our turf (Smyth, 2004). There is certainly an element of the guiding philosophy in multi-disciplinary practice settings that Nicholson, Artz, Armitage and Fagan (2000) discuss, in that "team members recognize the importance of contributions from other disciplines" (p. 65).

A key aspect of the HRYI is the close connection between government case workers and agency *community youth specialists* (CYS). We know that when youth buy in to services and risk engaging in a relationship, they typically want a lot of contact and have many needs. These two roles complement each other and allow more contact with the youth for more hours than the standard work day. While relationship-building is the primary role of the HRYI case worker, attending to a minimum of 15 high-risk youth as well as attending to the administrative responsibilities that come with the role creates a need to work as a team to help the youth get to appointments, attend court, register for school, look for a job, and connect with community resources. While both workers take on these tasks, community youth specialists have been able to be more flexible with time and often have a better sense of resources in the community from which the youth can benefit.

The roles are different but it is important to highlight that there is no hierarchy, as the CYSs do not work for the case worker. Communication is very frequent, and decisions are made as a team, which also includes the youth and other significant people involved with the youth. It has been important in the HRYI to periodically review the roles, to put any grievances on the table, to have a conflict resolution process, to ensure the common goal is meeting the needs of the youth, and to make sure that the youth has a support team who share the same agenda. This can also serve to avoid triangulation, as youth with attachment issues tend to work one against the other, which (as discussed in Chapters 2 and 3) can be an understandable way to keep people at a distance and take the attention away from themselves (Levy & Orlans, 1998).

Shifts are indeed being made to embrace equality, information sharing, and collective strength and power (Ricks et al., 1999). A successful partnership between these two roles can help define community practice in child welfare as far as working with high-risk youth. Also involved is an education piece so other case workers, service providers, and community members can appreciate how the child protection system can work differently and how collaborative practice can benefit the youth (Smyth, 2004). Also helping with finding common ground and developing a collaboration mentality is the fact that training for the HRYI brings together government case workers and agency staff, allowing for dialogue and gaining new knowledge from a variety of perspectives and mandates.

Another way the government and the community comes together in the HRYI is through the *High Risk Youth Multi-Disciplinary Consultation Team*, which has been operating since 2006. This offers a chance for case workers, community workers, parents, caregivers, or probation officers to talk about a youth who is presenting serious challenges. Significant people in the youth's life and the youth are invited. The youth attend the consults about 25% of the time (the expectation is they are invited but they may decline, cannot be located, or are confined). This is undoubtedly an intimidating environment but the team makes efforts to make them comfortable. Most of the youth settle quickly and become active participants in the consults. Feedback has been positive, with comments reflecting the youth felt it was worthwhile and that they were heard. The team is made up of people with experience working with high-risk youth, including government workers from child protection services, addictions and mental health, education, and justice; a psychologist; an Aboriginal liaison worker for First Nations, Metis, and Inuit (FNMI) youth; a police officer; and community workers from outreach programs and shelter resources. Recommendations are made by the team, most of which are non-traditional practice ideas that fit with the *Get Connected* practice framework and philosophy, including challenging punishment-consequence interventions and promoting relationship-based approaches. There is a focus on engaging the youth, flexible placement options, counselling opportunities, addictions, cultural connections, confronting issues of sexual health and sexual identity, education and employment, building on interest and hobbies, and safety. This process can serve to further build a network of safety under the youth so they have options if in a crisis, if they are not safe, or if they need to reach out to a safe adult. The consultation team meets for one afternoon each month, accommodating three consults.

Another example of community collaboration is the multi-disciplinary committee that assembled to organize the first High Risk Youth Conference in Alberta (if not Canada) for well over 440 participants. The conferences held in 2014 and 2016 highlighted progressive theory and practice for working with high-risk youth, and included a youth event also involving youth from the community. These illustrations of multi-disciplinary practice are important and have worked well, but it should be pointed out that the public institutions of child welfare, health, education, and justice do not always have similar perspectives on how to serve youth, and this can be further exacerbated when adding a community service approach that may overtly challenge government policies. An example is the use of a harm reduction approach that is still not accepted in many areas of public service. However, effective intervention requires the co-ordination of services from multiple sources that do not relate easily (National Scientific Council on the Developing Child, 2008). As multi-disciplinary collaboration becomes a standard way to meet the needs of service users, it will hopefully become more natural to relate easily and find common ground.

To help build a sense of community I find it is helpful to attend events agencies organize because, in part, the youth and the staff take notice and it further helps build credibility. It continues to amaze me how accepting the youth are – sometimes even more so than some of the agency staff. The youth will share much information and even tell me how they do not trust the child welfare system. When I remind them I am a part of that system, they are fully aware of that fact but tell me they see me differently. This has little to do with my skills as a social worker, but rather speaks to how being present and aware of one's position in the community helps build relationships with agencies and communities, which in turn helps foster relationships with the youth in those agencies or communities.

The importance of community partnerships is noted repeatedly in the literature on harm reduction (Maté, 2008; Taylor, 2010, see Chapter 4) and resiliency/strength-based practice (Madsen, 1999; Ungar, 2004, see Chapter 5). It incorporates the understanding that empowering communities and improving the quality of life in the whole community will help individuals as well (Hudson, 1999; Taylor, 2010). There is wisdom in the community, and service providers and agency staff may know the youth, their families, and indeed multiple generations of the family. Community partnerships between child protective services and the formal and informal resources within communities often provide valuable opportunities for the child welfare staff to better understand both the families and their communities (Anderson & Seita, 2006). We are remiss if we ignore this knowledge, as with it are possibilities for resources, safe places for the youth to stay, positive connections that can be fostered, and opportunities to make positive changes. It is suggested that social workers, as representatives of the state, "would be more effective in promoting equity and human rights if they shared discursive power with their communities" (Ungar, Manuel, Mealey, Thomas & Campbell, 2004, p. 552). It is particularly relevant for this group of youth called "the disconnected" (Smyth & Eaton-Erickson, 2009), as "community development exists because it has a value-based commitment to working with the excluded of society, those people who are too poor, too oppressed or too alienated to be confident about getting involved in community activities" (Henderson, 1997, as cited in Wharf, 2002a, p. 15).[2]

Collaborating on collaboration

A system of care recognizes that different agencies or systems have specific roles and mandates, but that rather than operating as a fragmented collection of services, a collaborative approach that holistically serves the needs of the individual is needed. Therefore, an integrated system of care is a local system that addresses the needs of individuals through the co-ordination and integration of programs, services, and resources from planning through to delivery (Homeward Trust Edmonton, 2015, p. 33). Perry and Szalavitz (2006) emphasize that children and youth need a healthy community environment that surrounds and supports them, especially one that increases the number and quality of a child's relationships and allows them a sense of belonging. We need to keep trying to build a healthier society, as

[t]he world we live in now is biologically disrespectful; it does not take into account many of our most basic human needs and often pulls us away from healthy activities and toward those that are harmful. . . . People without any relationships were believed to be as healthy as those who had many. These ideas contradict to fundamental biology of human species.

(p. 232)

Maté (2008) echoes how everyone needs to belong. Important for any youth is "to be invited into communities that can offer them acceptance, belonging and value" (p. 138). As Ungar (2007b) points out, youth may belong in any number of communities simultaneously: the community where they live; the cultural community with which they identify; their community of peers; or a community formed by exclusion. We know some youth may gravitate to gang involvement to find acceptance and belonging, or may seek other socially excluded people to create their 'street family,' if feeling alienated from their own family and if they sense they are not welcome in various groups within mainstream society. Aboriginal and immigrant/refugee youth facing racism and LGBTQ (lesbian, gay, transgendered, bisexual, questioning) youth facing homophobia and transphobia know this painfully well and are particularly over-represented with respect to addictions, mental health challenges, suicide and attempts and completion, being homeless, dropping out of school, being unemployed, and being victims of sexual and physical violence (Blackstock, 2008; Choi, Wilson, Shelton & Gates, 2015; Hunter, 2008; Poirier et al., 2008; Quinn, 2002; Quintana, Rosenthal & Krehely, 2010). Youth with poor self-esteem, and who carry around a chronic sense of failure and shame, tend not to find peers who are confident and feel a high sense of acceptance and belonging. They find their way to other youth who have a similar view of the world as they do. This re-emphasizes how all youth want connection and will seek it out in negative ways if healthy options are limited (Smyth, 2013). Social connectedness can be enhanced if workers from various disciplines and organizations are on the same page and giving consistent messages that allow the youth to feel valued and worthy (Perry, 2009), can put aside their judgements, and are aware of their own biases and views of the world.

Yet, high-risk youth who are street-involved, homeless, Aboriginal, and/or LGBTQ do not have a sense of belonging among their peers or society in general and feel marginalized and excluded from many of the institutions that most youth take for granted, such as school, community programs, shopping malls, public transportation, health centres, and parks (Abramovich, 2013a, 2013b; Anderson & Seita, 2006; Baskin, 2013; Gaetz, 2004; Nicholas et al., 2015). Some organizations are recognizing that alienating particular groups in society from public spaces cannot be justified (see Box 6.1) and are acknowledging the work of outreach agencies that specifically address the needs of the marginalized populations. These agencies are increasingly reaching out to each other to expand the range of services they can offer youth, including mandated government services, which is helping build wider safety nets under the youth. Some agencies invite other organizations onto their sites, offering an office or space to engage youth and do their work, while others are hubs that have many agencies (government and not-for-profit) in the same building using a one-stop-shop or wraparound concept. Opening the doors to collaboration with formal and informal services helps create a web of social care, offers more choice to the youth, and illustrates the safety and wellbeing of the youth as a "whole-of-community" or "whole-of-society" responsibility (Lonne et al., 2009, p. 149). With such a diverse range of services available, youth are able to access shelter beds, get food or bus tickets, get hand-held support to get to appointments while being emotionally supported, get clothing, get immunizations, get legal advice, learn life skills, get connected to jobs and school, access employment preparation, access emotional support that goes beyond government hours, get addictions counselling, access help for court, learn an instrument, express themselves through various art forms, access crisis intervention, get support with parenting, get a safe haven from violence, have birthdays celebrated, get the chance to celebrate Christmas with a turkey dinner (or other religious holidays), access tutoring, access outreach school, receive a smile, and get a hug.

Box 6.1   Libraries reaching out

On the surface, one would think libraries and high-risk youth do not have a lot in common. How would these two worlds come together? Intentionally, as it turns out. In Edmonton, Alberta, one of the main hang outs and meeting points is the downtown Stanley A. Milner Library. Over the past few years more and more youth ask to meet at the library or ask to be dropped off there. It took a while to figure out why this was the case. Our youth are not always quiet and they do not typically express their desire to study in a quiet place. In fact, most do not own a library card (that's for "geeks," after all). Even so, this phenomenon started spreading to other libraries around the city. What's up?

In a more unusual – though valuable – community initiative, the libraries have been making a point of reaching out to everyone, including high-risk youth. These youth have as much of a right as anyone else to using this public space. When youth are used to being excluded from many places in the community, this approach was challenging such thinking with a conscious effort to be inclusive. As would be expected, some library staff were nervous at the launch of its Safe Communities Initiative, but there are many advocates for the youth within the library system. In addition, Edmonton Public Libraries have hired three outreach workers to help support marginalized populations accessing the library. They advocate for clients, provide emotional support and connect them to community and government resources.

Library staff are also reaching out to other organizations in the community because, rather than fear these youth, they want to understand them. They are asking for advice on how to interact with street-involved youth and how to support and help them. Library staff continue to attend training sessions and have participated in community partnerships made up of social service organizations. They are hoping to be involved in more in-depth training for staff all over the city. Instead of pushing this population of youth away because of fear and a lack of understanding, they are trying to be creative, flexible, and welcoming. And the youth have responded. Libraries are becoming part of their routine and social life. They may not see much beyond being able to catch up on their social networking with the free access they have to computers, but studying, researching, getting a library card, and checking books out may be the next step. At least they know they are welcome to do these things now.

> *These efforts have not been lost on people outside of Alberta. In 2014, Edmonton Public Libraries was named Library of the Year by* Library Journal *and Gale Cengage Learning. This was the first time a Canadian library system has received this award. This initiative was one of the significant contributing factors.*

Conclusion

If we do it by ourselves, we have failed . . . because we failed to engage the talents, the passion, and wisdom of the broader community.[3]

Community is simply a collection of relationships. By defining community this way, it can be inferred that "more important than the designated space or location of the community is the relational nature of community members" (Ricks et al., 1999, p. 32). From a community development perspective, "a *partnership* is a relationship where two or more parties, having compatible goals, form an agreement to work together in a mutually beneficial manner, often doing things together that might not be possible alone" (Goldblatt, 2007, p. 4). The purpose of *collaboration* is to "develop shared vision, build inter-dependent system to address issues and opportunities and share resources" (Goldblatt, 2007, p. 6). These terms fit well for working with youth in the community by focusing on relationships, working together for a common cause, and finding common ground to create opportunities for the youth. Yet community development work remains undervalued, especially in government, but also among some agencies as well. There is a lot of talk about partnership and collaboration, but all too frequently the action piece is missing.

While child welfare systems might encourage such practice, there is no allowance made in the workload (Hudson, 1999; Wharf, 2002a). Some initiatives are starting to change this, but engaging with the community must become the way practice is done, especially if it results in better outcomes for the youth. We know traditional child welfare services have not been meeting the needs of the youth (Herbert, 2007; Smyth et al., 2005), but being able to build relationships with community agencies, other government departments, and community stakeholders, and being able to build a support network around the youth, is helping make services more relevant in the High Risk Youth Initiative. Therefore, community engagement remains a key aspect of the *Get Connected* practice framework and philosophy.

Carrying out the statutory responsibilities of child protection does not have to prevent or threaten relationships in the community. In fact, community practice, with collective problem-solving with the youth and families, can reduce the need for court orders and children and youth being brought into care. Working as partners can also help all involved to appreciate the need for such intrusive steps needing to be taken when necessary, because people have the same information and are working from a shared perspective. When difficult decisions have to be made, it can be far less conflictual, leading to a less traumatic experience for the family members. The community gets to know the statutory role and trust can be built (Hudson, 1999). This has been the case with the High Risk Youth Initiative. Youth and families who have had a good experience with the child welfare system are more open to risk building relationships with case workers because credibility increases when workers step out of their offices and into the community.

In short, greater integration between child welfare and the community is required to complement, reinforce, and support one another (Hudson, 1999). This drastically improves communication and helps build a common language, further opening doors to be able to work together. This fosters trust and creates an atmosphere of mutual respect, enabling partners to learn about each other's values, work, and concerns. Open communication provides a platform to air and resolve disagreements and provides partners with avenues to respond to changes and emerging problems (Goldblatt, 2007; Horwath & Morrison, 2007). Striving for this kind of relationship has been critical for the case workers and community youth specialists in the High Risk Youth Initiative as they evolve the partnership and work through traditional power dynamics. While always learning and improving, it has helped in appreciating the skills and value that each role brings to the youth as an equal partner. As Ricks et al. (1999) emphasize, "When a learning orientation is put into practice, it becomes apparent that there are no experts, only learners. People position themselves as learners and are excited by their potential and the potential of others" (Ricks et al., 1999, p. 82). Being involved in the community and building relationships continues to reinforce that this, indeed, really is the way child welfare work should be done.

Discussion questions to consider for Chapter 6

1   Is it realistic to be engaging in community development work when also trying to manage a full caseload?

2   Can youth truly see child protection case workers as part of their community support?

3   When children need to be brought into care, or parents must be served with court documents, can case workers still be seen as a resource rather than a threat?

4   How likely is it that community workers will be seen as betraying their youth and families if perceived as working too closely with case workers?

5   With case workers having a legislated mandate, and given government often funds the community agencies, how equal can partnerships really be? Is it necessary that all things be equal in community partnerships?

6   When case workers are engaged in the community, is it always appropriate that the decision-making process is shared? Are their circumstances in which it should not be shared? Why or why not?

7   What can case workers learn from the community to enhance their practice? What can community workers learn from the child welfare system to enhance their practice?

8   If a case worker is in a community agency and there is a difference of opinion in the direction that should be taken when working with a family, who should have the final say if a consensus cannot be reached? What are some strategies that could be adopted for resolving conflicts and coming to a consensus on various issues?

Notes

1 From the book, *Child Abuse and Neglect: Attachment, Development and Intervention* (2005, pp. 274–275).
2 In his book *Community Work Approaches to Child Welfare*, Brian Wharf is citing: Henderson, P. (1997). Community development and children. In C. Caanan & C. Warren (eds.), *Social Action with Children and Families: A Community Development Approach Child and Family Welfare* (pp. 23–42). London: Routledge.
3 This quote is from the Institute of Public Administration of Canada (IPAC) Conference in Winnipeg, August 2007.

Chapter 7

Getting connected
The profound importance of relationship

It's hard to keep living when you don't have anyone that loves you.
A high-risk youth in Edmonton, Alberta, March 2014

Talking about relationship reverberates through every section of this book, but that is because it lies at the heart of every aspect of the *Get Connected* practice framework and philosophy. Relationship can be transformational for high-risk youth, and given the poverty of relationships that is typically their experience, we must at least offer this population of youth the opportunity to risk making connections. It is my experience that things do not change for youth unless they are in a positive relationship. Healthy relationships allow the youth to give some thought about their circumstances and open the door for taking risks. Without this, understandably, youth remain in *survival mode*, not allowing people into their world and not risking more rejection and abandonment. If they are using negative behaviours to get their needs met and to create their identity, without the opportunity of being engaged in a relationship, where will the motivation to change come from? If the youths' environments do not change, and they do not get the chance to be supported in navigating and negotiating resources they need, how is the expectation of being one of society's throwaway kids going to be diminished? So while this relationship theme is key throughout, it warrants a separate focus to highlight the most important piece of the child welfare system puzzle that requires changing: We cannot expect youth to make changes simply by emphasizing their deficits and pointing them to programs; they need to experience relationship before they even start to think about making changes in their lives. As Perry and Szalavitz (2006) tell us: "Before they can make any kind of lasting change at all in their behaviour, they need to feel safe and loved" (p. 244). And, even before this, there is a need to understand and appreciate the struggle this is likely going to be for the high-risk youth and the worker, given nurturing and supportive relationships are what youth desperately want and need, but also what they often fight hard to resist. While there is the fear and anxiety of loneliness and abandonment, there is a parallel sense of danger that if the youth commits to a relationship the risk will be overwhelming (Giller, Vermilyea & Steele, 2006; Kagan, 2004; Maté, 1999). There is a need to journey in partnership, going at the pace that is comfortable for the youth to establish a sense of safety. If navigated properly, a relationship can be beneficial and rewarding for both the youth and the worker.

Transforming systems, transforming practice, and transforming relationships

---

Box 7.1   Crystal's story: who is to blame?

A child welfare case worker is meeting with 'Crystal' (15), as she has recently been assigned to his caseload. Crystal has not being staying in any placement for longer than a few days. She is not attending school, she is on probation for assaulting a peer (but refuses to follow her probation order), she is using hard drugs a number of times a week, she was recently diagnosed with an STI, and she is periodically running to her mother, despite being apprehended due to ongoing verbal and physical fights. The worker confronts Crystal about the lack of follow through and her lack of motivation to make changes in her life. He tells her that she cannot stay with her mother and that she will be reported to the Attendance Board if she doesn't start attending school. He also announces his intention to talk to her probation officer, adding she is likely to be breached and sent to the young offender centre. The worker tells Crystal this might be best, as she needs to see a doctor and he does not have any faith she will go to a clinic voluntarily. The youth is denied bus tickets, condoms, and a grocery voucher because they will be wasted. The youth escalates and tells the worker, "you don't give a shit, I don't need your help" before storming out of the office, slamming the door behind her. The worker discusses the situation with his supervisor and states that Crystal is manipulative, defiant, and uncooperative. He recommends her file be closed because it is not likely that any progress will be made in the near future.

The situation described in Box 7.1 is all too frequently played out in child welfare, as evidenced through my experience of reading through many files of high-risk youth, hearing numerous stories from the youth themselves and case workers, and seeing this reported in surveys of youth who have been involved with the system. To the worker, the actions of the youth appear irrational and illogical. After all, the worker might rationalize that he was offering Crystal a way out of her destructive behaviours and teaching her to take responsibility for her actions. However, one could also argue that it was the worker who acted irrationally and illogically in expecting Crystal to accept what he said, to follow his demands, and to be intimidated by his threats, all before he has taken the time to get to know her, understand her, and attempt to build any kind of relationship. Crystal comes from a traumatic childhood. She has a deep mistrust for any adults, especially those in authority. She has been rejected and abandoned repeatedly. She feels a deep sense of shame that she does not have a stable family. She feels stupid and sees school as a set up for failure. She got an STI after her ex-boyfriend raped her; she was too scared to report it but was charged for physically assaulting her attacker. Crystal does not believe anyone cares about her or that anybody would bother to waste their time on her. She believes that she can only rely on herself and that the world is a lonely and frightening place. Crystal is a survivor and knows better than to let anyone into her life who will threaten her independence and control.

By understanding such dynamics, her response to her new case worker does, indeed, appear quite rational and logical. The case worker simply reinforced everything she believes about the world. This is supported by Leeson (2007), as he points out that youth are "frequently labelled as badly behaved rather than having their reactions understood as an expression of distress and a sense of powerless" (as cited in Lonne et al., 2009, p. 79).[1]

Despite being aware of the background information of the youth on their caseloads, many case workers continue to use traditional practice methods in which building relationships is secondary to administrative duties (Herbert, 2007; Lonne et al., 2009; Wharf, 2002a). Interestingly, this idea that traditional methods are ineffective is not a new concept. Brendtro and Ness (1983) point out that the issues in child welfare relating to over-bureaucratization, fragmentation, the inability to adapt to changing times, and issues of alienation, indifference, and powerlessness were identified in the literature in 1972. Yet the struggles continue. We continue to wrestle with high case-loads, time-consuming administrative practices, and an over-reliance on punishment-consequence models that prevent us from engaging youth effectively. Despite these barriers, we are still inclined to blame service users when engagement does not occur, seeing them as defiant, uncooperative, and manipulative. We generally continue to struggle in shifting from a system-centred approach to the client-centred approach (Madsen, 2007; Ruch, 2010a), and we still see programs developed to meet the needs of the government department or agency rather than focusing on the needs of the youth. It seems we are also still climbing out of the brokerage model, or contractual and service-oriented approaches to practice, a hole that was pervasive in the 1980s and 1990s. Such practice reinforced that the *case manager* (rather than *case worker*) remained in the background directing traffic while agency workers did the face-to-face work and reported back to the faceless bureaucrat in the background. While we like to believe we have emerged out of such an impersonal practice method, it has not been eradicated and far too many examples of this are evident. There are ethical challenges to making decisions, and presenting evidence to the courts that could have a life-long impact for children, youth, and families, when there is little or no relationship established. Rather than trying to reduce risk and help families, service providers have been used, at times, to monitor families in an effort to add to the evidence against them in court. This fed into an organizational risk-management focus which became more and more pervasive, making practice increasingly black and white and reducing flexibility, resourcefulness, and problem-solving by workers that could otherwise help alleviate stress for the youth and families (Lonne et al., 2009).

We know, given the vulnerable population we are working with, that eliminating risk is impossible, and perhaps could tempt us to not open files and avoid working with extremely high-risk youth because of the level of risk with which they come to us. However, I would argue that child welfare could and should be measured by how it enters the uncertain and precarious world of high-risk youth knowing there are few solutions and answers, but also knowing that we can offer something they are desperate for – healthy and significant relationships. There is starting to be an acknowledgement that life inevitably comes with some level of risk. Adopting the harm reduction philosophy within the High Risk Youth Initiative (HRYI) is evidence that we need to work with risk rather than continuing to waste energy in engaging in the futile exercise of removing risk – energy better used in engaging in relationship.

Munro (1999) questions if the child welfare system is doing more harm than good given the "little appreciation of the pain caused to families by assessment procedures" (p. 117). This was reinforced again in Munro's (2011) review of the child protection system in England in which she recommended a shift from "a system that has become over-bureaucratised and focused on compliance to one that values and develops professional expertise and is focused on the safety of children and young people" (p. 6). Munro (2011) noted that the demands of bureaucracy have reduced the capacity of practitioners to work directly with children, young people, and families, and concluded that instead of "doing things right" (i.e., following procedures), the system needed to be focused on "doing the right thing" (i.e., checking whether children and young people are being helped) (p. 6). Often workers are measured (or audited) on how caught up they are on administrative duties; it is hard to measure the benefit of a caring relationship to a youth, as this takes time and is rarely observed by supervisors consistently.

Over the years, however, I have never been thanked by a youth for having their file up to date and in order, but a lot of times I am surprised how just minor relationship-based activities or comments were appreciated and created a lasting memory. While having a file up to date can be helpful to the system in the case of a tragedy, and certainly helps accountability, there is no evidence that having a file in order is going to help a youth overcome trauma, rejection, and abandonment. While documentation is necessary and important, systems have become driven by it at the expense of critical face-to-face contact. When social workers were asked what they value most about their practice, it was face-to-face interaction (Doel, 2010), yet workers in the child welfare field often say they feel chained to their desks filling out forms and answering emails.

In a documentary highlighting the importance of the shift in child welfare practice toward a focus on building relationships with the youth,[2] one youth made a connection between a willingness to work around policy and rules and feeling the system was actually working on her behalf, resulting in a sense of worthiness and value which was different from her previous experiences. She commented how it felt good that someone was willing to be different and "break the rules" on her behalf (Office of the Child and Youth Advocate, 2007). This adolescent also (confirming research) spoke to how youth resent not having a say in the decision-making process (Blundo, 2001; Brendtro & du Toit, 2005; Luckock & Lefevre, 2008; Ungar, 2006). Lee and Charm (2002) confirm the importance of the worker-client partnership in determining the success of the helping process. They found that success goes beyond the worker's positive attributes and includes the "provision of opportunities for active participation of clients, such as expressing opinions, asking questions, making choices, sharing information, and working together in a helping process" (p. 91). This can help youth avoid feelings of exclusion and discrimination, and help workers challenge structural dynamics that reinforce such feelings. So, while clearly still disadvantaged, the message is that youth are not left to fight for what they need on their own (Lonne et al., 2009; Luckock & Lefevre, 2008; Mullaly, 2007, 2010; Strega & Sohki Aski Esquao, 2009). The more clients feel that power and authority are shared, the more likely they are to form a positive working relationship, leading to better outcomes (Lawler, Shaver & Goodman, 2010; Lemma, 2010; Luckock & Lefevre, 2008).

This bureaucratic and compliance-driven focus has been a theme across most Western nations, given the contemporary dominance of neo-conservative social attitudes and neo-liberal values that guide social welfare (Baines, 2007; Lonne et al., 2009;

Mullaly, 2010; Ungar, 2004). The primary cultural behaviour is the legally sanctioned use of authority and overuse or abuse of power, making the collaborative ideal difficult to achieve and the ideal of worker-client relationship unlikely (Altman & Gohagan, 2009). Indeed, "there seems little doubt, generally speaking, we now live in a harsher and more punitive social environment . . . based upon blaming and judgemental social attitudes" (Lonne et al., 2009, p. 59),[3] reflecting a move away from the concept of social care in favour of the notion of social control (Lonne et al., 2009; Mullaly, 2010). Though being challenged more now, this remains dominant in child welfare practice, leaving social workers limited to maintaining the status quo rather than challenging the structures that oppress the very clients they are supposed to serve and support. This results in social workers feeling they had no choice but to compromise their professional ethics and values (Lafrance & Bastien, 2007; Mullaly, 2010; Strega, 2007).

Traditional child welfare practice serves to reinforce to the youth that adults punish, which is not conducive to developing a relationship (Altman & Gohagan, 2009; Lawler et al., 2010). Rather, it serves to push children and youth away, which can be interpreted by the youth as further rejection (Batmanghelidjh, 2006; Howe, 2005). The goal with children should be drawing the youth in through understanding and kindness, rather than adopting 'tough love,' tactics that are short-sighted and harmful and can serve to alienate the youth even further. In our behaviourally focused society, the be-all and end-all is the behaviour itself. If we gain compliance, we deem the method successful. However, while tough love tactics may remove the problem, it is short lived. When the conflict ends and separation is restored, the aggression will return with greater force, with the added fuel coming from the attachment frustration that has just been provoked. Most approaches to discipline are devoid of any sensitivity to emotional vulnerability, lacking in any consciousness of attachment, and possess little understanding of the dynamics of development. Once we factor in attachment and vulnerability, we see that "punishment creates an adversarial relationship and incurs emotional hardening. . . . Tough love is not designed with attachment in mind" (Neufeld & Maté, 2004, p. 271).

While Neufeld and Maté (2004) are speaking to parents with younger children, their advice of "use connection, not separation" should also be kept in mind by workers working with youth to avoid irreparable damage being done to the relationship or making it virtually impossible to establish one. When workers use separation as punishment (such as kicking youth out of placements, closing their files, or not allowing them to see family members), youth can respond aggressively, being unable to express their hurt appropriately. In such situations I have heard youth call workers all kinds of names, state they would like to harm the person, and then be more resigned, saying it confirmed that the person never really cared in the first place – it confirms their negative beliefs about adults and thickens the walls they have built around themselves. Though perhaps not intentionally, traditional approaches also serve to reinforce or trigger a re-living of the traumatic experiences they have suffered throughout their lives, as captured by Batmanghelidjh (2006):

> For this type of [traumatized] child, punishment is not an effective learning tool. The terrorized child has had experiences of extreme violation and horror. There is nothing more one can do to them which would frighten them into behaving

better. . . . The violated child is emotionally too disorganized to make the necessary connections and learn from the infliction of punishment. The violated child
lives in a different emotional universe from the rest of us. Their sense of personal
damage is so profound that mild threats of damage like punishment do not register with them. . . . Punishment is experienced as rejection, which deepens the
child's resentment. . . . Once these children feel contained and consistent love,
they will not want to lose it.

(p. 101)

This is seen is the use of the 'three-strikes' approach to the behaviour of youth in
group care or foster care. When there is an incident, as inevitable as it is, the youth
is told this is strike one, thus they are threatened that if there are two more incidents,
they will be discharged[4] from the placement. As high-risk youth do tend to see punishment as rejection, and given their profound sense of failure and shame, the first strike
often triggers emotional responses, behaviours escalate, the youth becomes more and
more unable to regulate themselves, and the next two strikes come in quick succes-
sion. So, what is a three-strikes rule is essentially a 'one-strike' rule for these youth.
This contributes to them cycling through numerous placements or, moreover, building
a reputation so no placements will take them.

The youth is blamed for their behaviour, but rarely are questions being asked about
the appropriateness of such rules and the approaches used by staff. In placements with
resources that shifted away from this approach to more relationship-based practices,
youth were staying longer, more often buying into the programs, and making better
connections to staff.[5] Such change is also helping ensure that "corporate parenting is
personalized and given a human face" (Luckock & Lefevre, 2008, p. 2).

Granted, at times, there may be safety issues that need to be taken into consideration and safety of workers and other youth is always paramount. However, we must
be very sure that our attitudes and actions are not triggering attachment and rejecting behaviours before we heap more blame on the youth and conclude they are out
of control. More likely, it is the stressed relationship which case workers and service
providers play a significant role in creating that pushes them into escalating their
behaviour. We should know that they will not be able to access their executive, or
rational, parts of the brain when escalated; thus they will rely on their more primitive
brain, likely resulting in poor decisions being made. In a futile attempt to maintain or
regain control, we can confront and bark orders all we like only to create a potentially
dangerous situation for everybody. Children and youth who are not in control lack
the ability to recognize the impact of their behaviour or to anticipate consequences.
Sadly, it is not uncommon for workers, in frustration, to make the youth feel more
shame, and reinforce that there is something wrong with them, by letting them know
their behaviour was selfish, insensitive, and inconsiderate. In reality this is disrespectful behaviour on the part of the worker given "acts that disrespect youth fuel disrespect and defiance" (Brendtro & du Toit, 2005, p. 28). If we are more thoughtful and
intentional about our practice, and appreciate where the youth have come from, we
can avoid this altogether and give the youth a sense that we are with them, not against
them (Neufeld & Maté, 2004). This is essential if we are going to continue down the
road of developing a relationship. This approach not only builds the support network
of the youth, but it offers the chance to co-regulate – keeping us calm and helping the

youth learn to calm themselves. This cannot be done in isolation, as the child or youth will otherwise rage until they tire out rather than having the nurturing and connection to help bring them down. This may not even require any words, as the reassurance they are not being rejected and abandoned, and that the worker is not angry, can be accomplished simply by close silent proximity.

As if you didn't know by now, it's the relationship . . .

The adult, ideally, must have "the presence of mind to create a mental space so that he or she can continue to serve as a secure home base, a refuge in the storm that can be life, so that the adolescent knows that a safe harbour always exists."

Daniel Siegel[6]

Experience and research again and again demonstrates that youth are wanting relationships with healthy and supportive adults in which there is a sense of equality rather than power-and-control dynamics. They do not want to be judged, they value mutual respect, and they want their voices to be heard. Herbert (2007) concluded that youth wish for "opportunities to form personal attachments with their social workers in order to repair damaged trust" (p. 241). Young people growing up in care ask that social workers take the time to get to know them, to listen to them, to not give up on them, and to be better advocates on their behalf. In addition, social workers should be attentive, available, caring, flexible, knowledgeable, real, and trustworthy; they should be "someone who cares about me," be "someone who is interested in me as an individual person," and be "someone who will call me back even for a two-minute conversation when lonely" (Herbert, 2007, pp. 241–242). Without establishing empathic, caring, and compassionate relationships, effective intervention is impossible and personal change and development are unlikely (Lonne et al., 2009, p. 139). From the youth themselves, they have said they do not cooperate with workers with whom they have no established connection (Brendtro & du Toit, 2005, p. 66). This echoes my experiences of repeatedly hearing youth question why they should talk to workers, or do what they say, when they do not even know them or perceive that the worker has not bothered to get to know them.

Over the years, the theme I have heard most consistently from youth with respect to what they value most from case workers and service providers is not to be judged. Though we tend to act like they are not aware, they are, in fact, painfully aware that they do not always make the safest or healthiest choices for themselves. But, they continue to want a better life (unless they have completely given up and are numb to emotional pain and humiliation, which happens but is uncommon). Feeling judged adds to their shame, damages their self-worth even further, and causes them to worry about losing the little support and help they have in their lives (see Box 7.2).

Box 7.2   Fear of being judged

I received this poem in a card from 'Sarah' on Valentine's Day, 2008. At the time she was in Secure Services, a locked facility where youth are placed when they are judged to be in danger to themselves or others, need immediate attention, and nothing less intrusive can alleviate the crisis. Sarah was not happy initially, but came to appreciate she was feeling unsafe and out of control. Sarah repeatedly told me she appreciated that she did not feel judged for the choices she made, and later regretted, in her life.

> *Thank you for always being there,*
> *To listen and understand me.*
> *I appreciate all you did for me,*
> *And all you still do*
>
> *Thank you for making me feel whole again,*
> *For putting my pieces back together.*
> *I appreciate you putting my life back together,*
> *You saved my life*
>
> *You may not understand,*
> *Why I do what I do.*
> *But you never criticized,*
> *You just helped me through*
> *I knew I could come to you when I was down,*
> *'Cause I knew you'd always be there*
> *To pick me back up*
> *And say everything will be okay*

Other key traits they tell me they look for include genuineness ("no bullshit"); for workers to show they are caring ("doing this job because you give a shit"); honesty ("won't stab me in the back"); flexibility ("I like that they don't always go by the book"); respect ("don't think they're fucking better than me"); being heard ("nobody listens to what I have to say, and it's my life"); and that their professional support team follows through on what they say ("don't blow smoke up my ass"). Of course, this would not just apply to high-risk youth. Everybody would like to be treated this way! Similarly, Thomas (2008) states the most important factors for engagement are a willingness to listen, a non-judgemental and non-directive approach, humour, straight talking, and trust and confidentiality. Doel (2010) cites research from the early 1990s that highlights what service users value in a relationship: sensitivity, patient understanding, friendliness, reliability, regular contact, attention to detail, and openness – all speaking to the presence of a caring person.[7] Howe (2014) writes of the idea on the "virtuous person who receives uncanny support from clients whose views, when sought, give high praise for workers who are available, reliable, fair, empathetic, and honest" (Howe, 2014, p. 184).

While the youth have responded positively to the HRYI with respect to having a connection to their workers, being heard, and feeling supported (Steering Committee, High Risk Youth Initiative, 2007), there have also been challenges. These challenges include the ongoing intensity of the work in being available to the youth as frequently as is necessary once a connection has been established; maintaining a work-life balance given the seemingly never-ending demands of the role; the ongoing exposure to the traumatic stories of the youth; the fear of a tragic incident given the high-risk lifestyles of the youth; the need to be constantly vigilant about maintaining limits and boundaries given the youth have typically experienced such profound boundary violations throughout their lives, leaving them extremely vulnerable (Reamer, 2012); and finding a balance between attending to the needs of the youth and maintaining the administrative duties that are part of the child welfare system (Lonne et al., 2009; Ruch, 2008). These systemic challenges may, in part, explain that while a therapeutic alliance would obviously serve to better facilitate positive working relationships between case workers and the youth, traditional practices are still the norm (Batmanghelidjh, 2006; Brendtro & du Toit, 2005; Lonne et al., 2009). These are systemic problems that the youth did not create and for which they should not receive substandard care. When they are ready to make a connection, workers must be able to respond, and the system needs to allow the time to make this happen. After all, the child welfare system was set up to keep children and youth safe, as well as to help and support children, youth, and families. Workers also need a system (government and agencies) that supports this challenging work and looks after the workers who take it on, potentially at a personal cost.

Wired for connection

Healing is not found in emotional coldness.

Camila Batmanghelidjh[8]

Despite the fact humans are wired for connections to others, it is my overwhelming experience that case workers consistently underestimate how much the youth they are working with actually want to be in a relationship with them. If aware of this drive for connection, workers could more effectively help youth navigate this relationship-building process appropriately. However, given the assumption that youth are more invested in being defiant, manipulative, and uncooperative, we are consistently missing the youths' "bids for connection" (Brendtro et al. 2009, p. 48), including when they are testing us to see if they will risk allowing us into their lives. At these times when the youth is "inviting us to cross the intimacy barrier" and we fail to acknowledge this, or we are too busy, we need to be aware that this opportunity may never happen again. Alternatively, if we are missing the signs and cross the intimacy barrier too quickly, we can expect an abrupt (i.e., "fuck you") reaction, leaving the worker feeling frustrated or rejected (Perry, 2010, lecture). These lost opportunities are too frequent because we do not value, or do not make or have, the time to be attuned to the youth on our caseloads. With this, lost is the chance for youth to heal their trauma-related problems as, according to Perry (2009), ultimately it is healthy relational interactions with safe and familiar individuals that can create the safety needed for this to occur. Youth need to be able to trust the worker and feel safe before they can "move on and address specific problems, whether those problems are intrapersonal, interpersonal or to do with the business of just trying to live and cope" (Howe, 2008, p. 181). Simply stated, relationships are the 'active ingredients' of the environment's influence on healthy human development. Positive change occurs in the context of authentic relationships – people need to know someone cares and will be there unconditionally (Hammond, 2010; National Scientific Council on the Developing Child, 2004a).

While Perry and Szalavitz (2006) state that recognizing the power of relationships and relational cues are essential to effective therapeutic work and, indeed, to effective parenting, caregiving, teaching, and just about any other human endeavour, the authors also discuss how some of the most therapeutic experiences do not take place in 'therapy,' but rather take place in naturally occurring healthy relationships. Research on the most effective treatments to help buffer child trauma "might be accurately summed up this way: what works best is anything that increases the quality and number of relationships in the child's life" (p. 80). This fits with what Siegel (2003) refers to when speaking of how "relationships can nurture and heal the mind" (p. 3) and what Howe (2005) means by one relationship being able to counteract trauma.

Without such connection the youth miss out on experiencing and learning about healthy connections with others, and thus could persist in engaging in negative personal relationships. There are many youth who go from relationship to relationship, whether intimate or as 'friends' (as these people are typically more acquaintances who also tend to be deprived of deeper meaningful relationships). These connections remain superficial, as the risk of being emotionally intimate, fear of losing control, and loss of self are simply too much (Maté, 1999). These relationships, as we often see with our high-risk youth, can often end up in violence given the lack of ability to communicate effectively, understand the emotions of each other, or regulate their own emotions or that of their partner. As discussed, "people will form relationships with others exactly at the same level of psychological development and self-acceptance as their own" (Maté, 1999, p. 264). Those who have been maltreated are often anxious and fearful of direct mind-to-mind communication. Such communication only takes place if there is a sense of feeling safe in the relationship, eventually allowing for the exploration of painful and difficult emotions (Howe, 2005). Workers can provide such safety, allowing our youth to break the cycle of going from one problematic relationship to the next and avoiding the common misconception of love becoming equated with sex, leaving the relationship unfulfilling and superficial. Workers can help youth understand that there are different kinds of relationships, including those that can be emotionally intimate, without being physically intimate. This can help the youth to start changing their natural instinct of pulling back and to start testing their ability to be vulnerable during meaningful communication that can help them heal (Howe, 2005; Maté, 1999).

When high-risk youth suffer from a dearth of naturally occurring or informal relationships, the best substitute can be the professionals, if we take the time and are flexible, shifting between our mandated roles and just hanging out with the youth and getting to know them. Indeed, this has therapeutic value for the youth, as case workers, community workers, and group home staff who are flexible in their roles can attest. The quality and number of relationships can be increased as the service team is built under the youth as a safety net. Once the youth are less intimidated by having caring and nurturing people in their lives, work can start on transitioning to less formal supports who can be invested in the youth over the long term and beyond the mandate of child welfare.

It is important for youth to learn that reaching out for help can be a sign of strength, rather than weakness. However, we need to help them create the safe space and find the safe people so they can keep moving forward rather than returning to old ways of coping. If feeling isolated, the chances of regression increases. If shame and guilt resurface, the chance of the youth asking for help diminishes. Sadly, in the absence of informal relationships, many youth must rely solely on the formal professional community for positive support. This being the case, we must respond accordingly and adjust our child welfare system to allow the time to 'hang out' with youth and get to each other in a less formal but significant way. We know many high-risk youth cannot rely on family in a consistent way, as this is where their troubles started. For some youth, inconsistent family relations can be very damaging (see Box 7.3) and leaving them to find their own 'street family' can be dangerous, as it can possibly lead to gang involvement, criminal activity, violence, and sexual exploitation. If we cannot be flexible enough, and genuine enough, to engage the youth and work with them so they can be emotionally safe, we can be sure that others will fill the void – quite possibly pimps, johns, or abusive partners. It is disturbing that pimps can do a better job of engaging youth than case workers and service providers but not altogether surprising given that the experiences of our young people do not always allow them to distinguish between exploitation and genuine caring. Our government and community organizations must give workers the flexibility and time to get to these youth first.

Box 7.3   Rejection and abandonment treadmill

As supervisor of the High Risk Youth Unit for seven years, a disturbing trend was observed with youth who were having a lot of trouble with their parent(s). The most common dynamic was between a female youth and her mother. Many high-risk youth were estranged from their parents and, while facing many challenges, they could understand the limitations of their parents and that it was not realistic that they would be moving back home any time soon. This didn't stop them wishing things could be different and grieving this loss but, to some degree, they appeared to know where they stood.

For those youth whose parents remained involved, different dynamics were noted. At the risk of generalizing, the mothers often had come from dysfunctional family circumstances themselves and struggled with stability in their own lives (moving frequently, addictions issues, financial hardships). They had difficulty with relationships so there were frequent boyfriends and much of their energy appeared to be put into needing to be needed, focusing on meeting the needs of their partner, and trying to find a sense of belonging – much like the female youth they had raised. The mothers and daughters wanted to be together and be part of each other's lives, but conflicts were inevitable if they were living under the same roof. This becomes a cycle of the mother inviting her daughter to live at home with the message that they could work out their problems. The daughter, being desperate for a sense of acceptance and belonging, and receiving acknowledgement and nurturing from her mother, would return home feeling hopeful. However, within two weeks or so, the daughter was being kicked out again, leaving her devastated. While she would say she expected this to happen, it did not stop this cycle from playing out over and over again. The youth would be stuck in this cycle of hope→conflict→rejection and abandonment→self-loathing/

self-harm. When the home situation would break down, it was observed that these young women would react against themselves with extreme drug/alcohol bingeing, cutting themselves, and/or being very promiscuous. It was as if they did not care what happened to themselves, such was the loss and heightened feelings of shame, anxiety, and sense of worthlessness. However, at the first sign of their mother wanting to reconcile, the daughter was back on the treadmill, with their support team helping to pick up the pieces once again.

This is a very difficult cycle to break. Telling the youth they should avoid contact with their parent is futile, as the mother and daughter are then likely to align against the case worker and the service providers. Maintaining a connection with the youth is essential given the need for intervention when the situation at home erupts into a crisis. Fortunately, many youth seek out support at this point, though a lot of damage can be done in the meantime. Fitting with the practice framework and philosophy of the Get Connected *model, and knowing that heaping more shame and punishment on the youth for breaking rules is unhelpful even if intended to break this destructive cycle and protect them emotionally, it is important that the support team is immediately available. The youth is particularly vulnerable at this time and will need the support to avoid these self-destructive behaviours. Over and above this, the connection offers ongoing emotional support, an opportunity to discuss this unhealthy cycle (with the mother as well), the chance to develop a safety plan, and the chance to gain insight as to how the next time could have a different outcome. Hopefully, the mother and daughter will be open to counselling but, at this volatile time, they typically want nothing to do with each other. When in the reconciliation phase they do not feel they need the counselling. Though it can be difficult for the support team to witness this destructive dynamic, it is critical the youth has someone to turn to when the hurt becomes overwhelming enough that they turn to harming themselves.*

Challenging youth; challenging ourselves

> Inasmuch as helpers hold a leadership position in the relationship, a collaborative partnership begins with our finding ways to cooperate with clients and make our work relevant to them, rather than simply expecting them to cooperate with us.
>
> William Madsen[9]

As Tammie's story in Chapter 2 illustrates, high-risk youth are not always easy youth to work with; thus workers must be self-aware, reflective, and, critically, reflexive.[10] It is not just about looking back and seeing how we could have done things differently, or how our words may have further marginalized a youth or damaged the relationship, but thinking of these potential dangers in the moment. As rewarding as this work can be, there are certainly times we can feel overwhelmed, frustrated, and even angry, making one feel inadequate as a worker and as a professional. I remember in the mid-1990s, when working for child welfare in a school, a youth asked me, *as long as I was trying to control everything he does, would I be telling him when he could breathe?* Inexplicably, I told him that was my goal. I do not know whether he smiled because of my absurd answer, the fact he knew he had me rattled which gave him control of the situation, or both. I had lost focus, was not reflexive, and put myself into a power struggle.

Especially earlier in my career, I saw apologizing and admitting mistakes as a sign of weakness and an admission that I did not know how to handle situations. Now I see being humble not only as being honest with myself and acknowledging I do not have all the answers, but also as a window to talking about relationship as a way to highlight that, at this point in time, we are part of each other's lives so let's get to know each other. It is a way of levelling the playing field, though the youth and the worker know the relationship can never be equal just by the fact that workers are in a position of authority and the involvement is typically mandated (though less so for a community worker). In addition, if the youth is not in a position to contribute to the decision-making process, decisions will be made for them and we expect to know many of the intimate details of the lives of the youth, which is hardly reciprocal. Despite these imbalances, we can do much to minimize this hierarchy, to give youth a voice, and to empower them to be making decisions in their own lives. We can help build a partnership.

In fitting with the harm reduction approach, and practicing in a strength-based way, being aware of the impact we have on our youth can make our work and our role less oppressive and foster opportunities to engage youth in a meaningful way. By being self-aware and understanding our trigger points and biases – as well as appreciating how our personal, systemic, and cultural values, as well as our privilege – can influence the way we practice, we are more likely to be thoughtful about what we say and how we say things. This can foster engagement and give youth fewer excuses to pull away and remain isolated. However, if we are rigid in our approach, address problems facing youth in a formulaic manner, react defensively, and engage in power struggles believing we know what is best, we can anticipate that the youth will not see us as relevant in their lives and the opportunities for a relationship will remain remote at best. The given is that the youth will test us – rightfully so – to see if we will be a safe person or a rejecting person (see '*Working through testing behaviours*' in Chapter 9). Why would any of us want to connect with another person who is acting in a dismissive and rejecting manner?

As workers, we must always appreciate that the youth are giving us the privilege of being invited into their lives. This is obviously not in the sense that we have a mandated duty to work with a youth whose file has been assigned to us, but rather when the youth and the worker perceive that the engagement process has started. Again, it is amazing when reflecting on how many people may have let this youth down that they are here taking this significant risk. How do we respond to honour such a step?

Madsen (2007) discusses the use of an anti-oppressive strategy: collaborative inquiry. This involves getting to know the youth outside of the problems that have quite possibly identified them up to this point. It is about learning about their goals and dreams for the future, what is getting in the way, and what is needed to help them reach their destiny. Rather than making assumptions, or falling into the trap of thinking we know best and believing we understand what is happening for the youth, we adopt a 'not-knowing stance.' This stance assumes we are genuinely curious about the youth, that we can never fully understand another person, and that we are always in a state of being informed by the other; that we always can learn more about what has been said or not said (Madsen, 2007, p. 157). This does not mean we abandon professional knowledge, as we have wisdom from our own experiences and in our work with other youth, but it tells the youth they are unique and are appreciated as an individual. It is not uncommon for youth to react to assumptions by saying – or shouting – at their worker, "you don't know me" or "you don't understand me." They are right, but we can ask questions and learn in a collaborative way, which promotes understanding, creates a sense of safety, and helps build relationship. Turnell and Edwards (1999) write that "the most empowering and caring activity we can engage in is to ask questions of those we serve" (p. viii).

In my current role, I am typically asked to consult in situations because the case worker, community worker, group home worker, or foster parent is in conflict with the youth. The adult here is frustrated and the youth is reacting because they are experiencing stress in their relationships (Perry & Szalavitz, 2006). As discussed previously, there may be a power struggle; the youth may feel threatened by having people caring about them and losing control; there may be a fear of imminent rejection; the youth may be feeling guilt, shame, and a sense of unworthiness; or perhaps the worker or the caregiver is using a tough love approach. But whatever the reason, there is a sense of disconnect. Missing is a sense of alliance that the youth needs to feel supported and valued, as well as have a sense of belonging, even temporarily. The difference between situations that are conflictual and those that are co-operative is partly the result of workers and clients forming an *alliance* in the crisis stage of contact (Turnell & Edwards, 1999). Such opportunities arise quite frequently as, with all they have going on in their short lives, high-risk youth are often in crisis. Madsen (2007) writes that his "preferred *relational stance* with families can be described as one of an *appreciative ally*" in which we position ourselves in an alliance with the client so they experience us as "in their corner" or "on their side" (p. 22). Being an ally also helps give the message that it is possible to deal with life's crises without panic, pandemonium, and despair and that positive human relationships are what makes this possible (Ruch, 2010a).

Simmonds (2008) explains how such a connection speaks to the essence of the work with youth, allowing for a level of communication that is meaningful to them and sustains a relationship over time (Simmonds, 2008). This is the comfortable level of relationship that, depending on the youth, can take from months to years to establish. It is the phase that we can indeed get to in which conversation can be less about crises and the immediate need to be safe and more about future dreams, goals, sense of place in the world, spirituality, and other meaning-of-life-type topics that other youth may share with their parent(s). Such chats can take place during drives (often a useful way to chat openly without the pressure of making eye contact), going for walks (another parallel-positioned way to converse), or over coffee (perhaps for a youth this is seen as a more adult way to talk). These settings also provide opportunities to be casual and joke around with the youth to show a more human side (Lemma, 2010). This is the phase where 'just being there' as a stable and reliable presence is important, even if face-to-face contact is not happening as much as it used to (Cook, 2008). This suggests the fears of rejection and abandonment are diminishing and there is an emergence of a trusting relationship. Just a presence and being attuned to a youth "helps build a more coherent, integrated mind, and helps overcome the sense of inevitability that others will be unavailable to you, punish you, reject you or abandon you" (Howe, 2005, p. 274). As this sense of self develops, youth begin to feel more connected with those around them and are more open to engaging in more meaningful relationships with people beyond their case worker and community worker, increasing their sense of belonging (Howe, 2005).

The one caution is to not allow complacency to set in. Such a comfortable relationship can be very pleasant for members of the service team, but this can increase the risk of creating co-dependency or dependency for the youth, which could threaten the progress that has been made and increase the anxiety when, inevitably, the youth's file should close. This can decrease the confidence the youth may have gained with respect to moving on to the next phase of their life and take away the opportunity to celebrate this transition.

Another idea that can make workers more reflective and mindful in their practice is writing letters to the youth. This can be done when it is particularly challenging to engage the youth on a face-to-face level, to help them through a difficult phase in which they are withdrawing, or when the relationship is coming to an end. A letter gives the youth something to hang on to and reflect back on whenever they want. A letter at the end of the journey can summarize their accomplishments, point out the barriers they have had to overcome, and recall the good, bad, and ugly turns of the relationship between the youth and the author of the letter. Such a letter can acknowledge mistakes made along the way on both sides, but also how the relationship was strong enough to endure. The letters can also highlight a sense of moving forward and help reflect back on the therapeutic journey (Madsen, 2007). Batmanghelidjh (2006) writes letters to youth that reflect their challenges and successes, and includes how society and the child welfare system (and her own work at times) has let them down. While initially worried about making the youth feel ashamed or exploited by writing the letters, this was not the case. She writes that a profound thing happened when she read them her letter. They were "deeply moved, as if for the first time their story was told with the emotional significance it deserved" (p. 153).

While not in a formal therapeutic sense, my experience with the few times I took the opportunity to write such a letter was also that the youth had a very emotional reaction and the youth very much appreciated that I had taken the time to write to them. It appeared to reinforce that they had value as a person; that their thoughts, words, and opinions were validated; that they could face future challenges; and that they no longer had as much of a fear of allowing other healthy people into their lives. When writing the letters, it became very clear to me how many risks the youth had taken to allow a connection to happen, and how far they had come from the days of being hostile and pushing people out of their lives and sabotaging through their belief that they were undeserving (Noshpitz, 1994). For the youth, their worker over time can become an invaluable source of memories. Again, this tends to be an area workers underestimate, but writing letters can help workers reflect on how they have been a positive influence. A letter can also be a chance to acknowledge and thank the youth for contributing to the worker's own personal development and learning. Every situation provides an opportunity to learn and improve practice, and the uniqueness of each individual means the learning is a never-ending journey. I think our youth are pleased to know how they contributed. Writing a letter when the formal relationship is coming to an end can be an appropriate time for consolidating work with the clients to help them identify their strengths, recognize their growth, and build up their confidence in facing the future (Lee & Charm, 2002).

Having established credibility and connection, most high-risk youth want us to be a big deal in their lives and, despite what workers might think, many youth will miss them once their file closes. This speaks to the need for ceremony once youth are moving out of the child welfare system. It can be damaging if workers simply disappear without a word. While this would seem very bizarre, the number of youth reporting such an event is disturbing. Some youth have told me over the years that they did not know if they had a case worker or whether they had an open file *even though they were permanent wards of the government!* This is, I hope, not done intentionally but, again, speaks to how workers assume they hold little value in the eyes of the youth (McMahon, 2010; Solomon, 2010). Of course, there is also the possibility that the end of the relationship is hard for the worker and they therefore avoid having this critical 'goodbye' conversation with young person on their caseload (Solomon, 2010). This can potentially undo much good work that has taken place. As McMahon (2010) points out, "the defended worker who argues that avoiding making close relationships lessens the service user's pain when they leave (and implicitly their own too) is denying their humanity and potential for emotional growth" (p. 161).

For all the efforts we might make; feeling we are giving a lot; that we are making ourselves vulnerable; that we risk struggling with vicarious traumatization, secondary trauma, or compassion fatigue/burnout (rather than compassion satisfaction or post-traumatic growth);[11] that perhaps we have even lost some sleep worrying about a youth; that we have gone out of our way, gone the extra mile, and gone beyond the call of duty . . . what does the youth owe us? Nothing, of course. We need to be mindful of the fact we do this work to collaborate with, support, and help youth. Typically, we do get something back, as once a connection is established the relationship can be satisfying on both sides, even with the ups and downs that are inevitable. However, this should not be expected and, at times, a youth will give very little back, which can leave workers feeling disappointed, disillusioned, or even resentful. I have heard workers complain that a youth on their caseload does not appreciate anything they are given or that is done on their behalf. Again, this is an issue for the worker rather than the youth. The youth are responding to their circumstances as best they can. It has been pointed out a number of times that making a connection is a big risk for a youth, having experienced relational trauma that makes them fear getting close to others (Howe, 2008). Workers cannot lose sight of this, thus the ongoing need to be self-aware and understand where such personal feelings and thoughts might be coming from. Sometimes our youth may simply not show appreciation throughout the time we are involved with them. As Batmanghelidjh (2006) tells us:

> They feel too ashamed to admit to using and needing the help they are given. The admission of vulnerability is too painful and shaming. The client who recovers often wishes to forget the organization and the people who helped because to remember is to be reminded of how vulnerable they were.
>
> (p. 117)

This avoiding and shame can also go both ways, as workers who feel unable to solve the challenges presented by the youth may feel "de-skilled, rubbished and ashamed. Unwittingly avoiding a youth, especially avoiding face-to-face contact, can be a reminder of 'mutual hopelessness' " (Batmanghelidjh, 2006, p. 117). Of course, we do not have all of the answers, and working with high-risk youth very much highlights how true this actually is. But, we have the youth, being experts in their own lives, to help us. Most youth, if the worker has credibility in their eyes, do not expect their worker to have all of the answers. We just need to be open enough, and courageous enough, to say "I don't know," "I am out of ideas," "I'm sorry," "I made a mistake," and "What do you think?'" or "What would you suggest?" If we are intentional about our practice, and open to being vulnerable in our relationship with our youth, we will be able to ask such questions. However, it can be surprisingly hard when we are tasked with, or people look to us, as always having the solution. This is not easy work, but with strong and informed supervision, and being self-aware, self-reflective, and mindful, workers can keep things in perspective, avoid burning out, and remain appreciative of the gift youth give to us by allowing us to be part of their lives.

Conclusion

> We need your love. . . . We look up to you more than you will ever know.
> A youth talking to a room full of case workers (2016)

I am guessing that when people are thinking about a career in working with children and youth they are not likely to be thinking it would be a good opportunity to punish kids into compliance to help them reform, see the error of their ways, and not be a burden on society. The thinking is probably more in line with wanting to build relationships, help others, perhaps help people avoid the struggles they themselves encountered, give back to society, and contribute to making the world a better place. So at what point, in child welfare at least, does this idealism take a back seat to the role of being an agent of social control? When did we start allowing relationships to become secondary to proceduralism, start spending our time in front of a computer rather than meeting with the youth, and start punishing youth for mistakes rather than helping them heal? While policy and procedures and accountability have their place, the focus must be less about "what we do" and more about "who we are being when we do it," as this will have the greater impact in the lives of our service users (Maté, 2008, p. 380). Indeed, what draws us into working with youth in the first place is more about *who we are* than about the mechanics of *what we will be doing*.

Thankfully there has been a shift and organizations are starting to appreciate the need to support relationship-based practices. Being trauma-informed and coming from a relationship-based perspective, we might be less likely to ask, "What is wrong with this youth?" and more likely to ask, "What is happening in my relationship with this young person that does not work for them?" (Gaughan & Kalyniak, 2012, p. 100). Inevitably, this will make us self-reflective and mindful in our practice, leading us to be less judgemental and more genuine and flexible in our approach to youth. Relationship-based practice is helping us reclaim our role as helper, support person, advocate, facilitator, and even friend and to let go of our role as the authority.

Working with high-risk youth is, indeed, not for everyone working in the area of human services. A rotation system of assigning files to workers does not tend to do a lot of favours for high-risk youth. While the benefits of specialization are debated in the child welfare system, and in academia, my experience is that these youth need workers who are passionate, will hang in for the long term, who are open to new ways of doing things, and who want to get to know the youth and understand where their lives have taken them. There are no quick fixes when working with youth impacted by early trauma. The truth is that very disturbed children take a very long time to provide visible outcomes (Batmanghelidjh, 2006). However, the journey is worth it! Even for older adolescents, it is crucial to connect each youth with persons who will actively and consistently check on him or her, follow up, monitor, exercise authority, and "hassle the youth enough to show they care" (Kagan, 2004, p. 300).

Discussion questions to consider for Chapter 7

1   Batmanghelidjh (2006) argues that a committed worker "is perceived as too involved, as if feeling is somehow an indicator of incompetence, or inferiority or weakness. Our structures are failing children because we are scared of love. The expression of our humanity terrifies us into political cowardice" (p. 157). While maintaining appropriate boundaries, can you be too committed to a youth?

2   Is it possible to be a worker and a friend to a youth? What are the limitations? What is the potential?

3   Can you think of situations in which proceduralism took precedence over relationship-based practice?

4   Are there times when you witnessed relationship-based practice take precedence over proceduralism?

5   What is a reasonable amount of time for child welfare to be involved with a youth?

6   What characteristics might be required for a service provider interested in working with high-risk youth?

7   Can formal supports (i.e., paid supports) be as influential and meaningful as informal or natural supports such as mentors, coaches, extended family, peers, etc.?

8   What might be some other reasons why workers continue to underestimate that youth value being engaged in a relationship?

Notes

1 Lonne et al. (2009) is quoting Leeson from, Leeson, R. (2007). "My life in care: Expereinces of non-participation in decision-making processes." *Child and Family Social Work*, 12: 268–277.

2 The documentary, *The Word on the Street*, was produced by the Child and Youth Advocate (2007), Alberta. Three youth, all labelled 'high risk' due to the life circumstances and the dangers that threatened them emotionally and physically, and three social workers (including this writer) were interviewed independently about their experiences in working together under the practice framework and philosophy of the High Risk Youth Initiative.

3 Reamer and Siegel (2008) point out that while the punishment orientation continues to be challenged currently, criticism of such approaches dates back to the Second International Penitentiary Congress in Stockholm in 1878, at which time it was resolved that "delinquent children should not be punished but educated so as to enable them to 'gain an honest

livelihood and to become of use to society instead of an injury to it' " (Platt, 1977, p. 50, as cited in Reamer and Siegel, 2008, p. 5); and again in 1879, when the Illinois Board of Public Charities noted, in referring to youth removed from their homes, that "the object of reformatory institutions is well stated; it is not punishment for past offenses, but training for future usefulness" (Platt, 1977, p. 106, in Reamer and Siegel, 2008, p. 5). Platt, A. (1977). *The child savers: The intervention of delinquency* (2nd Edition). Chicago, USA: University of Chicago Press.

4 There is often the use of medical and military language in group care and child welfare. Terms such as 'discharge,' 'terminating' placements or 'terminated from the program,' or 'going AWOL' are frequently used, and imply a need of *power over*, discipline, and the threat of punishment. This is another example of needing to change the language to reflect more relational and strength-based language.

5 This was noted in a number of shelters (rather than formal group homes) in Edmonton, Alberta, that changed their programs and adopted harm reduction and strength-based approaches. There was a significant increase in the length of stay by many youth, including a number of youth who had previously been denied placements in formal group care, and who had not shown stability in placements as youth (age 12 and older).

6 From the book, *Brainstorm: The Power and Purpose of the Teenage Brain* (2013, p. 198).

7 Mark Doel (2010) is citing a study done by Cheetham, Fuller, McIvor and Petch in 1992 (Cheetham, J., Fuller, R., McIvor, G., & Petch, A. (1992). *Evaluating Social Work Effectiveness*. Buckingham: Open University Press).

8 From the book, *Shattered Lives: Children Who Live with Courage and Dignity* (2006, p. 53).

9 From the book, *Collaborative Therapy with Multi-Stressed Families*, 2nd edn (2007, p. 34).

10 Gillie Bolton (2014) 'demystifies' *reflection* versus *reflexivity*: "*Reflection* is learning and developing through examining what we think happened on any occasion, and how we think others perceived the event and us, opening our practice to scrutiny by others. . . . *Reflection* is an in-depth consideration of events or situations outside of oneself: solitarily, or with critical support. The reflector attempts to work out what happened, what they thought or felt about it, why, who was involved and when, and what these others might have experienced and thought and felt about it. It is looking at whole scenarios from as many angles as possible: people, relationships, situation, place, timing, chronology, causality, connections, and so on, to make situations and people more comprehensible. This involves reviewing or reliving the experience to bring it into focus. Seemingly innocent details might prove to be key. . . . Reflection involves reliving and re-rendering: who said and did what, how, when, where, and why. *Reflexivity* is finding strategies to question our own attitudes, thought processes, values, assumptions, prejudices and habitual actions, to strive to understand our complex roles in relation to others. To be reflexive is to examine, for example, how we – seemingly unwittingly – are involved in creating social or professional structures counter to our own values (destructive of diversity, and institutionalising power imbalance for example). It is becoming aware of the limits of our knowledge, of how our own behaviour plays into organisational practices and why such practices might marginalise groups or exclude individuals. And it is understanding how we relate with others, and between us shape organisational realities' shared practices and ways of talking. Thus, we recognise we are active in shaping our surroundings, and begin critically to take circumstances and relationships into consideration rather than merely reacting to them, and help review and revise ethical ways of being and relating" (p. 13).

11 These concepts of *vicarious traumatization, secondary trauma, compassion fatigue or burnout, compassion satisfaction, and post-traumatic growth* will be discussed in Chapter 12 on boundaries and ethics in practice with high-risk youth.

Chapter 8

Broken spirits

Addictions and high-risk youth

The question is never 'Why the addiction? but 'Why the pain?'

Gabor Maté[1]

The great escape: addictions and high-risk youth

There is a correlation between adverse childhood experiences (ACE) and addictions and poor physical and mental health. Dr. Vincent Felitti's significant study of thousands of Americans from all walks of life demonstrated this in the ACE study (see Chapter 3 for more details on this study), leading him to conclude:

> Addiction is not a brain disease, nor is it caused by chemical imbalance or genetics. Addiction is best viewed as an understandable, unconscious, compulsive use of psychoactive materials in response to abnormal prior life experiences, most of which are concealed by shame, secrecy, and social taboo.
>
> (2003, p. 9)

So, addiction is more likely in people who have experienced trauma and lack of attachments. This is arguably 100% of high-risk youth and is supported by the fact that a snapshot of 55 high-risk youth showed 93% struggled with some form of addiction.[2] We want them to emerge from their addictions and from the hurt and pain they have known all of their lives. However, the way the child welfare system has traditionally dealt with this issue is to tell the youth they cannot use drugs or alcohol, be promiscuous, or self-harm or they will lose or be denied access to supports and services. While there may be tough challenges and fear from case workers and service providers in having to manage youth with addictions, this is another example of relying on punishment-consequence methods to try to bring about change.

Youth with addictions are often kicked out of foster homes and group homes, possibly locked in a residential facility, or denied access to supported independent living (SIL) programs because they are not seen as being stable or acting responsibly. If a youth is consumed with addictions or is putting themselves at an intolerable level of harm, there may indeed be a need to confine them (perhaps more than once) just to try and have the youth clear their head and be more aware of the risk they are to themselves. However, this *should* also provide an opportunity to start conversations around what good things they are deriving from their substance use, or behaviour, and what are the things they do not like about it. This can be done in a compassionate way without lectures (Ungar, 2006). These relationship-building conversations can be more productive than drug testing youth in an effort to catch them breaking the rules of a program. This not only is counter to building trust, but puts the emphasis purely on the addiction rather than on the underlying causes. Workers fail to consider what purpose the drug must be serving for the user (Maté, 2003). Indeed, we send the youth for drug testing but we do not always explore their pain.

Workers fail to realize that once the youth are told to stop using they then are forced to face their trauma and terrifying memories clean and sober. Turning to self-destructive patterns of behaviour may be the only coping strategy they have at this point in their lives. The thought of having to abandon this method of coping may be frightening and overwhelming. Before making such demands of the youth, workers must talk to the youth about how they are going to cope with their traumatic memories and what can be put in place to support them and develop alternative and healthier coping strategies. If youth continue to feel unsupported, marginalized, and isolated, the chances that they will find the strength to overcome their addictions when it is serving a purpose to the point of survival is quite remote.

As talked about as a theme in this book, tying cessation of addiction-related behaviours into worthiness to receive services typically sets the youth up for more failure and contributes to further feeling of shame, guilt, self-hatred, and self-destruction (Noshpitz, 1994). Youth are not giving in to their addictions to torment or hurt those trying to help them, but rather might be driven by their attempt to bolster their sense of personal control (Ungar, 2004) or avoid terrifying flashbacks. They might self-medicate to escape distress, and perhaps to self-regulate, as a way to get reprieve from the chaos in their head. They try to make their lives livable, even if this means "jeopardizing their lives for the sake of making the moment livable" (Maté, 2008, p. 28). While the youth in the HRYI often say they are desperate to shake their addictions, most are aware of their need for substances or behaviours as an "emotional anaesthetic" (Maté, 2008, p. 31). Traumatized people who cannot dissociate from their trauma use alcohol and drugs to produce the same numbing effect that dissociation produces; it becomes a way to reduce emotional, psychological, and spiritual pain (Bastien, Sohki Aski Esquao & Strega, 2009; Noshpitz, 1994). Maté (2008) refers to the pull of the drug having "wonderous power to offer the addict protection from pain while at the same time enabling him or her to engage the world with excitement and meaning" (p. 39). It allows the opportunity to escape spending "alone time" with their minds for fear it will be filled with bad memories and anxieties (p. 37). Maté (2008) writes:

> To expect an addict to give up her drug is like asking the average person to imagine living without all her social skills, support networks, emotional stability and sense of physical and psychological comfort. We must provide an island of relief. We have to demonstrate that esteem, acceptance, love and humane interaction are realities in this world, contrary to what she, the addict, had learned all her life.
>
> (p. 305)

Addiction is a response to life experience, not simply to a drug. We can order youth into treatment or lock them up to try and stop the cycle of self-destruction. This typically serves to make them angry more than help them realize they need to deal with their addictions. Workers can take away programs, opportunities, resources, or connections, but until they feel safe and supported, and their need to belong and be cared for is established, the system will continue to make them feel bad about themselves and reinforce their sense of failure. Maté (2008) cautions that coercion into treatment creates more problems than it solves, but inviting youth "into communities that can offer them acceptance, belonging and value" (p. 308) is likely to do more to help youth to enter a treatment program or at least meet with an addictions counsellor.

It is important that case workers and community workers always keep the door open to various addictions programs that might meet the needs of the youth. In the meantime, harm reduction-based safety plans can encourage the youth to reduce the amount of drugs or alcohol consumed or from engaging in other addictive behaviours, help them to access outreach addictions counsellors, help them find safe places to use, or help them access clean needles. Ideally, when the youth decides to take the next step, a plan can be put in place in a timely manner. The challenge is there are not always enough treatment beds for youth (in Alberta) and programs tend to rely on traditional methods, meaning a majority of youth end up being kicked out for attitude, behaviours, verbal aggression, or engaging in relationships with peers. Again, such rigid expectations are not a fit for high-risk youth and, adding to their stress, "chronically and mercilessly can in no way promote their capacity for healthy transformation" (Maté, 2008, p. 302). From an Aboriginal perspective, Bastien et al. (2009) also are critical of deficiency approaches, which, for indigenous people, replicate the process of marginalization that are at the core of their trauma. Consequently, treatment interventions often re-traumatize people.

It is not that there are no success stories. Many high-risk youth have overcome their addictions and consistently talk about the support they had and the belief others had in their strength to conquer their demons. However, it is not uncommon for young people to be in treatment a number of times and require intense and consistent support in between to get there. The question is how patient and understanding systems are to allow youth to try over and over to get clean and sober. Mysteriously, professionals tend to be hard on youth when they do not deal with their addiction upon request, despite the fact that high-risk youth lack an array of alternative coping strategies through no fault of their own.

Substance use can give youth a sense of identity and belonging within their defined community, yet we may disrespect this in favour of having them conform to societal norms that have not worked for these youth in the past. Some former high-risk youth who have been clean and sober for years needed many chances; they needed a chance to redefine their community and a create an identity and a sense of place away from the one that served this purpose before, albeit in a more harmful way (Ungar, 2004). When they failed they were hard enough on themselves without more criticism from those who were supposed to be helping them and encouraging them, or from people in society who may see substance abuse as a moral failing (Farmer, 2009). Others with addictions such as smoking, overeating, gambling, shopping, sex, hording, or collecting are more likely to be forgiven for failing to overcome their addiction on the first or second try, as these addictions are more mainstream and may even be entertainment in our reality TV world . A youth with addictions can be re-traumatized over and over again by ostracism and harassment as we fail to acknowledge they are locked into an addiction not only by their painful past and distressing present, but equally by their bleak view of the future.

Those with addictions often "cannot envision the real possibility of sobriety" despite the desperation to escape physical and mental suffering (Maté, 2008, p. 300). This has been reinforced by youth in active addiction and also when clean and looking back. While it can be a source of pride to reflect on how they overcame their addiction, they still clearly remember how it felt hopeless at the time, even when they knew it meant possibly losing their supports, their programs, their access to money, or even their child(ren). Maté (2008) points out that people with addictions are unable to develop compassion toward themselves and, again, it is common for high-risk youth to articulate that they have little love or respect for themselves. This fits with how they carry with them the burden of shame, guilt, and failure. Overcoming an addiction can start a change of how they perceive themselves, so it is important we are close by to "relieve their stress" (Mate, 2008, p. 300), be in their corner to encourage them not to give up, and to show them compassion. This can be achieved through using harm reduction approaches, which, of course, originated in the addictions field but tends to be absent in treatment programs (see Box 8.1).

Box 8.1   Rhonda's story: expectations

'Rhonda' finally agreed to go to treatment for her addictions. The 17-year-old mother drank frequently and used drugs periodically until she found out she was pregnant. Her daughter was born healthy. While there were some concerns about Rhonda's capacity to bond with her child in the hospital initially, this had improved over the three days she was kept in the hospital while tests were run to ensure the baby did not have drugs in her system. However, at the age of seven months Rhonda's daughter was apprehended and placed in a foster home. The police and child welfare services had intervened when Rhonda got into a fight with her partner when they were both drinking. The baby's father had threatened to take their daughter to his family out of town where Rhonda would not be able to see her. She attacked her partner and they both ended up with bruises and scrapes. Neighbours had called police due to the yelling and swearing and hearing a baby crying. The child was apprehended and both parents were warned to stay away from each other until the next day, at least. Rhonda had been hysterical at losing her daughter and called the case worker first thing the following Monday saying she would do anything to get her daughter back. Rhonda readily agreed to attend a residential voluntary youth addictions program.

Rhonda was very nervous entering the program, though staff welcomed her and helped her settle. She participated well in the group sessions, though was quieter in the individual counselling. During the second week, the youth were able to spend the Saturday with family, though were required to return by 9:00 p.m. Rhonda spent the day with her mother and sister, and had a two-hour visit with her daughter. She arrived back at the treatment centre by taxi just before the curfew. She rang the doorbell but there was no answer. She had been told the doorbell was temperamental, so also to knock in case. She did knock as she could not hear the doorbell ring. This went on for 20 minutes, to the point she was not sure what to do. She was getting anxious as she was now past the curfew time. She banged on the door harder, becoming more frustrated. Eventually a staff member answered the door and confronted Rhonda for being so aggressive in banging on the door. Rhonda said the doorbell was not working and explained she had been outside waiting and wondering what to do for 20 minutes. She was told to calm down and cautioned about her attitude. More staff came to the scene and saw that Rhonda was angry and upset. Rhonda said she just wanted to go to her room, calm down, and go to bed. Staff insisted she deal with her attitude, leading Rhonda to say that if the "fucking doorbell was working this would not have happened." The staff still wanted to deal with the situation rather than allow Rhonda to remove herself and calm down. Rhonda walked away, bumping a staff member aside as she headed to her room. The following day, Rhonda was discharged from the program for aggressive behaviour.

Addictions and pregnant youth

Pregnancy can shift the dynamics for youth struggling with addictions. In a meta-analysis of six studies on homeless adolescents, the mothers took the opportunity of pregnancy and childbirth to re-invent themselves, distancing themselves from their past behaviours, including substance abuse, which studies and experience have shown declined by 70% to 85% (Hathazi, Laankenau, Sanders & Jackson Bloom, 2009; Hunt, Joe-Laidler & MacKenzie, 2005; Sarri & Phillips, 2004). In short, pregnancy then can become a turning point away from street life and often toward finding their own place, going to school or work, and participating in youth programs (Hathazi, et al., 2009; King, Ross, Bruno & Erickson, 2009). This allowed them to focus on providing a stable and healthy environment for their children.

This shift in lifestyle and the ability to abstain from alcohol and drugs among pregnant and parenting youth has been noted with consistency over a decade of working with youth with high-risk lifestyles. While almost 25% of the female high-risk youth are pregnant or parenting at any given time, about 80% stopped using drugs and alcohol upon learning they were pregnant. Consequently, these young women gave birth to healthy babies. This was beyond the expectation of the case workers and community youth specialists. While the support and planning with these youth throughout the pregnancy could have contributed to making healthier choices, the belief is that such decisions went well beyond external resources. Much of the efforts made to help the youth deal with their addictions pre-pregnancy typically failed. However, learning they were pregnant was transformational for this 80%. Ceasing the use of drugs and alcohol, or reducing the use of hard drugs down to occasional marijuana use – not ideal but much better – seemed a natural and obvious thing to do. Perhaps the distraction of being pregnant helped them from having to face their trauma and their past clean and sober, replacing the drugs and alcohol. For many young moms, being pregnant helped them realize they had a responsibility beyond their own needs, that they did not want their children to have the challenges they faced as children, and shifting to a healthier lifestyle provided opportunities to reconnect with family who offered support and helped them cope (Hunt et al., 2005; King et al., 2009; Smyth, 2016). The young mothers reported being treated as adults. Becoming a mother was seen by some as a rite of passage to adulthood, with motherhood being a valued identity, one which commanded respect and allowed them to make decisions, possibly for the first time (Hunt et al., 2005; King et al., 2009; Siegel, 2013). For many street-involved girls "there is no quicker way to grow up" (Anderson, 1991, in Hunt et al., 2005, p. 362).[3] Many young mothers have used the supports provided and thrived as moms, appearing to break the multi-generational cycle of child welfare involvement. However, for others, once the novelty of being a mew mom wears off, tiredness sets in, and the reality of being a parent catches up with them after three to six months, protection issues can surface. They are still young and their trauma, lack of family support, limited freedom, and stressful relationships can cause a return to old and destructive ways of coping.

The biology of addiction

Lacking the chemistry of love, many pursue the love of chemicals.
Larry Brendrto, Martin Mitchell & Harman McCall[4]

Benoit (2006) outlines a situation in which a mother who is addicted to drugs and/ or alcohol has a primary attachment to the substance that gratifies the pleasure centre of the brain. That mother is less likely to derive pleasure from the caretaking of a dependent and demanding infant, and thus her attachment to the infant will be compromised. Aside from the likelihood that the mother may not be able to respond to the needs of her child, and that children growing up in households with a substance-abusing parent demonstrate impaired development and more adjustment and behaviour problems (Anderson & Seita, 2006; Howe, 2005), the child also sees how substances can become a coping strategy for stress, sadness, relationship issues, and loneliness. We know high-risk youth and street-involved youth often come from homes consumed with substance abuse, and running away or escaping into alcohol or drugs offers a way try and deal with their sadness and stress (Howe, 2005). The problems and the stress, however, can start well before the child emerges into the negative home environment. Combined, this external environment and brain development in the uterus is the single most important biological factor in determining whether or not a person will be predisposed to substance dependence and to other addictive behaviours. In the sense that a child's pre-disposition to addiction in their early development was programmed, "their brains never had a chance" (Maté, 2008, p. 187).

In adolescence, changes are taking place in the brain's reward and pleasure centres, resulting in routine activities becoming less satisfying. Youth shift from being parent focused to peer focused and they tend to take more risks. While from an evolutionary sense, this has helped in finding mates who are not close relatives, risking taking and ignoring routine, combined with immature judgement, can make teens more prone to addiction (Farmer, 2009). Add to this early trauma, brain development challenges in which accessing the rational brain is overshadowed by chronic stress and hypervigilance, experiencing what Perry (2010, lecture) refers to as a "poverty of relationships," and possibly blaming oneself for the loss of such connections, and the risk for abusing substances increases dramatically.

Abusing drugs can pathologically change one or more of the more common neurotransmitter systems in the brain. The key one is dopamine, as drugs induce large and rapid increases of this 'feel-good' chemical, which is the chemical messenger in the brain's reward system (Farmer, 2009). This creates a sense of euphoria – much like the natural high when dopamine and endorphins (natural opioids) are released during the process of human bonding and when experiencing love and care. This, of course, can be particularly appealing when life is a constant struggle; the rewards of the social contract are non-existent, causing a great emptiness; and there does not appear to be much to look forward to in life (Batmanghelidjh, 2006; Brendtro et al. 2009; Farmer, 2009; Perry, 2010). However, after repeated drug use, the reward system is less able to respond to behaviour that would normally produce large amounts of dopamine, such as food, sex, and humour. According to Farmer (2009), "The result is an addicted brain in which the reward circuitry malfunctions or becomes dysregulated, and even larger amounts of the drug are required for a person to feel a reward" (p. 142). The drug takes over the brain's dopamine system. Cognitive processes and reasoning become impaired, meaning traumatized youth are even more unable to self-regulate and even less capable of making sense of their behaviour. It makes sense that when the frontal cortex, or executive brain, is damaged, youth with addictions become unable to stifle inappropriate responses to their environment or learn appropriate social behaviours (Maté, 2008). As Maté (2008) writes, the brain systems involved in addiction are among the key organizers and motivators of human emotional life and behaviour; hence, addiction's powerful hold on human beings.

Maté (2008) further explains the relationship between the orbitofrontal cortex (OFC) and addiction due to its special role in human behaviour and from its abundant supply of opioid and dopamine receptors. This results in the brains of people struggling with addictions defaulting to short-term thinking rather than looking toward how their choices will impact them in the long term. The OFC

> is powerfully affected by drugs and powerfully reinforces the drug habit. It also plays an essential supporting role in non-drug addictions. . . . The OFC is the apex of the emotional brain and serves as its mission control room. . . . [T]he OFC is among the highest arbiters of our emotional lives. It receives input from all sensory areas, which allows it to process environmental data such as vision, touch, taste, smell, and sound. Why is it important? Because it's the OFC's job to evaluate the nature and potential value of stimuli, based on present information – but also in light of previous experience. . . . The OFC also contributes to decision-making and to inhibiting impulses that, if allowed to be acted out, would be harmful – for example inappropriate anger or violence. Finally it is linked to our capacity to balance short-term objectives against long-term consequences in the process of decision making . . . [T]he OFC works abnormally in drug abusers, showing malfunctioning patterns in blood flow, energy use and activation. No wonder, then, that psychological testing shows drug addicts to be prone to "maladaptive decisions when faced with short-term versus long-term outcomes, especially under conditions that involve risk and uncertainty."[5] Due to their poorly

regulated brain systems, including the OFC, they appear programmed to accept short-term gain – for example, the drug high – at the risk of long-term pain: disease, personal loss, legal troubles, and so on.

(pp. 170–171)

The stress of the disruption of important attachments means these children will not have the same biochemical milieu as children who have secure attachments. The outcome is that their experiences and interpretations of their environment, and their responses to it, will be "less flexible, less adaptive, and less conducive to health and maturity. Their vulnerability will increase, both to the mood-enhancing effect of drugs and to becoming drug dependent" (Maté, 2008, p. 192). High-risk youth are constantly under stress because they are prone to the five factors, in research literature discussed by Maté (2008), that universally lead to stress: uncertainty, lack of information, lack of control, conflict that the organism is unable to handle, and isolation from emotionally supportive relationships. Again, a brain pre-set to be easily triggered into a stress response is likely to assign a high value to substances, activities, and situations that provide short-term relief (Maté, 2008).

Most of the high-risk youth in the HRYI struggle with multiple addictions. For most youth the most prominent one is drugs and alcohol, but other addictive behaviours are now better understood. Three that would be described as destructive activities despite the fact they serve a purpose for the youth are *cutting* (i.e., *self-harm* or *self-mutilation*), *sex*, and to a lesser degree, *crime*. These are being discussed more openly and more frequently as addictive behaviour. These interchangeable addictions will activate the same brain systems as drug addiction. Maté (2008) writes that personal history and temperament of the individual will decide which activities produce this effect for any particular individual, but the process is always the same. For someone with a shortage of dopamine receptors, it is whichever activity best releases extra quantities of this euphoric and invigorating neurotransmitter that will become the object of the addictive pursuit. In effect, "people become addicted to their own brain chemicals" (Maté, 2008, p. 216).

Criminal activity

With respect to crime, youth have talked about how they have become addicted to stealing cars. It gives them a rush of excitement and a sense of control, certainly two things they are not feeling in their lives in general. A female youth noted how she would tremble walking by parked cars as her mind was going through the motions of how to steal it. If the need (or craving) became too much she would steal it, often going through a number of cars in a night. This also resulted in her becoming less careful and getting caught. Unfortunately, other youth have talked about the same rush and sense of control when fighting. Another female youth, who was otherwise calm and passive when not drinking, said she felt powerful and in control, like she could finally fight back against the world. However, this sensation also appeared to overwhelm or overload the brain, as during the escalation of anger or the violent episode she frequently blacked out, leaving her with no memory once the fight or assault had started. Her body was left trying to cope with a high-stress situation as well as a sense of euphoria simultaneously. Escaping the real world of self-loathing and feeling a sense of helplessness and hopelessness, even momentarily, can be very reinforcing, though the harm they do is not excusable.

Self-harm

> Because the truth is that when I see my blood running, it's about the only time I feel relief. It's about the only time I feel anything at all.
> Michael White interviewing a youth about cutting (2007)[6]

It is common for high-risk youth to cut[7] themselves. They may also use other self-harming methods, but cutting is by far the most frequent ritual and the most obvious. I have seen many youth with healed slashes all over their arms. With those I know better, when they show me the damage they have done, I will run my hand over their arm telling them it makes me sad that they felt a need to do this to themselves. They do not recoil and do not show embarrassment. While they may or may not hide it in public, they know that I am aware of their pain, and that the hurt and anxiety becomes overwhelming at times. I tell them of my fear they will cut too deeply and they confirm that they do not want to kill themselves, but need a release from their torment or a way to gain sense of control when they feel anxious, out of control, and helpless.

From a harm reduction and resiliency perspective, this is better than attempting or committing suicide – though they know if they accidentally slice too deep and lose too much blood, people will assume they committed suicide anyway. Sometimes they also cut their legs, stomach, or other places on their body. Some eventually stop cutting, though the urge to self-harm is always present. Perhaps some may feel ashamed of their scars but others may come to see the scars as something to be proud of, in that they have gained some sense of power and survived the battles in their lives (Batmanghelidjh, 2006). Other youth, boys more so than girls, will give themselves crude tattoos which appears to be self-harm, though some youth may disagree. Regardless, the youth are not horrified at their actions. They see it as part of who they are; they just wish things did not have to be the way they are. It serves a purpose and helps them cope with life even though they know it is destructive and they will, literally, bear the scars forever. Most appropriately, Pipher (1994) calls self-harming, "psychic pain turned inward in the most physical way" (p. 158).

Cutting can be soothing because it provides even momentary escape from anxiety caused by revisiting traumatic memories or the stress of surviving day after day. People can become so disconnected from reality that they move into dreamlike consciousness where nothing seems real and they feel little emotional or physical pain (Perry & Szalavitz, 2006). Such experiences are linked with "the release of high levels of opioids, the brain's natural heroin-like substances that kill pain and produce a calming sense of distance from one's troubles" (Perry & Szalavitz, 2006, p. 189). Youth may find that cutting produces a dissociative state, giving them a *safe space* away from overwhelming stress, in much the same way others may use drugs and/or alcohol to escape or self-medicate to avoid dealing with traumatic events in the lives. With the release of brain opioids (endorphins) that self-harming brings, it is especially attractive to those who have been previously traumatized and found relief in dissociation (Perry & Szalavitz, 2006). Although anyone who cuts will experience some degree of opioid effect, the experience is far more likely to be perceived as pleasurable and attractive to those who have a sensitized dissociative response from previous trauma and are in emotional pain (Perry & Szalavitz, 2006; see also Howe, 2005, 2008).

The relationship a youth has with self-harming can also be to stop flashbacks or painful affect coming into consciousness. Self-harm may be a way of feeling physical pain as a confirmation of being alive, or distracting awareness from intra-psychic pain by what is experienced as more tolerable physical pain. This behaviour can also be a powerful and disturbing way of expressing rage at oneself and others (Howe, 2005). Indeed, with an absence of coping strategies, hurting the self becomes a way to calm down. However, with time, and with no intervention for such behaviours, the habit of inflicting harm on the self becomes more ingrained (Pipher, 1994), especially given the sense of calmness achieved after they have harmed themselves (Clare, 2009; Howe, 2005). An act of violence can be a substitute for youth who may feel too ashamed to cry; "they may experience crying as defeat. . . . .When crying is too difficult, the release of blood through self-harm can be seen as a substitute for tears" (Batmanghe-lidjh, 2006, p. 56). Cutting can also be a form of self-punishment for individuals who experience excessive self-blame (Howe, 2005; Regehr & Glancy, 2010).

It is hypothesized that those who experience the rush of endorphins that self-harm brings get temporary help to escape inner shame, fear, and despair (Howe, 2008). Given this, on the one hand, we need to acknowledge the helpfulness of self-harm in managing and organizing emotions (Batmanghelidjh, 2006). Self-abuse has been called a "friend" by youth "because it stops you from hurting others and from killing yourself" (Noseworthy & Lane, 1998, p. 29). Workers need to tune in to the youth and not see self-harming as a play for attention, or trivializing it as an act of rebellion. Counselling, when the youth is ready, can be helpful in weaning away from self-harm and in finding better ways to cope with their trauma and pain. Narrative approaches can play a key role in giving adolescents the opportunity to find their voice and per-haps re-author their dominant story line of self-hate that leads to a sense of feeling worthless, useless, and deserving of what she or he gets (White, 2007).

Sex addiction

Sexual contact also promotes the presence of dopamine and provides an escape. Maté (2008) states that the female sex addict is not addicted to sex at all, but to the dopa-mine and endorphin rewards that flow from the feeling of being desired and desirable. Sex addiction is a stand-in for the nurturing the person was deprived of. The dopa-mine and endorphin rewards that love is meant to provide are obtained by having sex, but, as with all addictions, it is only temporary.

The craving for contact is, perversely, accompanied by a terror of real intimacy because of the painful instability of early relationships. That is why a relationship with a sex addicted person will not last, as the need to avoid having to face their deepest fears is too much. By moving from one partner to another, a sex addict avoids the risk of intimacy while still getting the dopamine hit of the novel and the new. With most youth from the HRYI, love and sex is hard to separate and are typically seen as interchangeable. If they are sexually active they are being loved, and will state that they love their partner, even if they have not known each other a long time. This can be repeated over and over.

As Maté (2008) points out, the promiscuity is not perversity but the "outgrowth of a childhood adaption to her circumstances" (p. 234). These youth were typically sexually abused so their perspective of what love means is distorted. The love they learned was associated with violence, manipulation, and empty promises. They may have been told they were being loved but felt abused and dirty. The only escape as children was to dissociate, something they continue to do when behaving in a promiscuous way (Batmanghelidjh, 2006). Nevertheless, while being exploited, even in a dissociative state, the concept of being held and cuddled is so important to people that love can be associated with whatever gives us that warmth and contact. If a person feels wanted only sexually, as an adult there may be a tendency to look to sex to reaffirm that he or she is loveable and wanted. Even feeling unloved and undesirable – without being sexually abused – they may look to sexual contact as a quick source of comfort (Maté, 2008).

High-risk youth do talk about how they go from one bad relationship to another. A few will share that they are scared to get close to their partner, but the 'intimacy' keeps them going back. It is not unusual for female youth to repeat that they would do better without a boyfriend but they fear being alone and lacking someone in their bed at night to act as a protector. One gets the sense it is more about having someone there than it is about a specific person. Given their experiences of sexual abuse, they may be terrified of sexual contact and not be able to integrate loving feelings into sexual encounters. They may be phobic of sexuality, while simultaneously promiscuous (Batmanghelidjh, 2006). Youth may turn to alcohol and/or drugs (particularly crystal methamphetamine and ecstasy) as a way to cope with these risky sexual experiences, though this increases the likelihood of high-risk sexual behaviour, including increasing the possibility of sexually transmitted disease, sexual assault, and pregnancy (O'Hare, 2001), all of which are frequent outcomes among the high-risk youth population (see Box 8.2). There is, of course, the risk of HIV/AIDS as well, though this is not generally considered by these youth. High-risk youth crave physical contact, the dopamine rush, and the need to feel accepted and loved, no matter how remote this may be between two people whose experiences have provided them with minimal knowledge of what these terms actually mean.

Box 8.2   The seduction of crystal meth

The drug of choice at the present time is crystal methamphetamine. It is a nasty, mean-spirited drug that appears to have the power to turn youth into people they do not want to be. These synthetic materials wreak havoc with the youth, who end up losing weight, ceasing to care they exist, and, after being awake for a few days straight, crave sleep as much as they crave meth again. Meth builds walls between the youth and the people who care about them as they pull away, get angry, and feel they are being judged, which typically has more to do with how they feel about themselves than it does about their support team judging them. It turns youth against themselves and appears to highlight their sense of failure, shame, and guilt even more – if that's even possible. Youth on meth lose their placements, get kicked out of programs, and are expelled from school, and if they had family involved, they likely lose them too. Youth can 'tweak' like they are having mini seizures when they are coming down, which in public is not a good thing when they are already feeling paranoid. One youth I worked with would put up to 16 sugars in her coffee (I counted as I stood there stunned) when coming down off meth. Youth who swore they would never use needles are using needles to shoot meth. This brings with it risk of infection, Hepatitis C, and HIV/AIDS, but they don't think of this when they are using. The young kids are not aware of the hierarchy that is now being eroded as drug smokers trying needles can no longer look down on drug shooters. They just jump in to using needles, thinking how much better this is than using stolen cough and cold medicine.

The youth are getting lost in meth, adding to their need to get lost in life and escape. It's a potent combination. Some girls told the executive director from a youth-serving agency that they felt using crystal meth was safer than using the socially acceptable substance of choice – alcohol. They reasoned that with crystal meth they don't pass out or fall asleep when using it. These features of drinking to excess means they are at high risk to be sexually assaulted or raped. It is incredible that this bizarre level of harm reduction and resilient thinking actually makes some twisted sense, as the high-risk lifestyle does significantly increase the risk of being violated. But, there again, nothing about this drug is rational. I hate it. I hate what it does to the youth. I hate that it gives them a way out of having to think about their challenges and their future. I hate that it gives them a sense they can conquer the world, then mocks them by attacking their souls when they are coming down.

Conclusion

Whether dealing with various substance or behavioural addictions, physical health, or mental health issues, the optimal intervention remains the same: compassionate, relationship-building care that does not punish, isolate, exclude, or marginalize the youth or reinforce their sense of shame, guilt, failure, and self-loathing. This requires a willingness for workers, caregivers, health care professionals, and anyone coming into contact with the youth to view situations in which the youth find themselves with a different lens and to change practice accordingly. There is a need to learn more about engaging and working with this population, as well as to provide the resources to help and support youth through their fear- and anxiety-inducing experiences. There is a call for those in the helping professions to resist seeing substance abuse, cutting, being homeless, and talking about suicide as personal deficits, weaknesses, or even criminal activities, and understand how these behaviours are perhaps a way to self-medicate, help youth cope with trauma, silence the noises in their head, or fill the void of having no one to love them and care about them. Such a perspective may go much further in having youth overcome their sense of helplessness and hopelessness.

In addition to helping youth adopt better coping skills, by adding more appropriate addictions and mental health resources, the outcome could result in significant cost savings. Positive connections and experiences can result in youth being more open to talking about and attending to their addictions and physical and mental health issues instead of waiting until they are in a serious state requiring longer-term hospitalization and longer follow-up care. Obviously, stressed youth with poor coping skills and an inability to look after their own wellbeing become adults who are stressed and demonstrate poor coping skills. These youth will require ongoing support in the adult system, where they may face even less compassion and more isolation, exclusion, and marginalization. Emotional isolation, powerlessness, and stress are exactly the conditions that promote the neurobiology of addiction in human beings (Maté, 2008).

We should not fear creating dependency, and we should refrain from putting unrealistic expectations on youth to navigate systems that they are unfamiliar with or that may even be openly hostile toward them. Hand-holding youth when needed and appropriate can go far beyond getting them to appointments and helping deal with their overall wellbeing; it demonstrates people are concerned and care enough to make sure they will be okay. After all, this is all anybody would want.

Discussion questions to consider for Chapter 8

1 *What might be the best way to work with a youth who is up front about not wanting to stop using drugs and/or alcohol?*

2 *Should youth be able to participate in programs when they are in an active addiction? Does this set them up for failure? What are the safety implications?*

3 *How does a worker create a safety plan with a youth who is frequently cutting and who is at risk for accidently killing themselves? How would you cope as a worker if a youth was unwilling or unable to stop cutting themselves?*

4 *How would you approach a youth about a possible sex addiction if they appeared unaware that this was an issue in their life?*

5 *When might 'hand-holding' cross the line to creating dependency?*

6 *How can workers help youth work through their fears of going to see a therapist?*

7 *What are possible challenges that may arise when trying to implement suggestions outlined in this chapter?*

Notes

1 Taken from the book, *In the Realm of Hungry Ghosts: A Close Encounter with Addiction*, by Dr. Gabor Maté (2008, p. 34).

2 This number was taken from a snapshot analysis of the files of 55 youth receiving services through the High Risk Youth Unit on October 3, 2011.

3 Hunt, Joe-Laidler and MacKenzie (2005) are quoting: Anderson, E. (1991). Neighborhood effects on teenage pregnancy. In C. Jencks & P. E. Peterson (eds.), *The Urban Underclass* (pp. 375–398). Washington, DC: Brookings Institution.

4 Taken from the book, *Deep Brain Learning: Pathways to Potential with Challenging Youth* by Larry K. Bendtro, Martin L. Mitchell and Herman J. McCall (2009, p. 49).

5 In this passage, Dr. Gabor Maté is citing: London, E. D., Ernst, M., Grant, S., Bronson, K., & Weinstein, A. (2000). Orbitofrontal cortex and human drug abuse: Functional imaging. *Cerebral Cortex*, 10(3): 334–342.

6 Taken from the book, *Maps of Narrative Practice*, by Michael White (2007, p. 47).

7 Cutting is also referred to self-harming or self-mutilation. In this chapter 'cutting' is used interchangeably with 'self-harm.' Deliberate self-harm involves the destruction of body tissue or inflicting pain and/or injury on the body without suicidal intent (Inckle, 2011; Regehr & Glancy, 2010). *Moderate self-harm* (as opposed to *stereotypic self-harm* such as head banging and biting oneself, often associated with developmental delays, autism, neurological disorders; or the rare *major self-harm* involving self-castration or amputation and usually associated with psychosis) is the most common; typically involves cutting and skin-burning; and is usually associated with Borderline Personality Disorder, dissociative states, complex PTSD, and eating disorders (Regehr & Glancy, 2010). In addition, self-harm can also involve scalding; inflicting blows or banging the body; scratching, biting, and scraping; inserting sharp objects under the skin or into body orifices; interfering with wounds; pulling out hair; scrubbing away the surface of the skin (sometimes using chemicals); and swallowing sharp objects or harmful substances, including overdosing on medications and/or drugs (Inckle, 2011).

Chapter 9

Strategies for engaging and working with high-risk youth[1]

> Unfortunately, children's saviours must sometimes be found among the professionals paid to help them.
>
> Michael Ungar[2]

By now we have an understanding of how early childhood experiences – including repeated rejection, abandonment, abuse, and neglect – impact brain development and the ability of youth to self-regulate, to form trusting relationships, and to feel cared for and valued. We know relationship is crucial in helping youth navigate through their many barriers and cope with feelings of marginalization and exclusion. We know that they are more vulnerable to addictions and potentially emerging mental health issues. We also know that a harm reduction approach can be more effective in engaging youth and getting more genuine buy-in for accepting supports and services. We have learned to focus on strengths rather than highlighting deficits and reinforcing the profound sense of failure of high-risk youth. We know that an understanding of resiliency can assist in making service planning and connections more meaningful. We can also appreciate that collaborating and being a part of the safety net under a youth can be key in achieving long-term success. But how does this translate into the actual essence of our work – the one-to-one interaction, the actual striving toward building a connection, the profound experience of being a part of the life of a youth and them being part of yours? We start with a case study (see Box 9.1) that will take you through the strategies, as we leave theory behind and focus on the more intimate action steps of this important work.

Box 9.1   Jessica's story[3]

I was introduced to 'Jessica' while visiting a street outreach agency in Edmonton, Alberta. She made it clear in the beginning that she hated "fucking social workers" before walking away in defiance. At 15 years old, she was trying to make her way in the world, unable to rely on either her mother or father, who were in an on-again, off-again relationship. Jessica presented as tough, gang affiliated, and anti-authority. It took me eight months to engage her in any kind of meaningful conversation that wasn't full of sarcasm or wasn't a lecture on how useless social workers were when it came to helping families and kids. Despite the many challenges she faced, she did not see child welfare services as relevant to her situation and, in fact, believed 'the system' had made things even worse for her.

Jessica's first few involvements with child welfare came as an infant due to alleged drug use by her parents, lack of supervision, and being left with inappropriate caregivers. The family was very transient and Jessica, with one parent or the other, often found herself staying at run-down motels, typically with little food. Left alone on many occasions, Jessica, even at the age of five or six, adopted the role of caregiver for her two older sisters and younger brother. Jessica's father drifted further away from the family and the mother struggled and remained emotionally distant. There were some mental health problems and gambling became a factor, meaning there was often little money to maintain a place to live or have enough food available. School was very inconsistent, as little effort was made to ensure the children attended. The children were brought into care on a number of occasions. However, typically the mother would engage with the case worker and cooperate in helping to find a relative who would take the children. Eventually they would return to the care of their mother, though the family remained transient after repeated evictions.

During a stay with extended family at age eight, Jessica was sexually abused by a babysitter. While she did not disclose the abuse, Jessica's behaviours escalated until the children were no longer welcome. After further spells in motels, the father got a stable job, allowing him to rent an apartment for himself and the children. Eventually, the two older sisters went to live with their mother while Jessica and her brother stayed with their father. While this brought a small measure of stability for Jessica, her 14-year-old brother started drifting away and engaging in criminal activity and drug use. Jessica had been using marijuana and drinking since the age of 10 or 11, and by age 12, she was spending many nights out of the home, staying with friends or boyfriends who were in their late teens. At 16, Jessica was living with a man in his late 30s, a relationship that involved much verbal and physical violence. She had dropped out of school completely.

Child welfare continued to become involved periodically, but her father would say there were no issues and his daughter was welcome to return home. If Jessica could be found, she would say very little or tell the investigating worker to leave her family alone. Jessica would check in with her father and brother once in a while to see how they were doing, clean the apartment, and ask for money, which her father would give her. She was having very little contact with her mother or sisters, who were all drinking a lot. She would see her sisters on the streets at times, making her feel guilty that she was not able to help them.

Through some street friends, Jessica started spending time at an inner-city youth agency. Staff there reported that while she was hard to get to know and shared little about her situation, she needed help given her drug use, deteriorating health, lack of stable housing, and anger management issues. Despite this, she was respected by other youth and clearly stood out as a leader even among youth years older than herself. Jessica feared and hated cops and social

> workers, and she continued to make it known that she was fine and needed no help with anything. The community agency monitored her to try and get a sense of whether she was in danger, but she was adamant she lived at home. When it became apparent that this was not the case, and that she was also using crystal methamphetamine, agency staff called the High Risk Youth Initiative.
>
> Despite her initial hostility, when I met Jessica, it was clear that she felt quite independent and could certainly manipulate her environment in order to get her needs met. Thus, she clearly possessed strengths and skills from which to build upon. However, it was also clear that she was not going to let any adults into her world without a fight, demonstrating that any outsiders were a threat to her. This left her with few, if any, safe people for her to reach out to if she was in danger. A balance was needed between learning more about Jessica and trying to protect her from harm on the one hand, and being too intrusive, leading her to be angry and avoid any contact on the other. Such intrusiveness could also result in community agency staff losing a connection with her, and with it the ability to at least check in with her and assess whether she was safe. Also gone would be the ability help her out with food, basic necessities, and emotional support.
>
> One day, when taking another youth for lunch, Jessica agreed to tag along. Her hostility had not been enough to make me give up on her and she observed other youth being responsive to me as a child protection worker. She would say later that that she had become curious and at least wanted to see what she could get out of me as far as food, clothing, and a bus pass. She remained very guarded, but the window had opened a crack.

In a traditional child welfare system, if youth demonstrate they are what Dr. Michael Ungar refers to as *dangerous*, *delinquent*, *deviant*, and *disordered*, and are resistant to help, we can cut them loose and justify our actions by saying they did not want help. We can further justify this by stating that we allowed them to be autonomous and independent. However, we know better and closing files due to lack of cooperation typically ignores the fears and risks of the youth in making connections. It is far more likely that these youth are lonely out there on their own. "[W]ithout belonging somewhere, they risk becoming nameless and lost" (Ungar, 2009, p. 11). This is far from uncommon for our high-risk youth. Ungar (2009) tells us that his work with children and youth demonstrates

> that our children want to find a place in their communities where they are heard and feel they belong. Denied those experiences, behaviours make a satisfying substitute. . . . They want to know they count. . . . So much of what they want can only be found when adults who care for them are part of their lives. . . . our children need their attachments with adults to create a secure sense of who they are. . . . they want real connections.

(pp. 18–19)

The following strategies aim to makes these connections real. As noted throughout this book, this is challenging, demanding, and emotional work. However, if this is our passion, and if we got into the field to help others and work with people, we need to pay attention to how we can best engage and work with the youth. The strategies below are not a definitive list and all of us come with who we are, our skills, our experiences, and our view of the world that can add to how we make connections with those who struggle to do the same. While I emphasize that I certainly do not have all of the answers, sticking to traditional practices that the youth say are not meeting their needs would appear futile, and arguably is oppressive and unethical. The following strategies were developed incorporating and honouring the voices of the youth.[4]

The strategies

Youth have spoken to me repeatedly about the importance of their relationships with their case workers and the impact these relationships have on the services that are offered to them. Recognizing that the formation of these relationships is essential to youth, and in efforts to provide some feedback to practitioners who sought clarification into how to build these relationships, Arlene Eaton-Erickson and I developed a number of strategies that would articulate some values and principles that could assist in helping youth feel safe, allowing them to actually take a risk of letting others, even paid professionals, into their lives. These strategies have been shared with youth over the years and have been validated by their feedback.

Youth are valued and worth the effort

* *The voices of the youth will be heard, and there is a commitment and a passion in being creative and flexible.*

This is not the only strategy that appears obvious; yet it needs to be stated. Let those who are passionate about working with high-risk youth, work with high-risk youth. We know our youth are, sadly, particularly attuned to who is 'real' and who is not because of their repeated experiences with rejection, abandonment, and loss. They will be aware of nuances that we do not know we are even putting out there – subtle body language, tone of voice, excessive blinking, perhaps. It will be hard enough for them to risk making a connection at the best of times, but if their worker is not genuine, there is no hope of a connection. In the general child welfare system, file assignments may work on a rotational basis. If the worker is fearful of youth, finds youth frustrating or too challenging, or simply believes they are not well suited to working with youth (fair enough!), why would they be assigned youth? Yet, this is not unusual, even though it is hardly in the best interest of the youth. This could lead the youth to disengage, and possibly reinforces in the eyes of the worker and the supervisor, that the youth are defiant and uncooperative and do not want help. Many youth are clearly feeling that their case worker does not like them, does not have time for them, or that the system cannot handle them. In short, they do not feel valued by their worker or the system, or society in general. This increases their perceptions of feeling marginalized and excluded in society (Gaetz, 2004; Gaetz et al., 2013). The High Risk Youth Initiative allows youth to be assigned to case workers who have chosen to work with this population. This has helped improve the opportunity for more youth to make connections even if their previous experiences with the system have been negative.

Believing that youth have value has to be the beginning. The soul-deep belief that youth *are* worth it – worth the acknowledgement that youth do fall through the cracks of a service system that does not adequately meet their needs – must drive our practice. We must search for the courage to speak of these system deficiencies and acknowledge *our* role in the creation or perpetuation of them. One must have the strength to let go of old and comfortable ways of doing things; believe philosophically that youth are the experts in their own lives; demonstrate the commitment to listen to what youth have to say; and be willing to do things differently and think and act outside of traditional practice. This can, and will, only be accomplished if there is a driving belief that youth are worth it (see Box 9.2).

Box 9.2   Jessica

As has been discussed, it is not uncommon for youth involved with the child welfare system to see case workers, or service providers, as uncaring and as "just doing their job." It is about getting a pay cheque, not about caring for them. Jessica had this perception, initially. Of course, if we are around long enough, this perception can change. While tempted to explain that working in the field of human services is not a fast route to riches, we bite our tongue and set out to prove we actually do care. It is hard to pinpoint the time that Jessica changed her point of view. She had been annoyed with me for some time, believing it was my job to make her miserable. I didn't get angry, didn't get frustrated, and didn't go away. When I was reasonably satisfied that she would not pull away too much, I could start telling her that she was important, that I cared, and that she had much value. To hear it is one thing, but when youth feel they have no value (which is fairly typical for youth trying to make sense of their perception that their parents don't want them), it is very hard to internalize this concept. Youth like Jessica do have a difficult time with this, but there is the potential to get to a point in which there is a mutual sense of value toward each other. This was evident when she would encourage other case workers or services providers to talk to me because I understood her and knew what she was about.

Be available

- *Accommodating youth when they are ready to work; being available both physically and emotionally.*

My experience and research clearly indicate that, for the most part, work with youth is done in their timeframe, not that of the worker. The case worker's desire to talk, address the issues, and move forward can only be accomplished if the groundwork of acknowledgement, connection, and comfort has been established with the youth. The worker's skills of engaging with youth and asking the right open-ended questions will not succeed if a youth is not ready to engage. Being available is about being available both physically and emotionally when the youth is ready to participate.

Youth have identified that a barrier to this availability is the regular nine-to-five routine of many professionals. Youth have made it clear that their lives do not move into this schedule very easily or successfully. Given the lifestyles of high-risk youth, whose schedules are more nocturnal, morning appointments and programming are not as successful, especially in the early stages of building a relationship. Youth often find themselves in crisis situations when service delivery systems are closed and express the need for workers to be available during these times.

This can pose a number of problems for case workers, outreach workers, and community workers, especially if they have families and are trying to establish a work-life balance. Within the youth's support team, there are times it is important to be able to expand traditional work hours, especially when in a crisis phase, to send a message they have not been abandoned, they are not alone, and they are valued. This role can be shared among the support team, and again, it is particularly important when the relationship is just being established. This is not to create a dependency, but rather acknowledges that the youth are still young, have had little guidance, and, like all of us, need a little hand-holding at times. A 16-year-old youth should not be expected to get themselves to doctor's appointments, dentist appointments, meetings with school personnel, or court on their own – yet this is done frequently. These are life events that we would never expect our own teenagers to navigate on their own. Case workers *are* the guardians for many of the high-risk youth. While we cannot be at all appointments, there is a level of flexibility and creativity that is required, and this is another area in which systems need to be more responsive to the needs of the youth. This is not to say we need to be at the beck and call of the youth indefinitely. As the connection grows and the worker establishes credibility, conversations can evolve and boundaries can be put in place. The youth do understand that we are not available 24/7 and they also appreciate that we work with many other youth who may need our time as well. My experience is that when the youth internalizes that we are still there for them without having to be physically there for them, they are not as demanding of our time. We know that when they buy in to the relationship, they buy in hard, but once they are reassured we are not going to abandoned them, we do not have to be on call.

In the HRYI, the youth do have the work cell phone numbers of their workers and community youth specialists. Again, this may be overused by the youth initially, but once boundaries are established, a vast majority of the youth are respectful and appropriate. They may leave messages such as a reminder of an appointment and to share their excitement of something good happening in their lives, but they typically would not expect an answer back during off hours. However, there may be times that special arrangements are necessary, such as when a pregnant youth goes into labour, when a youth is trying to leave an abusive relationship, or when a youth is out of town for treatment or visiting family. It can be important to introduce youth to workers at emergency services so they have an alternative should a crisis arise during the evening or night, or on the weekend. It is important for the youth to become knowledgeable about the availability of both formal and informal supports that exist in their communities. This wider support network allows youth to access help as needed, rather than only during standard work hours. Wharf (2002a) argues that these types of "community social work and community organizing are neglected but potentially powerful strategies for improving child welfare" (p. 9).

A lot of youth have reported to me that they typically see their workers "when I fuck up." In a deficit, problem-saturated approach, this makes sense. Planning often needs to happen when poor choices are made, such as when youth get kicked out of a placement, or risk losing their schooling, job, or program. However, like all kids and youth, it is a big deal when somebody from their support team (and case workers as guardians in particular) shows up for events they see as important in their lives. They may have a part in a play, be performing at a music or dance event, or be on a sports team. They may be 'marbling out' of their treatment program or graduating from a program or school. I have had a number of youth who are anxious for me to meet their partner, their biological families, or their teachers. If you want to see how big of a deal this is to the youth, show up unexpectedly and look into their eyes. For youth who grew up feeling like nobody cared for them, there is no better time to *be available!*

Being available emotionally is also important – to be intuitive about what a youth is feeling and thinking, and when they need support and reassurance. When a youth is ready to engage, it is crucial to be present, to be responsive to the youth in the here and now. In theory, this sounds simple, but experience has highlighted some practicalities to consider when with a youth, such as turning off cell phones, pulling over if driving, and putting off the next appointment if the youth is in crisis. Emotionally, this can be challenging. After a long week of work, at 4:00 p.m. on a Friday afternoon, it is difficult to be 'fully present' when a youth determines it is time to engage. Being able to communicate openly and honestly with the youth about where you are at energy-wise and emotionally allows the youth to adjust to the situation. As stated above, they excel in picking up on nuances, so emotionally hibernating is not likely to work (see Box 9.3).

Box 9.3   Jessica

Jessica, at age 15, had been living in a common-law relationship with a boyfriend who was 19, but significantly less mature than she was. He cheated on her and, when she confronted him about it, he kicked her out. She was devastated with the situation. Jessica was also angry and confused. However, she needed to get at least some belongings from the apartment, but was justifiably intimidated to go there by herself. She did not want to go with police, as this was even more intimidating and she didn't know whether or not she had outstanding warrants. As her partner only got home from work after 6:00 p.m. it was important for me to be available at that time to support her through this emotional confrontation. We went for coffee and debriefed, and she practiced what she would say to him. Once at the apartment, she had the opportunity to tell him how she felt before getting as many of her belongings as possible. She appreciated having this opportunity to tell him how his actions had impacted her. She felt safer that I was with her. While it was not overly comfortable for me to be in that situation, it was important to Jessica to have my support.

Go the extra mile

* *Doing small, thoughtful things (e.g., getting a youth a treat on the way to a visit) challenges youth to ask themselves why somebody cares about them and to adjust to this reality.*

Sometimes going the extra mile is as simple as finding out what a youth's favourite chocolate bar is and bringing it to them. Sometimes it is finding out about the music they like and learning about it. Sometimes it is a visit to a youth correctional centre on a weekend because a youth is lonely and sad. As we have discussed in earlier chapters, some youth believe that they are not worth spending time with. Others blame themselves for their situation and still others feel they are not worthy of being loved. Thus, small things can carry a lot of meaning, despite the youth's all too familiar "I-don't-care-anymore" or "whatever!" attitude.

My experience has shown that going the extra mile also can prompt the youth to ask, "Why is this happening?" Sometimes their reaction to the worker's additional efforts is a turning point in the relationship. At first, the reaction can be negative if the youth interprets the extra attention as having a hidden agenda or as a form of manipulation by the worker. A youth's isolating view of the world can be threatened by having a person show they care, but over time, the youth can take comfort in the fact that someone does in fact care about them. Having someone care is also something the youth cannot control and, while they can find this frustrating initially, it can become acceptable given that the youth do ultimately want connection. Going the extra mile can help give the youth permission to take the risk of entering into a relationship. Psychologist Dr. Richard Kagan (2004) challenges us "[t]o go above and beyond the expectations of a child" (p. 203) and to continue being the heroes "who keep on caring for others and helping others, even when they feel hurt, scared, lonely, or so mad they cannot think straight" (p. 278) (see Box 9.4).

Box 9.4   Jessica

Christmas is a particularly challenging time for youth, as it can highlight the fact they don't have family around, reinforces feelings of loneliness, and possibly triggers bad memories of drinking and violence during family gatherings. Jessica did not look forward to Christmas. She would ask me what I did for Christmas. As fortunate as I am, I would feel badly telling her, but she would challenge me if I distorted the truth. One thing we had in common is a particular brand of chocolate. For Christmas, I would get Jessica an oversized version of this chocolate with her gift. This became our tradition over a number of years. She would look forward to what was coming each year. I don't know if she remembers the gifts, but she does remember the chocolate.

Be self-aware

- *Workers must be aware of whom they are as people and professionals, especially with respect to their beliefs, values, judgements, and power. This can enable the worker to become an ally in the lives of youth. Given their life experiences, the youth typically have a keen ability to detect genuineness, truth, and integrity in others.*

Self-awareness is a critical aspect of all casework practice. It is especially important when working with youth. Youth have a keen ability to detect authenticity, truth, and integrity in others – in fact they grow up honing these skills. High-risk youth have stated that this skill is essential to have in order to survive on the streets – knowing who to trust, who not to trust, and when you are being 'played' – as it could mean the difference between life and death (Office of the Child and Youth Advocate, 2007). Youth have reported that they know whether their social worker cares about them or if they are "just another case" (Office of the Child and Youth Advocate, 2007). Clearly it is important that there is congruency between beliefs and actions when working with this population, as the incongruence is very apparent to youth. As a youth recently stated, "My social worker is awkward around me; I don't think he really likes me."

Youth present with a myriad of issues and experiences, and they report it is particularly important that they do not feel judged. When a youth perceives that they are being judged, an internal barrier rises immediately and a flight-or-fight response typically occurs. Youth either attempt to verbally (and/or physically) defend themselves from further feelings of pain and rejection, or youth will emotionally (and/or physically) retreat to escape the judgement. Either way, the youth disengages, making the helping relationship difficult.

Being self-aware means having awareness of your judgements. It is often heard that workers should be *non-judgemental*. However, it goes deeper than this because we all hold judgements. Rather, it is about managing our judgements and talking to the youth about them, as they inevitably pick up our reactions and know that we have issues or concerns. This can be interpreted as being judgemental. There have been youth whose career choice was to be a dancer in a strip club, often because it paid well and they did not believe they were smart enough to be in school. It is hard not to have judgements in such situations. However, there is a big difference in talking about the risks and dangers such a lifestyle can bring, rather than judging the youth for a poor choice and telling them you are not willing to support such a decision by maintaining services. The fact that the youth was honest about her future, and perhaps brought it up to have a discussion about it, is positive. If their character is attacked and the threat of abandonment is attached, it will inevitable reinforce feeling of worthlessness, failure, and shame.

It is critical that we are aware of whom we are as people and professionals; our judgements, beliefs, values, and power (Bishop, 2002). Each of these will affect what we believe about ourselves, about our youth, and how the relationship between youth and ourselves will be perceived. For example, a white, heterosexual man would be situated in a stratum of life that looks very different than where a two-spirited, indigenous young woman would exist. Being aware of these differences and acknowledging the power differential, privilege, and the diverse lived-realities of the two individuals allows for the youth to remain the 'expert' in his or her own life, and enables the worker to become an ally with them in accessing relevant and appropriate services (Bishop, 2002; Madsen, 1999). As discussed in the chapter on harm reduction (Chapter 4), the traditional *practitioner-as-the-expert* and *paternalistic* approaches run contrary to harm reduction values, rely on punishment, and result in judgements being made to determine if the youth is worthy of receiving services (Batmanghelidjh, 2006; Lonne et al., 2009). If the youth withdraws from the support and services, very often it was because they felt judged and could see that further rejection was close at hand (see Box 9.5).

Box 9.5   Jessica

At age 16, Jessica had a boyfriend who was 38. I had judgements around this relationship, though I didn't manage them well. Initially, I opted to keep my thoughts to myself and not be obvious about my opinions, but she quickly saw through this. She was thinking, "This is my boyfriend and he cares about me." I'm thinking, "He is immature and sexually exploiting her." I felt protective of Jessica and bad for her in that this relationship was not good for her. Not being open or having a conversation about the relationship was very stressful for Jessica and I could feel that she was pulling away. She was in a position that she felt she had to choose between the relationship with her boyfriend and the relationship with me, which had to that point progressed well. She came to fear that because I didn't approve of her boyfriend, I would withdraw my support, as well as the services she was receiving. At one point, when eating at a fast-food restaurant, she became very angry that I disapproved of her boyfriend. She started shouting and swept her food off the table and walked out. I caught up with her and talked her down. I apologized and we agreed to discuss this situation. I told her my fears; that I had concerns about him being jealous and controlling, and concerns about his drug use and his potential for violence. I was careful not to criticize her choices or tell her that I couldn't continue to support her as long as she remained in the relationship. I listened to her perspective in the relationship and learned she also had some fears but felt that the relationship was improving, and that they were working on their drug issues together. Jessica was able to tell me that I was judging him without getting to know him. I told her this was a valid perception, but added that this was more to do with being protective of her than it was about judging him. She appreciated this and was relieved to learn I had no intention of closing her file or no longer working with her. Once Jessica understood that we could have disagreements without it meaning the end of our relationship, her anxiety was significantly reduced and we were able to have more open communication.

Be consistent: "I will not give up"

- *The youth have experienced people giving up on them all of their lives, so will not expect the relationship with their workers to be any different.*

Youth need the assurance, before they will invest and engage, that the adults involved in their lives are committed and will not give up on them (Kagan, 2004; Levy & Orlans, 1998). Most of these youth do not believe that child welfare workers will be there for the long haul and that it is only a matter of time before the workers will give up on them. Many behaviours and choices the youth make test the case worker or agency worker in an attempt to have the worker prove that they are committed (Kagan, 2004, p. 187). The consistent message of "I will not give up on you," backed by visible actions, demonstrates to the youth both the consistency and commitment they need to begin to invest in the helping relationship. Sadly, in human services, we tend to blame our failure to make connections on the weaknesses of others, which can be our cue to declare the individual "untreatable" and give up on them (Dennis & Lourie, 2006).

While there are many dedicated workers, I have heard numerous times from youth that they did not know if they had a worker or if their file was open or closed. Others have stated they had had up to seven workers in a year or had not seen their worker in months. This *is* giving the youth a message that their worker has given up and that they do not care. While there may have been circumstances beyond the control of the worker, the perception is nevertheless the same for the youth. What is inexcusable is workers who leave with no explanation when it is in their control to explain to the youth what is going on and to end the relationship as positively as possible. Workers have said that they did not think the youth would care much, as there was not much of a connection established. This is highly disrespectful. As we learned in the first two chapters, if there is one thing our youth do understand, it is being rejected and abandoned, and they do care about this in a profound way!

A strange comment I have heard on a number of occasions from workers and caregivers is that it is not fair to get attached to children and youth, as eventually we have to leave the relationship and this will re-traumatize them. This could happen if the separation is not handled well. However, when the relationship is healthy and the goodbye is a *celebration* (though acknowledging the sadness too) the youth is left with not only positive memories, but also a blueprint for what a healthy relationship should look like. The more positive relationships the youth experiences, the easier it gets to take the risk of letting people in their world, even knowing this will not be a forever connection. It can reinforce to the youth that adults are not all unreliable and out to hurt them. Further, when care is unconditional, youth will "feel comfortable enough to try something in which they might fail, because they have the knowledge there will be someone there to catch them, help them up, and support them in trying again" (Dennis & Lourie, 2006, p. 23).

If we leave the youth with more capacity to make healthy connections, this can last a lifetime and help them have a more positive view of the world. If we do not appreciate their need for such relationships, we do them a significant disservice and simply reinforce their negative perceptions. As stated in the introduction to this book, our research showed that, so powerful is the relationship and the message that we will not give up on our youth, they come to see the whole child welfare system as positive (Smyth et al., 2005) (see Box 9.6).

Box 9.6 Jessica

Fairly early in building a relationship with Jessica, she went through a phase of feeling like she just wanted to give up. She said she didn't care what happened to her. Her boyfriend at that time had broken up with her and she ended up in and out of her mother's apartment once again. She refused to go to a group home or a shelter program. Jessica started to party frequently and her use of crystal methamphetamine (also referred to as crystal meth, meth, pint, jib) increased. She would disappear for days then call feeling badly. We would meet but she was more distant and disconnected, perhaps feeling she was letting me down. She would go back and forth between giving up and saying she wanted to change. When I told her that I was looking out for her, she would get angry and tell me I was interfering with her life. I would intentionally repeat that it was okay for her to be angry, but that she was too important for me to do nothing. I added that she may have given up on herself, but that didn't mean I would give up on her (while such comments may have been too threatening for Jessica when I was trying to get to know her, I believed that I had established enough credibility – though not trust – to be able to challenge her without her withdrawing completely). She continued to disappear with friends, but she would eventually call. I told her I was prepared to wait her out. She started to question why I still wanted to work with her and was not comfortable hearing me tell her that I valued our relationship. She also reacted to me telling her I worried about her, as if it was an attack on her independence. Over time, she tired of her lifestyle and would call more frequently. She was open to talking and accepting services, though addictions treatment and counselling were off the table. I didn't push it. Eventually, she did get her addictions under control herself and entered a supported independent living program. She didn't tell me at the time, but a couple of years later Jessica acknowledged that it had been kind of cool to have someone looking out for her and worrying about her. She was happy I had not given up on her.

Working through testing behaviours

- *Given their life experiences, high-risk youth have the right to be sceptical and suspicious. The youth will not easily risk being hurt again and will want to know if the worker will hang in there with them. Workers must avoid falling into the youth's scripts and reinforcing that adults cannot be trusted. "As annoyed and exasperated as we may become, we can remember that children are doing their jobs, testing us where it hurts the most, and highlighting their wounds and our own" (Kagan, 2004, p. 203). This is not poor behaviour but rather a sign of resilience.*

If a youth's past experiences have been negative, traumatic, or involved manipulation, they are not going to take the risk of forming a relationship with anybody without testing the waters first. Children and youth will test us "to see if we care enough to go the distance" (Kagan, 2004, p. 187). This is simply part of working with high-risk youth. A majority of youth in the HRYI have had negative experiences with child welfare workers and so are, rightfully so, sceptical and suspicious. As such, they will push, swear, disappear, argue, challenge, occasionally threaten, sabotage, lie, say they do not care, threaten suicide, cut (self-harm), use drugs and/or alcohol, run away, and/or hide. The youth will expect the 'power card' to be played; to be told what to do and when to do it or to face the consequences (perhaps file closure or residential treatment). This is reading their *script*. If they play their part, we fall into our part with the predictable ending. They successfully drive us away, relieving the pressure for them to make any connection. They have 'written' such scripts before and such practice allows them to refine their skills and respond to power struggles. It is a survival technique – they force the rejection before they get hurt again (Kagan, 2004; Levy & Orlans, 1998).

Often childhood trauma has made them wary of adults, so they become skilled at a young age in keeping people at a distance. The more adults read their script, the more reinforced the behaviour becomes. Youth have demonstrated that it is during this testing phase in which they often feel hopeless that anything will, or can, change. If the youth's belief that adults do not help and do not care is reinforced, they will perceive that there will be little to gain from working together. We as workers must pass these tests that youth throw at us and not assume that such behaviour means they do not want help or that they are attacking us personally. That they are taking a significant risk to test the relationship at all means they are contemplating making a connection even though there are no guarantees that they will not face further hurt. This shows resilience and courage, not defiance and manipulation. It is essential we understand this if the relationship is to progress (see Box 9.7).

Box 9.7   Jessica

At the risk of sounding like a sucker for punishment, I like the testing phase. Even though a youth might be angry, and perhaps verbally abusive, they are putting a lot of energy into the relationship. It is tougher when the youth shrugs their shoulders and says "whatever . . . ." This reminds me of the saying that the opposite of love is not hate, but indifference. The indifferent youth worry me more and take longer to come around, though hopefully they get to the testing phase as well. Jessica went through the indifference when she was engaged in her addictions, but she certainly tested me at times. She would tell me I am wasting my time, that she was just going to be a pain in the ass, that she didn't have to listen, and that she was not going to talk. She would miss meetings and refuse to answer her door when we had arranged for me to pick her up. Admittedly, these times were frustrating, though I was aware it was not a personal attack. Her behaviours made sense given her life experiences, so I resisted falling into her script and confirming her belief that I would not hang in there with her. Given her overt hostility at our initial meeting, I knew she would be testing me for a while. Like with many youth, I felt I was able to pass her test. Her behaviours and words, and the need to keep me at a safe emotional distance, dissipated over time.

Intentional interactions

- *Every action and conversation is done in a purposeful, thoughtful, and respectful way. Be tuned in!*

Relationships with youth should be intentional, significant, and purpose filled. A harm reduction approach helps ensure this is the case, as it focuses on the individual as unique, with unique experiences and needs. A common complaint by youth is they feel, at times, they are just a "file number" or a "case," reflecting a lack of respect and caring. Being intentional also pulls us out of a *formula mentality* in which we, as workers, are almost on auto-pilot in that if we see an issue in an individual we generalize it and reply with a standard response or service. There is no such thing as a 'one-size-fits-all' response to all of our complex youth. Such a "presumptuous or disrespectful" response is more in line with a medical model approach in which the worker acts in the role of expert (Mullaly, 2010, p. 310). Rather, relationships should be based on shared-power (Bishop, 2002). There must be a desire to learn and understand, and there should be specific goals and outcomes which are designed in partnership with the youth and others the youth identifies as significant in their lives.

Being intentional also means having a sense of timing. Often early in relationships we are tempted to assert to the youth what the expectations are and what rules need to be followed. We do this before we have even established any kind of relationship and then we are taken aback when the youth react negatively or aggressively. Refraining from laying down the law is not enabling youth to do whatever they want, but rather it speaks to intentionally striving to make a connection and establishing our credibility with the youth. Obviously, we will receive less resistance from a youth if we are patient and pick the appropriate time to nudge them in a direction in which they want to go, even if there is still a fear of failure or more disappointment. When approaching youth in this manner, it is not unusual for youth to articulate that they appreciated the push and felt the worker believed in them enough, which would not be the outcome if we are pushing our own agenda with no thought to timing. In a system that defines outcomes and sets budgets that can be tied into expediency, we can reduce the sense of satisfaction and success in youth because our focus may become meeting the needs of the system rather than focusing on the needs of the youth we are serving (Herbert, 2007; Lonne et al., 2009; Wharf, 2002a). Our research has shown that, in general, youth can understand the limitations of the system, the boundaries that exist, and the roles and responsibilities of the worker, but the only way to have discussions about such realities is in relationship. It is extremely important for youth to understand what they can expect from their social workers, as child welfare workers have specific provincial/territorial/national legislation under which they must work.

The workers need to be *tuned in* to the youth, which can make intentional actions and conversations easier to navigate. This involves reading their mood and body language; their readiness for heavy conversations; what may trigger traumatic memories; their propensity to dissociate; whether you position yourself for eye-to-eye contact (say over coffee) or parallel contact (such as walking or driving); and the surrounding environment (having a difficult conversation in school when they have to return to class versus in their placement where staff will be around to provide support after the meeting). All of this falls under being thoughtful and purposeful with the youth. We can joke, use personal disclosure, challenge, and share differing opinions, but there is a time and a place. Being tuned in to the youth will help guide workers and help the youth be tuned in to you (see Box 9.8).

Box 9.8   Jessica

At times, most likely when I am feeling stressed or overwhelmed, I enter a state I call 'child welfare brain.' At the risk of offending some, this is not a positive state of mind, as it reflects when I lose perspective of the relationship-based practice and slip back into punishment-consequence methods. On one such occasion I picked up Jessica from a friend's place and was driving her to a community agency. Walking in from the parking lot, I told her that her service plan needed to be updated. I asked her what she wanted in her new service plan and what should change. I reminded her – though she didn't need reminding – that she had not met many goals in the previous plan. I should have seen that she was not in a good mood and was doing her best to shut me out, but rather than asking her what was wrong, I persisted with my agenda. She stopped walking, turned to me and shouted "just be there." This shut me down effectively. For the head space Jessica was in, and for what was going on for her at the time, "just be there" was very valid for a service plan. Anything else was meaningless. I could have gone ahead on my own and done a lengthy service plan with a number of goals, lots of tasks, identified signs of progress and review dates, and suggested outcome deadlines. It wouldn't have mattered at all to Jessica at this time. I reflected on the lesson she had taught me and wondered why I kept pushing her and ignoring her cues. I apologized and we were able to reconnect. A couple of weeks later she called me and said we should meet and work out a service plan.

Gaining trust is not the main goal

- *Allow trust to evolve naturally. If the youth perceive this is a goal/agenda of the worker they may feel threatened and pull back. Some youth may not develop the capacity to trust in the time they are involved with child welfare services, so getting to the point that they know their worker will not harm them can still be significant and allow for progress.*

A large number of high-risk youth with attachment issues have learned to "trust no one, to block caring for others, and simply to do what they want to get what they need" (Kagan, 2004, p. 207). They are not going to trust workers easily and may not even possess the capacity to do so; such may be the damage done to them. Yet, we do tend to talk about getting the youth to trust, take satisfaction in telling people that we got a youth to trust us, or fall into the habit of telling a youth he or she "just needs to learn to trust me." As a *trusting* relationship is so important we allow ourselves to be single-mindedly driven by it at times. Indeed, trust is emphasized in much of the literature as a goal in any relationship with children, youth, and families. While perhaps counter-intuitive, I would argue that we should let it go. We may tell a youth, "you can trust me," but our "pushing [youth] to trust before they are ready ignores how frightened they are of connection" (Heller & LaPierre, 2012, p. 233). Children and youth who have experienced trauma want to trust but they are scared and angry (Heller & LaPierre, 2012). We know we are genuine and caring so we want youth to respond to this, even when they have not reached a point of feeling safe enough to take such a risk. These are youth who have gone through placement after placement, even with nurturing and loving caregivers, and have still not been able to let others into their world. We may be good workers, but trust is not about us and we cannot set this agenda. If we do, and the youth is not ready, the youth may withdraw (dissociate) or act aggressively. It could be that a youth was sexually abused by an uncle who told them "it's okay you can trust me" or whose boyfriend turned out to be a pimp but groomed his 'girlfriend' by telling her the same thing.

The word *trust* is a powerful but loaded word. It has meaning, but it can be abused. For a youth who does not have the capacity to trust, it can be meaningless or it can be overwhelming. By not making it an overt focus of the relationship-building process, it opens up possibilities for the youth and can allow trust to grow slowly over time. 'Jenny' (see Box 2.4 in Chapter 2) lacked a capacity to trust. Even after five years with the HRYI, she grew comfortable, but she could never trust me, as her worker, or other workers and service providers, regardless of how much time we spent with her. The first hint of disagreement seemed to reinforce to her that we did not care about her, that we would now give up on her, and that this outcome was inevitable. We would take the time to reassure her that this would not be the case and, while the situation would settle for a while, this pattern would repeat. While Jenny did not learn to trust us, over time she did accept we were safe enough to allow her to reach out when she needed help. This is important because good work can be done when there is *buy-in*. This is not the same as trust, but it is an acknowledgement that she eventually understood we would not hurt her, lie to her, or go behind her back. If I had told Jenny that she could trust me, she would have been very threatened by this, so trust simply did not become an issue. The worker sets out to support, advise, guide, help, and learn from the youth. If through this process a trusting relationship emerges, this is a gift and the connection will definitely be stronger. If it happens it certainly is something to be celebrated with the youth; it just should not drive the process (see Box 9.9).

Box 9.9   Jessica

Many youth frequently need reassurance that their file will close only when they are ready and this will not be a sudden decision. Even though we had worked together for years and had a good relationship, Jessica still feared that I might suddenly close her file, leaving her without support. I was surprised, as I had told her many times we would discuss her file closing together. I was coming from my assumptions about trust, rather than Jessica's experiences of not being able to trust others. I questioned why she thought I would do that, but this had more to do with my own confidence that I would never do something hurtful and disrespectful to her than it did about her anxiety and fear in taking the risk of allowing me into her world.

Create healthy confusion

- *By being attuned to the needs of the youth, and demonstrating that there are people who worry about them and care for them, their view of the world as lonely, frightening, and unsafe can be challenged over time, allowing for deeper conversations around relationships.*

Kagan (2004) writes:

> Traumatized children often act as though there is no past and no future, just the present. And, the present becomes a repetition of what children could not change, often, the script traumatized children came to believe about themselves. I am unlovable, undeserving, and deep down bad, damaged, or crazy.
>
> (p. 267)

As explained in Chapters 2 and 3, children with attachment issues and who have experienced trauma generally have poor self-esteem and, indeed, this becomes part of their script. Ongoing feelings of being unworthy and actions that push caring and nurturing people away remain strong for these youth. Also noted in the chapter on relationships, we tend to reinforce these negative feelings and thoughts – or scripts – through the traditional punishment-consequence interventions. Therefore, we need to be intentional about getting off the script, which causes a sense of confusion – but healthy confusion. My work with high-risk youth has demonstrated that such thinking, or scripts, can be challenged by doing things the youth do not expect, including being a safe, consistent, and genuine adult in their lives.

If the youth believes that nobody cares for them, that they do not deserve to be loved, that they have to be in control of themselves because they cannot rely on others, and that the world is essentially an unsafe, lonely, and frightening place, then our efforts must be focused on challenging the youth's negative belief system. An anonymous but wise person once said: "*Sometimes we put up walls, not to keep people out, but to see who cares enough to knock them down.*" The walls of our high-risk youth are thick indeed, but if we hope to get off of their scripts and foster change, we must be those workers who care enough to knock these walls down. By following the strategies noted above we can start to be the exception to their template of an adult, an authority figure, a social worker, a service provider, etc. If we are consistent and the youth start to sense we are not going away, this can lead the youth to question why we care. Perhaps it is more than simply because it is our job. Perhaps it is because someone genuinely wants to help. While this can be threatening to the youth, and we need to anticipate there may be times they withdraw to their personal safe place, it is important we do not get drawn back into their script. As Dr. Bruce Perry tells us, "the human brain likes things that are familiar more than things that are good"[5] (2014, lecture), so effort is required on both sides to journey down this unfamiliar path of giving up an ingrained belief system. We know the familiar place is the safe place on both sides, as the youth is allowed to avoid the inevitability of hurt and rejection, and, as workers may find, it less risky to take the path of least resistance. However, with persistence, the youth can be motivated since, as has been pointed out a number of times, *youth want healthy connection with adults.* It just takes much thinking and risk-taking on their behalf. If we simply reinforce that adults want to control, punish, and give up, the result is reinforced negative thinking rather than healthy confusion.

Challenging the youth must occur in a sensitive and respectful way (Levy & Orlans, 1998), as the tendency to push too hard results in the youth pushing back in a reactive, almost unconscious and automatic way, known as *counterwill*.[6] In such cases we end up back in the power-and-control relationship, with the youth being labelled uncooperative and defiant, and with very little progress being made. My experience has shown me that the youth will go at their own pace – one that is safe for them. If this safety is evident, then there is a better chance that they will allow their view of the world to be challenged. Again, this can happen without the presence of trust, as getting some level of buy-in already demonstrates some challenge of their view of the world. Creating healthy confusion can be a vehicle for moving beyond buy-in and into the realm of trust. This can also help in the future if the belief systems change enough that others can also be seen as an exception to the negative view of adults, allowing youth to take more risks and add to their support network (see Box 9.10).

Box 9.10   Jessica

Early in the relationship with Jessica, she was quite blunt in asking me why she should trust me as inevitably I would reinforce why social workers could not be trusted. I didn't claim otherwise, knowing that Jessica would have to live a new experience which would take time. She thought I was strange, weird, or freaky. I didn't see this as negative, as it showed that at least she was trying to figure out my motive for being persistent. As time went on and she grew more comfortable, I could use the times she disappeared (hanging out with friends and using) to tell her I was worried about her. As she was getting used to me being around, she would not be threatened enough to be angry, but she would change the topic or pretend not to hear my concern. Eventually, I asked her why she didn't like hearing that I worried about her. She said it seemed to make her feel dependent and not as in control (i.e., weaker). I told her I can't help but worry when I don't know where she is and knowing she is using drugs and could get hurt or be sexually exploited. She would tell me it is none of my business, but I said it could be as I cannot simply let her be in harm's way and do nothing as a child intervention worker. This got more of a reaction, but I also believe she saw that I 'had her back.' While her safety was a reality I could not ignore, it was still a risk telling her I may need to act without her consent if she was in imminent danger. I told her that my worrying about her and not wanting to see her hurt trumped me having the consequence of her wrath. After this she maintained more contact and would call if she was in an unsafe situation. There was a shift in her thinking, as I was now seen as a resource rather than simply an authority figure.

Explore the youth's motivation to change

- *Fear of failure and change can often be mistaken for lack of motivation. Labels can contribute to this in the form of learned helplessness. Hand-holding is often necessary at first, as is 'checking in' to ensure they feel safe.*

My experience indicates that it is erroneous to believe that youth do not want to change. They try and they try again. As previously stated, it is difficult to make changes without a sense of connection and support. High-risk youth often have little or no belief in themselves that change can occur. Setbacks are extremely difficult and reinforce the negatives they already believe about themselves. If these beliefs have not come from their family circumstances, they will arise from the labels that have been attached to youth as they encountered human service systems such as health, education, child welfare, and justice. They learn they are 'problem children,' that they have behavioural issues, are conduct disordered, have ADHD or ADD, are depressed, are learning disordered, are attachment disordered, are anti-social, and are *high risk!* They also hear it from peers and are labelled "druggies," "criminals," "psychos," "sluts," "hos," and/or "stupid." How does a youth find an identity through all of these labels? How does a youth find some measure of motivation through all of this deficit-based talk?

As my research and conversations with youth have shown, high-risk youth have very limited access to resources, little help to find resources, and a deep mistrust that such resources will result in a positive experience. A youth's mental health, internalized beliefs, and addictions may be barriers that prevent them from meeting their basic needs, such as finding a place to live, escaping hunger, and even arranging transportation to appointments. Poverty can have an impact on motivation for these youth, often resulting in homelessness, a sense of exclusion and marginalization, an inability to find work, and an inability to buy clothes or bus tickets to get to places such as school (Gaetz, 2004). Such a sense of disenfranchisement and a feeling of being different can have an impact on self-esteem, which does not help youth in engaging in mainstream activities in society. This cycle is not easily broken and in fact is reinforced when high-risk, street-involved youth are profiled, targeted, and judged (Gaetz, 2004, 2009, 2010). As an example, Gaetz (2009) states that research has demonstrated "that most homeless youth do not avoid work, but the vast majority face significant barriers to obtaining and maintaining employment" (p. 5). Therefore, we must be careful not to make assumptions that youth simply lack motivation.

It takes time working with the youth to get their permission to involve other resources whether a psychologist, a psychiatrist, school, a life skills program, a placement, a physician, or a dentist. It can be very much a 'seize-the-day' mentality in being ready to act when the motivation is evident – when the youth is feeling safe. As tough as the youth may be on the street, getting them engaged with much-needed resources can involve a lot of 'hand-holding,' otherwise the appointments simply do not happen. For most youth, being pushed into series of meetings means being put into a situation of repeatedly taking risks, and this can be overwhelming. Again, this does not necessarily reflect a lack of motivation by the youth, but rather it can be that the process is moving at the pace of the worker rather than the youth. We certainly want to see the youth be healthy, get relief from a tooth ache, finally get glasses so their vision is not blurry, start healing from their trauma, start using their talents in school, etc. However, if the youth is not ready, and cannot keep up with our enthusiasm for them and our belief in them, the youth can become discouraged or feel they are letting us down. This can do harm to the relationship on both sides and, ironically, may serve to reduce their motivation even further. This speaks to the need of constant 'checking in' with the youth to ensure they are feeling safe, have appropriate support, and can handle the speed at which events are unfolding. In short, we cannot be more future focused and want the help and support more than the youth. Such scenarios risk reinforcing their sense of failure (see Box 9.11).

Box 9.11   Jessica

I was very pleased when Jessica said she would like to go into the human services field. Obviously, it was something we could talk about and I could help her and give her advice. She knew it would be hard and that she would have to spend some time completing high school work before she could apply for the social work program at a local college. I knew she had the right thinking and people skills to do well. However, indifference from family, resistance from her boyfriend, and the fear of failing were all barriers. When Jessica was upgrading, she became pregnant and this delayed her applying for the social work program. I tried to maintain her enthusiasm but she had a lot going on in her life. Jessica believed it was important that she get a career going, especially in case she ended up a single parent. She eventually applied to the program but, by the time September came, she was overwhelmed and had to defer her studies. I didn't push her, but I sensed in her that she felt she was letting me down. I had obviously not tempered my enthusiasm that she would be a colleague one day and now there was a risk she was feeling pressured to follow through. We talked about this and I told her she had a lot going on and she must make decisions so her life was manageable. She has not let this dream die and she started taking courses the following school year.

Celebrate small successes – inspiring hope

- *Celebrate even the smallest successes and allow the youth to define success as experts in their own lives.*

When working with high-risk youth, it is essential to remain hopeful – to believe that youth are not 'stuck,' that change can occur, and that youth are strong and resilient. Working from a harm reduction approach is about being aware of what the young person sees as important and remaining focused on their individual definition of success. It is a philosophical shift to define success through the eyes of a youth and not as the 'expert' (Elovich & Cowing, 1993; Worden, 1999). It is important to celebrate the successes, no matter how small, and maintain communication to assess that progress is being made in a way that makes sense to the youth. For example, one worker I supervised had a non-traditional perspective when youth went absent from their group homes. She dared to question why youth were given consequences when they returned: loss of privileges, time out, missing fun activities, or losing visit times with family (which is unethical practice). The worker argued that rather than punish the youth, staff should welcome them and celebrate their return. She suggested they offer milk and cookies, and tell the youth they are glad they returned and are safe. This just made sense to her and she believed the youth would respond better. More recently, as the shift to relationship-based approaches takes hold, group homes are starting to re-evaluate their negative procedures.

These opportunities to notice successes will present themselves daily, giving workers the opportunity to remain intentionally focused on celebrating the small things and inspiring some measure of hope in all situations. As noted earlier, some youth state that they only see their case worker when things go wrong. This is not uncommon with a deficit-based mentality in which we can quickly list the youth's problems and may even see any accomplishment as an exception, an accident, or as having a hidden motive. At times even the smallest accomplishments can change the momentum and give them a glimmer of hope that things can be different. We see this in schools that welcome youth into their classrooms as opposed to those that feel they have no choice but to take the youth and are quick to find fault and start the process of suspension and, eventually, expulsion. If a youth lacks a sense of belonging and feels marginalized and excluded in the school system, they are set up for failure. Conversely, I have seen youth succeeding at some alternative schools when their mere efforts to attend are celebrated. Once they believe they can be successful, they take more risks and start seeking out help without fear of ridicule and rejection. A number of high-risk youth have graduated from high school and have entered post-secondary institutions. Feeling hope in one area can bring hope in other areas of their lives (see Box 9.12).

Box 9.12 Jessica

Jessica thought school was not for her. School represented failure, so, by grade eight, she had little motivation to return. Focusing on school when her life was in chaos and when she was frequently moving around made it hard to settle into a school. She did not receive help and thus fell further and further behind. Over time, Jessica felt frustrated, as she wanted to do something with her life but was now so far behind it seemed pointless to go back to school. However, as her confidence in herself grew, we had more and more conversations about how it was the barriers in her life that contributed to her lack of success at school rather than intellectual capacity or motivation. She returned to an alternative school program and started slowly. She received encouragement and support from school staff and was able to pass tests. She was encouraged to continue and dream bigger. She eventually believed she could get into post-secondary school to study youth work, though it still felt daunting to her.

Work from a strengths-based perspective

- *High-risk youth typically feel a profound sense of failure. Workers who place unrealistic expectations on them and use punishment interventions when they do not follow through can reinforce this sense of failure and can be perceived as one more adult in the life of the youth who is abusive, unintentionally or otherwise.*

At the risk of repeating information shared in Chapter 5, this section will be brief, but the fact that the need to focus on strengths is both a cornerstone of the practice framework and a strategy speaks to its importance. However, some workers continue to come "ready-made with a bias toward seeing problems and then trying to fix them by making suggestions to the client" (Blundo, 2001, p. 297). We tend to use 'problem-saturated' language (Hammond & Nuttgens, 2007; Madsen, 1999; Worden, 1999), which, again, conforms to the expectations of disconnected youth who have heard such language most of their lives.

To be blunt, as workers, we need to approach youth with a kind spirit rather making them feel worse about themselves and reinforcing the message that the world is an unsafe, hostile, and frightening place. Even though it goes against our values and ethical practice, I still hear, not too infrequently, that youth need to be set straight, that we cannot let them manipulate us and be in control, and that they need to be taught a lesson. Expecting high-risk youth to listen and respond accordingly to these messages is shocking and says more about the worker taking the actions and words of the youth personally than it tells us about the capacity of the youth to make connections. With a negative view toward a youth, it is challenging to find and build on their strengths. Perhaps we fear a loss of control, when in all likelihood the youth is simply trying to get by and survive (see Box 9.13).

Blundo (2001) claims that:

> Traditional social work practice is disempowering as workers use technical skills such as confrontation, overcoming resistance, and managing the "manipulative" client while at the same time manipulating the relationship to enhance compliance with professional decisions. . . . In contrast, from a strengths perspective, the "manipulative" client is understood as using considerable skill and thought for a purpose that is meaningful to that person. It is resistance only when these actions are perceived by the worker as the client challenging what the worker wants to take place.
>
> (p. 302)

Box 9.13   Jessica

Jessica had leadership qualities but she couldn't, or perhaps wouldn't, acknowledge them. When I pointed this out to her, she would change the subject or blow it off as if what I said was meaningless. It turns out it was meaningless to her. I was at fault for not explaining clearly how she was a leader and what I observed that allowed me to make this conclusion. Eventually, I confronted her on why she does not like me telling her this. Partly, she was not used to receiving compliments and this made her uncomfortable. The second reason was that it sounded phony to her. She had assumed that I told all of the youth I work with that they are leaders. She had concluded that it was part of my job to give youth such compliments. I explained to her that this would not be very ethical to simply tell all the youth I was working with they were a leader if it wasn't true. I told her this could potentially set up a youth for failure and embarrassment, or they could sense that I was lying to them, resulting in further damage to their fragile self-esteem and leading to irreparable damage to the relationship. I gave Jessica examples of how I had seen her use her leadership skills. This changed her perception and she was able to see how this made sense and that it was a strength she possessed. Jessica learned to be better able to accept compliments to some degree and felt a sense of value knowing this was not simply said as part of my social work script.

Be patient

- *The youth may have never been able to develop healthy relationships so this will take time. Most youth expect to fail and feel unworthy of help.*

Whether in government bureaucracies or small non-profit agencies, there is a demand to see positive outcomes and know that money is being spent effectively and efficiently. This is particularly prominent when programs are developed more to meet the needs of the system rather than those of the youth that are being served by the system. This can result in workers setting the pace rather than focusing on how much is manageable for the young people. We are dealing with a population that has been struggling with trauma for most, or even all, of their lives, yet we have expectations that youth follow rules, be motivated, accept help, and deal with their issues, or we may close their files for lack of follow through. There is also the tendency to expect that youth in the child welfare system be ready for independence at 18 (sometimes 16) even though they have had little guidance and mentoring in their lives, and despite the fact we would not have this expectation of our biological youth who have many resources, as well as mentoring and guidance. Even with respect to children, Dr. Bruce Perry discusses the "absurdity" of having a child with years of trauma and thinking counselling once per week will help – this is "arrogant and ridiculous" (Perry, 2014, lecture). While it certainly would appear irrational, why do we impose such deadlines and expectations? There is the cost argument, though we also know that homeless youth and traumatized youth are costing various systems a lot of money in physical and mental health costs, addictions, incarceration, and court costs. There may also be child welfare costs as youth become parents. In addition, these youth are not high contributors to the economy given lack of education and employment opportunities, which results from social exclusion, discrimination, and lack of resources (Gaetz, 2014b; Gaetz & O'Grady, 2013). Therefore, given the social return on investment of serving youth properly, the cost argument is very thin. Having patience is a minimal cost up front and potentially results in big savings in the future.

Being patient needs to be thoughtful strategy rather than simply a thought. This can help with knowing when to gently nudge the youth to take a risk and being okay with pulling back if this risk becomes too threatening. As we learned in the chapter on relationships, it can take an average of two years to build a genuine relationship, given the challenges high-risk youth face in letting people into their world. As much as we might be used to setting the agenda, the youth actually sets the pace. This does not mean we are passive, as this may foster dependency, but every youth is unique and comes with their own experiences around relationships. We need that internal dialogue in our heads to understand and appreciate where the youth is at, be respectful, and slow ourselves down if necessary. Indeed, 16, 17, or 18 years of damage and broken relationships cannot be unpacked and resolved in a matter of months (Lemma, 2010; Maté, 1999; Smith, 2004). We need to be present for our youth and being patient is part of being in a relationship if it is to be respectful, understanding, and genuine. It cannot be forced or rushed. If we are impatient and frustrated, this can trigger youth, reinforce that adults harm rather than help, and push them to rely on attachment behaviours such as keeping people at a distance and being defiant, uncooperative or manipulative. Impatience does not create safety and prolongs the process of making connections.

Even if we are patient in making a connection, it takes even more time to expand the youth's networks of support. If they have one positive relational experience there is the possibility they will be open to taking further risks with other healthy adults (Perry, 2006). But, there is no quick formula to rush the process. As Maté (1999) advises, "The best attitude to adopt is one of compassionate patience, which has to include the tolerance for failure" (p. 234). The worker must be willing to take the time to share in a "journey of discovery and progress" (Luckock & Lefevre, 2008, p. 6). If we create a safe environment progress will be made, but we just cannot dictate how fast this will happen. We must accept that we cannot control this for our youth (see Box 9.14).

Box 9.14   Jessica

As stated earlier, it took eight months of knowing Jessica to even have a super-ficial conversation. It would have been reasonable to conclude she was not interested in help or changing anything in her life. However, I also knew she was young and getting into potentially dangerous situations. It was hard to not be more intrusive and perhaps even prevent her from being on the street. However, such intervention would have been temporary and she was likely to return to the streets. Essentially, I would have closed the door on establishing any kind of positive relationship. Waiting her out was not easy, but it produced the best results. It gave her the space to question why I persisted in being con-cerned about her without overwhelming her or engaging in a battle for power and control.

Safety plan with youth

- *If youth can be engaged to actively participate in creating their safety plans, they are more likely to be invested and start to appreciate that others are concerned about them.*

All youth within the High Risk Youth Initiative are eventually asked to participate in completing a *safety plan*. It is their document, not ours, but is does help all those who are involved with the youth. It is not a service plan, but reflects that the youth are involved in decisions and that their safety is important. The goal is to reflect con-cern, but not control. Some youth write it themselves, while others talk while the case worker or service provider writes (many youth struggle with literacy). Some cannot think of what to say or write (or are nervous about saying the wrong thing perhaps) so prompting or making suggestions can help. The youth are never forced to fill out the form or threatened with a withdrawal of service for not cooperating. In my experi-ence, very few youth refuse as this form is done *with* them, not *to* or *for* them. Some may not be ready initially, but when they have had some time to assess the relation-ship, they eventually become more willing.

The first point is standard for all youth. The other three points are filled in by the youth:[7]

1   *Goal: I am safe.*

   That's it. Simply, it says all that needs to be said. It is not a service or work plan. It is easy for the youth to remember.

2   *What things/situations make me unsafe?*

   We may have lots of thoughts on this but it is the youth who will identify the level of safety. If they are struggling, we can prompt and ask if our suggestions make sense and whether they believe such a safety concern is true. A youth may be in an unhealthy relationship (and many youth have identified this) but they may not be ready to leave. They may identify concerns with drugs and alcohol, certain friends, family members, or hanging out in certain places. Typically, the youth will identify more superficial things initially, but as the relationships develop with their support team, the list will expand as they disclose more. The youth are taking a risk with this question, knowing that if they say too much it could prompt a case worker to have to act (being suicidal, boyfriend is actively violent, or they are being sexually exploited, for example). However, the youth may add things to the form to prompt further discussions and to get help with leaving dangerous situations and making healthier decisions. This makes it important that the safety plan is updated every few months or so. Friends and acquaintances come and go frequently in the lives of high-risk youth, so it needs to stay relevant.

3   *The best way for me to deal with this is . . .*

   Hopefully, this is an empowering statement for the youth. Some youth do not appear to have thought about this much, and will look at their worker as if begging to let them off the hook and tell them how to deal with unsafe situations. Assist and prompt but do not rescue! This can help the youth to give some serious thought about who they hang out with and what situations are actually dangerous; it can help them develop a thinking process around these areas. This perhaps sounds a bit idealistic, but, again, when building a relationship, this can evolve over time. I have seen youth start talking about the way they may deal with their unsafe circumstances, then stop and re-evaluate as if they are gaining insight at that moment. Youth can also return to this safety plan that *they* developed and signed, and ask what happened or why they are not accessing their supports in times of crisis. A challenge for workers is accepting some of the responses the youth identify. We may not like their solutions but we cannot ask them to work at this safety plan, then undermine them by thinking we know best. We need to remind ourselves about the harm reduction approach, bite our tongue, and thank them for putting their thoughts and ideas on paper.

4   *These are my placement options and supports I can call on . . .*

This is an opportunity for the youth to identify who the safe people are in their lives. It is very sad when a youth simply stares at the form desperate to think of one person. There are also interesting instances in which youth do not put their partner as an identified safe person. As time goes on, typically youth will identify their case workers and community supports, as well as system care-givers and various program supports. They may also identify family members (immediate or extended) who may not have been noted as a potential resource before. This could be a person who can offer accommodation in a crisis or be nurtured into being a longer-term placement. It can also help clarify how much value the youth puts on the supports identified. Again, this question can prompt conversations. There have been instances in which youth have listed a former partner, a john, or a pimp as an emergency placement option. While they know they may have to trade sex for a place to stay (survival sex), they may see this as a better option than a group home, shelter, or being on the street. It may also be a place where they can access drugs and/or alcohol. This can result in a discussion on what safety really means, as some youth would not see this as sexual exploitation as they are getting what they need (this may prompt a more mandated response depending on the legislation of a particular jurisdiction). This part of the form is also valuable for after-hours staff to have access to if alternative, pre-approved resources are listed. Without this, staff are forced to rely on traditional placement options, which are likely to create a conflict and result in the youth running away (see Box 9.15).

Box 9.15   Jessica

Jessica would often list her mother's apartment as a place she could stay in an emergency. This might beg the question as to why she couldn't live with her mother and her sisters. She cared for her mother, who would help her out finan-cially at times, but she was clear that she couldn't live at home. Jessica said her mother struggled with depression, was not often home, and she could not provide any emotional support. This hurt her in many ways. In addition, her two sisters would use the mother's apartment whenever they wanted, and they would often bring their boyfriends home and this created conflict. She also identified that if she was at home, she would be expected to clean the apartment, even though no one else appeared to contribute. What Jessica was able to state was that her mother's place could be an option for a night or two if she had nowhere to go and was faced with having to go to a group home or shelter. The safety plan helped start a number of conversations and provided much insight about her family dynamics.

Build relationships and community networks

• *It is critical that the youth has a support network built under them. The days of working in isolation and expecting positive outcomes are over.*

Given this was highlighted as a key area of the practice framework in Chapter 6, it is enough to state that, by extending our own networks of support, we inevitably expand the networks of support for the youth. The youth are part of the community, so we in child welfare services need to be part of the community. Outreach workers and service agencies are working with high-risk youth in the community. Child welfare needs to be partners in this human service community, as working in isolation, as the authority, can cause turf wars and conflict. The community represents an important resource for youth and is rich in wisdom, ideas, creativity, and supportive resources.

In interacting with outreach and agency partners in Edmonton, Alberta, community members (professional and non-professional) have proven to be invaluable in their role in bridging the 'disconnect' between the youth and the system. By developing partnerships with outreach and service agencies, there is the opportunity to expand the support network for youth to access a wider variety of services (mandated and non-mandated). It is also very important that the youth perceive their support people working together; that they have a team on their side, working in their best interest (see Box 9.16).

Box 9.16   Jessica

As noted earlier, my first meeting with Jessica was at an inner-city drop-in for youth. The agency, at the time, was small and was located in the basement of a run-down building. It was dark and an intimidating place to go. Also at that time, the police and child welfare workers were not welcome, as this typically meant youth were taken away, which upset other youth and staff and had the potential for explosive conflicts. It took a while but, having helped a number of youth from this agency, I established enough credibility to be able to drop by and talk to youth. An outreach worker, Wallis, acted as the bridge between Jessica and me. While Wallis was as distrustful of the system as any of the youth were, he would tell Jessica that he thought I was okay and encourage her to at least talk to me and see what I could offer. His words had an influence on many street-involved youth, as he had demonstrated he would not give up on them. While it took a long time for Jessica to get used to me and to talk, Wallis did not stop encouraging her to get help through me. If I was okay with Wallis, the youth were more willing to take a risk. By Wallis and me working together and giving consistent messages, I believe it gave Jessica permission to see what I was about. It turns out she didn't hate social workers as much as she thought!

Keep learning from the youth

- *The high-risk youth are a unique and diverse group of people who can teach us so much. Let them know how much you appreciate this and that this can serve to help other youth in the future. They are typically pleased to be able to help others, to 'give back.'*

It is profound when these high-risk youth get to the point of allowing us into their world, sharing their hurt, pain, dreams, goals, wishes, thoughts, and fears. How can we not learn from this gift? Our work gives us the opportunity for continuous learning, so while we are trying to help the youth improve their life circumstances, they are helping us in our practice and as people too. As Kagan (2004) writes, "Children keep me learning. Children also keep me humble, showing me day by day how little power I have as a practitioner" (p. 203). They can challenge us, frustrate us, overwhelm us, but also make us laugh, understand people better, learn from our mistakes, and give us better answers and solutions for high-risk youth we will meet in the future. The youth should know how much we appreciate this and how this learning always goes both ways. We can be specific as to what about the youth gave us the most learning and explain how this might help in working with youth in the future. It is not uncommon for youth to want to 'give back' and help other youth, even if their experiences of being raised in the system have not been particularly positive. They do not want to see youth going down the same path as they went, which can open the door for peer mentorship programs. While this requires a lot of supervision and debriefing with youth mentors, it can have a huge impact, especially for youth who show a lot of fear and anxiety toward authority figures.

I lead a program evaluation of a support and learning group at iHuman Youth Society for young, mostly Aboriginal, mothers, called Woven Journey. Aside from being optimistic about their futures and vowing to give their children better lives than they experienced – and despite their ongoing challenges with poverty, broken relationships with family members, and coping with their own traumatic experiences – all of the mothers wanted to give back and help other youth, especially those who were pregnant. They felt fortunate to be part of Woven Journey and that they had much to offer others who were struggling. I was struck at how natural this next step was for them – it was not some idea they could put into place, but rather the natural evolution of this cohesive group. Again, these young women had taught me a lot about resiliency and how, despite what they have overcome, they are not just surviving and coping but rather thriving and sharing (see Smyth, 2016).

It is also important to recognize such contributions from the youth. Going for lunch or supper and talking about the learning opportunities the youth provided can be a way to celebrate and reinforce that they are in a partnership with the case worker and others who make up the support team. This can make their contributions real and meaningful for the youth. Another idea is to write a letter to the youth thanking them and, again, reviewing the learning opportunities. These letters can be a valuable reminder that they have much value, that they have much to offer others, and that they are appreciated, intelligent, and insightful. Dr. William Madsen uses letter writing in his therapeutic work. He reports that when a client received letters, there was a sense of importance and warmth, knowing that someone was thinking about them. It was a reminder they were understood and respected, and that someone believed in them (Madsen, 2007) (see Box 9.17).

Box 9.17   Jessica

I have mentored a lot of students over the years. While I think I have something to offer from my years of experience, students always offer a unique perspective, so it provides learning opportunities for me as well. Students keep me grounded, as they tend to reinforce through questions and discussions why this work is so important and how rewarding it can be. As having a student can also involve the youth, I have engaged many of the youth in helping students get as much out of their placement as possible. I asked Jessica not only if it was okay that I involve a student in her life, but also if she would take an active role in helping the student learn. Of course, Jessica was a youth I knew well by this time and whom I felt would be interested rather than intimidated or overwhelmed. Jessica felt she could share her own experiences within the system and what she felt were aspects that worked well and what did not. This situation worked well, as Jessica had an extra support person involved and the student could engage in meaningful conversations about the youth's life and help develop his/her own practice. This was appreciated by the student and was a good experience for Jessica too.

Discussion questions to consider for Chapter 9

1   *What are some of the challenges you might face in your attempt to 'be available' for the youth? What are some strategies you might put in place for yourself to find an appropriate work-life balance?*

2   *Why does* not *focusing on trust sound so counter-intuitive?*

3   *How can being a self-reflective worker help with implementing these strategies?*

4   *Can you think of times in which you were obliged to follow policies that reflected a 'tough love,' 'three-strikes,' and/or 'zero tolerance' approach? How did this benefit/not benefit the youth? How did you feel about implementing such a policy?*

5   *Are there other strategies that you can think of that could be useful in enhancing your relationship with youth on your caseload?*

6   *What might be some boundary challenges in following the strategies in this chapter when working with such an emotionally vulnerable population of youth? As ethical and boundary challenges will, and should, be common if one is being thoughtful and intentional about practice, what are some ways to keep such discussions alive and out in the open among your colleagues?*

Notes

1   An earlier version of this chapter on strategies for working with high-risk youth appeared in the book chapter, 'Making the Connection: Strategies for Working with High Risk Youth' by Peter Smyth and Arlene Eaton-Erickson (pp. 119–142), from the book, *Passion for Action in Child and Family Services: Voices from the Prairies* (2009), edited by Sharon McKay, Dan Fuchs, & Ivan Brown;. Regina SK: Canadian Plains Research Centre (see also references section). The strategies have been revised and updated for this book.

2   From the book, *We Generation: Raising Socially Responsible Kids* (2009, p. 116).

3   "Jessica" represents the stories and experiences of a number of youth who were part of the High Risk Youth Initiative.

4 I am indebted to Arlene Eaton-Erickson, with whom I originally developed these strategies for training purposes and for a chapter we co-authored in 2009 (see endnote 1).

5 This can also explain why some children and youth will push and/or bait caregivers in various settings until they are punished, as this is familiar and predictable, and can help them avoid the risk of making connections and being rejected and abandoned. Staff in residential settings and group homes have told me that it is not uncommon for children and young adolescents, in particular, to display negative behaviours until they are physically restrained.

6 Gordon Neufeld and Gabor Maté describe this notion of reacting automatically as *counterwill*: "Counterwill is an instinctive defensive resistance to any perceived coercion. It can be evoked in anyone at any age, whenever a person feels controlled or pressured to do someone else's bidding and can be triggered even when no coercion is intended. It makes its most dramatic appearance in the second year of life and again during adolescence but can be activated at any age" (Neufeld & Maté, 2004, pp. 89–90).

7 Thanks to Jay Vandermeulen, a former colleague, who provided much of the wording for this safety plan.

Chapter 10

No room for error
Boundaries and ethics and high-risk youth

Taking a universal precautions approach to boundaries in the helping professions can avoid problems. If there is no touch, no sharing feelings, we can avoid misunderstanding and misinterpretations. We will not put ourselves in compromising positions which may threaten our careers. While this might work for us as workers, it could be argued that such practice could be quite unrewarding and mechanical. Moreover, it does not work well for high-risk youth, who tend to already have a view of the world that nobody cares. Having supervised students for over 20 years, this topic always comes up and I often hear the perspective of maintaining what I have come to call *uberboundaries*. Typically, when they hear that I do not come from this rigid perspective, there is often much relief. Being keen and still holding onto their idealistic view, the area of boundaries and ethics is very confusing for many students. I then have to break the news to them that it is not any less confusing even after practicing in the field for many years. This is not a bad thing, as we should always be thoughtful and intentional about all of the things we do and say to the youth with whom we are working. Relationship-based practice demands much thought and reflection (Ward, 2010). The bad thing is that, in government at least, we are not having discussions, symposiums, training, or much supervision around boundaries and ethics. It is as if everyone should know about the importance of these areas so there is no need to talk about them. This could not be further from the truth. The actual truth might be closer to the fact it is such a grey area, potentially messy and awkward, and given there are as many interpretations of appropriate boundaries and ethics within worker-service user interaction as there are social workers and community workers.[1]

Gross boundary and ethical violations certainly do happen. While they do an incredible amount of damage and are inexcusable, they are, thankfully, quite rare. However, as self-aware practitioners, we should be challenged with ethical dilemmas every day because we live and work in the grey, especially given this incredibly challenging population of youth. In many cases it is hard to determine the right course of action in a given situation that a youth might present to us. This means we must be intentional in everything we do: reflexive in the moment (what is the most ethical think I can do or say?), mindful about the youth (how will my decision impact the youth?), and reflective (debriefing with the youth and with colleagues after the fact).

What do we say to a youth with whom we have a very positive relationship when they say "love you" at the end of a phone call or in a text? What do we do if, in our office with nobody else around, a youth initiates a hug? How do we respond if a youth is having a very difficult time, has no money, and is pleading for a pack of cigarettes?

These situations all involve unique individuals and all have a context of their own so, again, the answers to these questions are grey rather than black and white. These are not life and death and do not involve destructive and intentional abuse of authority, engaging in a sexual relationship, exploitation, threats, violence, or withholding or denying resources to gain an advantage or maintain silence. Still, they are important and can help or hinder the relationship we may be trying to establish or have established. It is finding a balance of not compromising our ethics and values while also continuing to give the message to the youth that they are valued and that we care about them. We need to get to a point that if they misinterpret our words and/or our actions, we can communicate openly and work this out. Establishing boundaries and knowing where we stand with respect to our personal and professional ethics and values (see Box 10.1) is essential, but we must be able to communicate these with our youth in a compassionate, sensitive, and understanding way, and appreciate the impact our ethics and values have on the relationship. Indeed, the way in which boundaries are drawn, respected, and renegotiated is significant to the workings of any relationship (Doel, 2010).

Box 10.1   Defining *ethics* and *values*

Ethics . . . *are about matters of right and wrong in our conduct and behaviour. They look at our character in terms of qualities which are good and qualities which are bad. They consider how we should behave in relationships.*

Values . . . *are about what is regarded as valuable and worthwhile. Professional values consider how practitioners should treat their clients. . . . Professionals should strive to act in a worthy manner.*

Taken from: *The Compleat Social Worker*
by David Howe (2014, p. 156)

Boundaries are also necessary because they not only serve to foster the autonomy of the service user, they also allow the survival of the workers (McMahon, 2010). They help prevent professionals from taking on responsibility for what these troubled youth are doing, thinking, and feeling. Workers are committed to getting in touch with the inner world of the youth, knowing the pain they will find there, and perhaps within themselves, so they appreciate the need "to make warm relationships" (McMahon, 2010, p. 162). If workers do not pay enough attention to boundaries it can lead to much frustration and self-doubt and the relationship can suffer.

Our youth will search for boundaries if they are not apparent. Remembering that youth who have experienced early trauma and attachment issues can struggle in social situations, they cannot be expected to pick up cues and be aware of social norms. Not being clear on boundaries is like blindfolding a child, youth, or even an adult and leading them into a dark, silent room. This individual will put their arms out and keep feeling around, or pushing, until they find the boundary of the wall. They could very well become anxious and fearful, which could lead to anger or rage with the lack of direction and safety. If we do not set boundaries with our youth, we cannot fault them when they keep pushing and testing until they find their limits. They have not learned boundaries so it makes sense that they will need to push until they find them. There might be a youth that simply demonstrates a serious lack of regard for the boundaries of others, though experience informs me that among our high-risk youth this is very rare. If this is a concern it is typically due to serious mental health issues, which require intervention beyond worker–service user interaction. In short, accepting that workers are the ones who must set boundaries early as the relationship is evolving is better for everybody and allows for healthy discussion and valuable learning. Ungar (2002) reinforces this by telling us, "teens need more than just connection. They also need boundaries, rules and the feeling that someone gives a damn and is going to keep them safe and help them succeed" (p. 12).

Setting boundaries also means finding a balance. If they are overly rigid, we push youth away and perhaps reinforce to them that the world is a hostile and lonely place. As critical as boundaries are, I have seen social workers hide behind them as if afraid to risk being intimate on any level. If too casual or ambiguous with our boundaries, values, and ethics, we send confusing messages that could end in conflict, hurt feelings, and further disappointment and alienation (Taylor, 2010; Valios, 2001). Further, it could lead to serious boundary violations resulting in betrayal and life-long scars (see Box 10.2).

Box 10.2   Reamer on boundaries

Frederic Reamer is a professor at the School of Social Work, Rhode Island College. He is the author of *Boundary Issues and Dual Relationships in the Human Services* (2012).

- "Historically, human service professionals have not generated clear guidelines regarding boundaries for use in practice. This is partly because the broader subject of professional ethics – to which the topic of boundaries is closely tied – did not begin to receive serious attention in the scholarly and professional literature until the early 1980s" (p. 3).
- "Briefly, boundary issues arise when human service professionals encounter actual or potential conflicts between their professional duties and their social, sexual, religious, collegial, or business relationships" (p. 2).
- "[N]ot all boundary issues are problematic or unethical, but many are" (pp. 2–3).
- "A professional enters into a *dual relationship* whenever he or she assumes a second role with a client, becoming a social worker and friend, employer, teacher, business associate, family member, or sex partner" (p. 3, quoting Kagle & Giebelhausen, 1994, p. 213).[2]
- "A *boundary crossing* occurs when a human services professional is involved in a dual relationship with a client . . . in a manner that is not exploitive, manipulative, deceptive, or coercive. Boundary crossings are not inherently unethical; they involve boundary bending as opposed to boundary breaking. In principal the consequences of boundary crossings may be harmful, salutary, or neutral" (pp. 7–8).
- "A *boundary violation* occurs when a practitioner engages in a dual relationship with a client . . . that is exploitive, manipulative, deceptive, or coercive" (p. 6).

Looking after yourself, looking out for others

Box 10.3   How do youth make sense of relationships?

It is not uncommon to hear that a case worker has to maintain professional boundaries and that we are not friends and not parents (though we may be guardians to many children and youth). The other argument is that we need to role model healthy relationships and to allow emotional connections to develop. While we can control this on our end, we do not have as much control as to how youth make sense of the relationship.

In a documentary on the High Risk Youth Initiative called 'The Word on the Street' (Office of the Child and Youth Advocate, 2007), a youth described me as "father-like, which can be a pain in the ass, but he is there for me." She saw the connection with me, and her community worker, as "personal . . . they care [about me] like their own child, or friend, or whatever. Peter and Rebecca will go out of their way." Some may say this crosses a line, especially given that such relationships are relatively short term. However, the youth describes how the worker-client relationship can be important and helpful. In addition, the experience can result in positive memories – on both sides – and can help the youth in allowing other adults in their lives as a way of building their support network.

Throughout the years, youth have expressed to me that I played a fatherly role in their lives, or perhaps an uncle role. This is not due to confusion by the youth, but rather a need to have people in their lives who act like family. One youth called me "Daddy Peter," with the compliment that I was like the father she wished she had had in her life. This allowed for an exploration of this sadness and to clarify roles in a way that is not rejecting. Another youth saw me as a family friend because of my efforts to help the whole family. I have received "happy Father's Day" text messages.

The personal friend perception is trickier, as there are decisions that must be made. The relationship can never be equal, as a friendship should be. However, the youth typically use this term when the relationship has been established for a considerable amount of time (two to three years), when they are more stable, and when they are becoming more independent. I believe it serves many purposes, including: 1) the youth is not feeling the need for formal, more clinical services but wants to maintain a connection on an emotional level; 2) the youth is appreciative of the help they have received; 3) the youth see it perhaps a sort of rite-of-passage of joining the worker in the adult world; 4) that the working relationship is now voluntary, rather than mandatory, as when they were younger.

The life experiences of youth, positive and negative, will contribute to how youth define their relationships. As long as we are open to discussion when it does not feel right, the youth appears confused, or the youth is having difficulty letting go, then allowing the youth the space to make sense of the connection in their own way is important. Shutting the youth down or being critical of their interpretations can bring to the surface not only a sense of further rejection and abandonment, but also feelings of shame, anxiety, and guilt. It can reinforce,

> *once again, that adults cannot be trusted. It is on the worker to be thoughtful and reflective about what the youth says and how the youth acts. They need 'fathers' and 'mothers' to help guide them, 'aunts' and 'uncles' checking up on them, and 'friends' to help support them through life. As long as we keep it in perspective, the youth will keep it in perspective.*

We know that high-risk youth are an extremely vulnerable population. When the very people who should love you and nurture you as a child are unable or unwilling to do so, and further, they physically and sexually abuse you, how do you make sense of the world and understand love, caring, healthy touch, and appropriate boundaries? (See Box 10.3.) Our youth often feel they are not worthy of having people care for them or worry about them. This might threaten their sense of control or they might perceive this as a weakness. Many equate sex with love. Others might interpret any kind of touch as sexual in nature. With such a distorted perspective, it is critical that helpers establish and maintain their boundaries and help youth untangle the knotted mess that has been created for them. How will the youth learn to appreciate a caring adult, be in a healthy relationship, learn to love and be loved, understand the different levels of intimacy, and be able to distinguish between healthy and unhealthy touch if it is not discussed and demonstrated over and over?

This is a huge responsibility and can influence how our youth are able to build healthy relationships throughout their lives. The challenge for helpers is to be comfortable with their own boundaries so they can be thoughtful, mindful, and intentional when interacting with high-risk youth. Many people working with children and youth have experienced boundary violations in their own lives. Many get into the field because they want to help youth who have gone through the same struggles. I have heard social workers question how a person can truly help youth work through their trauma when they have not had such experiences themselves. There is no doubt that coming from difficult circumstances can add a dimension to a relationship with a youth that I cannot offer. However, being fortunate to not come from difficult circumstances, when a youth tells me that I can never truly understand what they have been through, that is the truth. I can be understanding and empathetic, feel pain for what they have experienced, and offer support and help, but I can never say that I understand what they are going through. To say otherwise would be unfair. I do ask myself if this is a barrier to engaging and working with high-risk youth and I do not believe it is. In the chapter on relationships, I discussed that youth look for workers to be non-judgemental, genuine, honest, and respectful. They do not typically ask to have workers who have been through similar experiences.

Being able to truly know what a youth has experienced by having gone through similar trauma can be a powerful part of a relationship *if self-disclosure is used appropriately, intentionally, and for the benefit of the youth*. It can be a helpful technique and has become more accepted over time. Reamer (2012) cites a study in which 69% of clinical psychologists reported that using self-disclosure in a therapeutic setting is ethical under many circumstances or unquestionably ethical. Only 2% stated that self-disclosure is never ethical. Whether the result is positive or negative, self-disclosure is a boundary crossing so it requires much reflection. To use self-disclosure, a helper must have worked through their own issues and be comfortable with who they are. They must not use their work in order to satisfy their own emotional needs or to try and resolve their own traumatic experiences. In short, the relationship is not for the practitioner's benefit (Turney, 2010).

Self-disclosure, when used with good judgement, can prove to be therapeutically beneficial to service users in certain circumstances (Reamer, 2012). Many addictions workers have journeyed through challenging times and often use appropriate self-disclosure to empathize and reinforce they do actually have a sense of what it is like to abuse substances. They know what it is like to use as a way to get through the day, numb out to escape the pain of their lives, self-medicate to deal with diagnosed or undiagnosed mental health issues, or cope with the chaos in their heads. This can also give hope to people with addictions – hope that their lives can change.

Some theoretical orientations, such as those from a traditional analyst perspective, may discourage the use of disclosure while those from the humanistic, existential, narrative, and feminist perspectives may engage in the use of this technique as a way to enhance transparency and promote a more egalitarian, nonhierarchical relationship (Reamer, 2012). As the practice within the High Risk Youth Initiative comes from an anti-oppressive perspective and uses a harm reduction philosophy, the use of self-disclosure is not discouraged. However, as the work takes place with such a vulnerable population, and as there is a focus on building relationships, workers must exercise caution. Ongoing discussion with colleagues and supervisors is essential. Workers should also be outlining their conversations in which self-disclosure was used in their case notes.

Indeed, while self-disclosure can be a good way to level the playing field, to be open and transparent, to show some vulnerability as a worker, and to demonstrate to youth that taking some risks is important, it can also be misinterpreted. In particular, a worker must avoid areas such as details of their own current problems or stressors, personal fantasies or dreams, and social, sexual, or financial circumstances. When not used thoughtfully, self-disclosure can harm the youth if they are struggling with their own trauma. If there is a connection, they will be looking to their worker to be the healthy adult to help them cope with emotional challenges. The youth should never be in a position of feeling responsible for helping their helper, which, understandably, could be very overwhelming. In such situations, self-disclosure may be occurring inappropriately because of the practitioner's own deep-seated emotional or dependency needs and perhaps, even unconsciously, as a way to establish a personal relationship with the service user (Reamer, 2012).

Unfortunately, there is no shortage of examples in which the mind can justify any kind of inappropriate action over time. There are decisions made because of past experiences, out of passion, due to being reactive, and all the way to being planned and executed over a period of time. The latter involves the most insidious boundary violations: the abuse of power, grooming, and exploitation. A worker being in a sexual relationship with a youth whom they are supposed to be helping and keeping safe is a violence that leaves a trail of destruction with, quite possibly, no end. I have seen the damage it does having worked with a young adult after her disclosure of an inappropriate and abusive relationship. She never believed that the worker, who was the one person she genuinely believed could save her, could turn out to be the one person to betray her. (This reinforces the importance of creating a support team with the youth rather than having to rely on one connection.) It was a long journey to place any level of trust in a case worker to start with, so her faith in others was justifiably shattered. An investigation revealed there was a grooming process; she was clearly exploited for the purpose of the person who had all of the power. The case worker also held the power over her funding, maintaining her support status within child welfare system and the services she did or did not receive.

Such actions also rock the confidence of colleagues, leaving everyone angry, frustrated, and with a sense of guilt. It leaves a stain on the system and the many professions that work with youth. While one can speculate on what drives a person to knowingly make the decision to violate a boundary in such an extreme manner, it reinforces that ethics and boundaries is not an area that anyone can be complacent about. These discussions – whether in supervision, one-on one with a colleague, and as a team – are critical. So is being self-aware and reflective. We work with vulnerable people, sometimes muddling through with our own vulnerabilities. Trying to convince oneself that troubling or awkward thoughts and feelings will simply go away is playing with fire. At times we cannot help what thoughts and feelings hit us, but we can do something to prevent acting on them inappropriately.

Workers must be constantly vigilant, as it is their responsibility to maintain limits and boundaries, especially given the often skewed view that abused youth have been taught throughout their lives. While such conversation can be difficult to have with a youth, it is also a learning opportunity. Workers can help youth sort out what are appropriate and inappropriate relationships not only with their service team members but also with family members, with partners, with co-workers, or with friends. If we close the door on ongoing discussions of ethics and boundaries, we risk a *conspiracy of silence* atmosphere such as what happened with the abuse in the residential school system in Canada that left a multi-generational trauma legacy for Aboriginal people. Every time we minimize or hide a gross boundary violation, we run the risk of allowing those periods of dark history to repeat. Vowing to never let such atrocities happen again cannot be meaningless, which it becomes if we are not keeping the conversations alive.

Again, such gross boundary violations are rare, but boundary crossings can also do harm. For instance, when a youth is being critical of their parents, do we validate their feelings in the sense of joining in their anger toward their parent because we feel they have been treated unjustly? Will this help the youth engage with us or will the youth feel we have no right to criticize their family? If we feel sorry for a youth on our caseload who is homeless after losing their shelter bed, do we consider taking him or her home? Because we believe the relationship has progressed very well, do we think it might be okay to share our home phone number? For good reason, child welfare systems and agencies have restrictions in these areas. Perhaps in some extreme circumstances there may be exceptions, though fuelling anger in a youth, taking them home, or sharing personal phone numbers are seen as significant boundary crossings.

How about meeting for coffee after a youth's file has closed? Allowing a youth to pay for coffee? Accepting a gift from a youth? Sharing one's own religious beliefs? Perhaps a youth is excited to meet their previous worker with an update about the positive things they are doing in their life and want to say how much they appreciated the help they received. Perhaps the youth wants to pay for coffee because they just received their first pay cheque and are very proud of themselves. Perhaps the gift was made during a craft night at a youth outreach centre and the youth has no family to share it with. Perhaps a youth was appropriately asking curious questions about their own spirituality and there was no intention by the worker to impose their own beliefs. While some may remain adamant that these scenarios are still inappropriate, they are grey.

In my experiences of allowing myself to cross such boundaries, overwhelmingly this has been a big deal to the youth. They are situations and conversations that we would not think twice about in family situations (how thoughtful is it if a 17-year-old youth took their mom and dad out for lattes after receiving their first pay cheque?), but we impose boundaries on system youth or former systems youth. Sometimes a youth whose file has closed calls me and leaves a voice message to say things are going well. Others may call when a difficult situation arises because while they may have better coping skills, they still perhaps have a limited number of support people they can call. My sense is that, having had relationships with youth over a significant period of time, they do learn boundaries. Reaching out in this way shows growth, that they have worked to overcome boundary violations imposed on them, and they have been able to "benefit from forming relationships with people who are emotionally available and responsive, intelligent and psychologically minded" (Howe, 2008, p. 161). The relationship has shifted from worker-service user to simple human interaction by two people whose lives have intersected. This does not happen often and I am aware that when it does it is a boundary crossing. It is one, however, that the youth appreciates, that I do not feel is a burden, and, most importantly, that does no harm.

With the above scenarios of a coffee meeting, accepting a gift, and talking about spirituality and the use of a term such as 'friend' can potentiality do harm that may not be anticipated at the time. These actions can potentially set up the youth, who is a current service user, to think they have special relationship with their worker that other youth do not have and that they can access extra resources. Later on they then may be devastated and angry if the worker then has to take steps to secure them in a locked facility for their own protection, report an illegal activity that was disclosed, or if the worker's employment status changes. This may also leave the youth assuming the friendship will continue indefinitely, contrary to the thinking of the worker. The youth can be left feeling rejected and abandoned all over again, possibly damaging progress the youth may have been making and reinforcing once more that adults cannot be trusted. There can also be a ripple effect, especially given the world of street-involved or high-risk youth is small and they talk. It is likely that if one youth discloses to others that they have a special friendship or access to a worker, another youth also connected to the same worker could feel slighted or feel that the worker is not genuine or honest. They may start to question themselves as to why the worker does not value them to the same degree. If the youth has a different worker, they may expect a similar level of connection from a worker who is less open to boundary crossing.

I have used the term 'friend' when having contact with a youth whose file is closed and if in a social situation where it is appropriate to introduce the youth, or young adult, to a third party. Not only might it come across as dismissive by identifying to others that this is a youth I used to work with, but it also breaches confidentiality and is likely to make the youth feel uncomfortable. If the youth adds that I used to be his/her social worker, that is fine, as this decision belongs to them. At this point in the relationship, there is no worker-service user hierarchy or authority and there is no direct control over the resources that the youth requires (though the relationship is still not equal because of this history). Meeting for a coffee is not an obligation (or should not be at a least) and it is to catch up and enjoy each other's company. This is very similar to a friendship situation, so I am comfortable introducing the youth as my friend. One definition of 'friend' is: *a person attached to another by feelings of affection or personal regard.*[3] As the attachment does not end when the formal child welfare status or agency contract ends, this definition makes the use of the term 'friend' appropriate. It is also useful to talk to the youth about why you perceive the connection as a friendship as a way to let the youth know they continued to be valued and to set boundaries.

Harm reduction strategies can make workers more thoughtful about boundaries. A youth perhaps is really struggling emotionally and historically copes by using drugs. He asks to borrow money for cigarettes, so a contract is made to use this to avoid drugs, while also agreeing that this will be the only time that lending money for cigarettes will happen. The worker had decided that arguing over cigarettes when the youth is trying to cope would not help the relationship and could result in much worse consequences, such as using drugs. This is not to say that this is right or wrong, but to highlight how these in-the-moment circumstances arise and it can be very difficult to determine the best approach. Documenting such decisions is important, as is, once again, debriefing with a colleague and/or supervisor.

Youth asking to "borrow money" is an ongoing boundary challenge, especially given they have very little of it. Generally it is not a good precedent to start, but again, we work in the grey. Generally, I tell the youth it is not a good boundary to cross as it could become an expectation. If it is the afternoon and the youth has not eaten all day, or quite possibly for a couple of days, I might give a youth a few dollars to eat but only if I do not have the time to take them to a restaurant or assist them to buy groceries using government or agency funding. I may also give a youth bus fare rather than see them walk, avoid paying for public transport (risking a substantial fine or being banned), stealing a bicycle, or hitchhiking. Using humour in such situations has worked as a way to avoid lending money while not coming across as rejecting (such as telling the youth I would be broke giving money to everyone I would like to help).

So, the general rule is to not give the youth money but to be open-minded and intentional about it if the need arises. Though there might be a temptation to do so as a 'teaching moment,' lending youth money as a loan is discouraged. Even if the youth makes this suggestion, high-risk youth do not have enough extra money to pay back loans. If they happen to have extra, there are always things they need that would fall under basic necessities. If they are struggling to pay the money back, they may feel guilty and possibly avoid contact, which is not helpful to the relationship. There is also the chance they may find even a small amount of money through troubling ways such as being sexually exploited, jacking another youth, or dealing drugs. My experience is that our youth are typically embarrassed to ask for money and they know the risk of being turned down. However, when a decision is made to give a youth money, they typically use the money for the purpose for which it was requested. I have had a few young mothers in tears asking for money to help feed their babies or buy baby supplies. If possible, I find it has been helpful to take them shopping, letting them know I can claim this back so they feel less guilty, or to connect them with emergency services. A young mom can feel very anxious asking for help feeding their baby or buying diapers, as it is admitting to a worker in the child welfare system that they cannot meet the basic needs of their child. However, it is important to point out that they had the courage to reach out for help and that they were putting the needs of their child before their own needs.

A good rule of thumb for those agonizing over ethics and boundary challenges is to think how this is going to look on a contact note on the youth's file. If a worker is feeling hesitant about being transparent and documenting the decision, that person should not be crossing the boundary and this should be explained to the youth (see Box 10.4). If a worker is comfortable documenting the discussion with the youth and the final decision, it can be a good indication that the person is on safe ground, can justify what they did to others, and that they acted with the youth in mind, not herself or himself.

Box 10.4   Janet's story: bringing Janet home

Christmas is a particularly difficult time for our high-risk youth. The youth do their best to make the best of the joyous season but, as we hear in songs and advertising, Christmas is a time for family. The holiday season can be an even harder time to shut out the fact that they do not have a family.

On December 23, 2004, I had spent quite a bit of the day with 'Janet.' She had been partying the night before and had crashed at somebody's house, though she did not know who, as a friend had taken her there but had left sometime after Janet had passed out. Janet was confident she was not sexually assaulted but some money and bus tickets were taken from her purse. A bus driver had let her ride for free after she explained she needed to get to her case worker's office. Janet arrived looking very rough and inadequately clothed for the below-zero weather. We went for breakfast then she slept for a few hours on a sofa in the youth lounge.

Janet was 16 and had signed her own voluntary agreement so she could get help from the child welfare system. There was a significant amount of conflict between Janet and her mother, and this escalated when her mother's boyfriend moved into the home. He had decided there were going to be rules and, if Janet did not like them, she could "get the hell out." The boyfriend took on the disciplinary role, as he was frustrated at the way Janet treated her mother. He made no attempts to get to know Janet or accept her input into what the rules or consequences would be. This was destined to fail, so Janet was in and out of shelters, while also staying with friends periodically. She refused foster care and believed staying in a formal group home would be like home with all of the rules. Janet believed she could look after herself. We had a good relationship and she would make contact frequently to let me know she was safe. She admitted to feeling depressed and was angry that her mother chose her boyfriend over her. However, she did see her mother once in a while and was told that if she showed more respect and followed the rules, she was sure that things could be worked out with the boyfriend. Sadly, the mother would make arrangements to have Janet visit but typically cancelled them because her boyfriend was tired, not up for a visit, or had had a bad day at work. The two would meet for coffee once in a while but Janet would get frustrated that her mother could not stand up for herself or her daughter.

Her mother had promised Janet that she could come home for Christmas Eve and Christmas Day. Janet felt she could make it work for a couple days, as she really wanted to be with her mother and sister for Christmas. After going to get some appropriate winter clothing for Janet – rather than risking a big family argument about who should pay if Janet chose not to live at home – I continued to try and find a place where Janet could stay the night before going to her mother's, as she had run out of friends to stay with at this time. Shelters' beds were all full, as were group homes, though Janet could not bring herself to go to such a placement right before Christmas. I called her mother and requested that Janet be able to return home a day early. Her mother was not opposed but there needed to be a conversation with her partner. Janet and I went for supper while waiting for a call back. It got to 8:00 p.m., so a call was made to the mother, who said her boyfriend was very busy but she would talk to him when he returned home within the hour. She was hesitant though agreeable to the suggestion I bring Janet by the home at 9:00 p.m. so we could talk and make a plan should things get tense. I told her that her daughter really wanted to make these few days work.

I drove Janet home but we were met at the door by the boyfriend, who was angry and felt everyone was making plans behind his back. I explained that Janet really wanted to be at home for Christmas but he replied that he was not going to allow this "disrespectful little bitch" to ruin Christmas. He slammed the door closed. Janet was sobbing. She was also upset that her mother had not come to try and rescue the situation. I was vibrating with anger too, trying to keep myself under control. I rang the doorbell in an attempt to talk to Janet's mother but there was no response. Janet and I sat on the front steps of the house while she cried and wondered what she was going to do for Christmas now. I had trouble not tearing up, seeing how devastated she was. This was shaping up to be her most miserable Christmas yet.

My last option was to take her to the After Hours Unit in the hope that some other youth had not returned to their shelter bed. Perhaps she could sleep on a sofa at After Hours Unit, though we ran the risk of a lecture about how this office is not a shelter for youth which, of course, it isn't. Janet was terrified at the thought of having to be around strangers after such a hurtful event. With my emotions playing a bigger part than I might like to admit, I told Janet I was taking her home with me. I called my wife and let her know. She would move the two of my four kids that shared a room in the basement upstairs with us. I knew Janet was exhausted and that we would be up and out of the house early. I did not call the After Hours Unit, as I felt I would be talked out of the plan, which at this moment would not have helped Janet. Janet was thankful and very appreciative. She knew workers are not supposed to do such things and that I could get in trouble. I told her this was true but that I would talk to my boss first thing tomorrow. She stayed in the basement by herself and got up with no problem the next morning. We headed to my office. She stayed in the youth lounge while I explained the situation to my manager, wrote up the details for Janet's file, and once again started looking for a placement. My boss was understanding but reinforced that this crossed a boundary in a significant way and that it could not happen in the future. A shelter bed was found for Janet. She was very sad and knew that she would spend Christmas with staff and youth she did not know. However, she was also understanding and thought it was cool she stayed in her case worker's home. I strongly suspected she would tell other youth that knew me what had happened. I could tell them that this was a particular situation and then I could hide behind confidentiality.

In over 27 years this was the only time I made such a decision. I have no feelings of regret, as it seemed this was the right decision for Janet in that moment. However, I still wrestle with whether this was the right thing to do from a professional and ethical perspective. If I didn't know Janet well, or she had been angry with me, or under the influence of drugs or alcohol, I would not have made such a decision. But, feeling the pain of someone who had just been rejected right at Christmas did not allow me to put some space between my emotional reaction to what Janet was experiencing and my ethical decision-making process. It reminds me how grey and uncertain this work can be.

Touchy subject

Compassionate touch encourages our capacity to connect, abusive touch corrupts it.
Michael Ungar[4]

While the Canadian Association of Social Workers (CASW) does not specifically address physical contact between a worker and service user in its *Code of Ethics*,[5] it does address protecting the vulnerable and disadvantaged from injustice and violence and the threat of violence, placing the needs of others above self-interest when acting in a professional capacity, and striving to use the power and authority vested in them as professionals in responsible ways. Social workers are also required to "establish appropriate boundaries in relationships with clients and ensure that the relationship serves the needs of clients" (Canadian Association of Social Workers, 2005, p. 7). However, this area is covered more specifically under the CASW *Guidelines for Ethical Practice* (2005):

> Social workers avoid engaging in physical contact with clients when there is a possibility of harm to the client as a result of the contact. Social workers who engage in appropriate physical contact with clients are responsible for setting clear, appropriate and culturally sensitive boundaries to govern such physical contact.
>
> (section 2.5.1)

The Child and Youth Care Association of Alberta (2014) has two sections that can cover physical contact:

> Members are responsible for ensuring that their relationships with their clients are therapeutic to those clients. In a situation where the relationship is of no

benefit or is detrimental to the welfare or wellbeing of the client it is the duty of the member to terminate the non-therapeutic relationship and refer the client to other professionals.

Members will not violate legal or civil rights of clients or others with whom they come in contact with in the practice of the profession. Nor will members take any action which is inconsistent with the maintenance of dignity and worth of their clients or other affected by their professional actions.

(p. 1)

The National Association of Social Workers (NASW, 2008) in the United States does have a section in the Code of Ethics specifically covering physical contact:

> 1.10 Physical Contact: Social workers should not engage in physical contact with clients when there is a possibility of psychological harm to the client as a result of the contact (such as cradling or caressing clients). Social workers who engage in appropriate physical contact with clients are responsible for setting clear, appropriate, and culturally sensitive boundaries that govern such physical contact.

Again, this is a grey area, as the NASW distinguishes between appropriate physical contact and the need to set clear boundaries and when such contact could cause psychological harm.

Reamer (2012) recognizes that touch can enhance therapeutic relationships and progress. The value of touch is recognized by social workers, as just over 83% stated that hugging or embracing a client can be appropriate. Touch can also come in many different forms depending on the situation. It can be the standard accepted *gestures of greeting and goodbye*, though a youth who is comfortable in the relationship tends to do this through hugs. Again, in my practice, I don't initiate but will accept hugs, assessing the situation and being thoughtful and intentional. When a youth would come into the office (i.e., "youth lounge") and some rapport had already been established, I would typically touch a youth on the arm, shoulder, or back as a welcome, perhaps out of concern that I had not seen them in a while. Some youth were having a difficult time and would initiate a *comforting hug*. It is common to give youth a *reassuring touch* to demonstrate that they are doing okay or not to worry. A *playful touch* – which I might use to push their shoulder with my fingertips as if trying to tip them over – can show that not all contact must be deep and heavy, while also demonstrating no hidden or exploitive agenda with playful teasing or joking. *Grounding or reorienting touch* on the hand or arm is intended to help reduce anxiety or dissociation. *Celebratory or congratulatory touch* (whether a pat on the back, hand on the shoulder, or a hug) can reassure youth that there is a belief in them and that they have someone in their corner cheering them on.[6] It must be recognized that some clients may feel uncomfortable with physical contact (Heller & LaPierre, 2012; Reamer, 2012). We must be aware that touch is a complex therapeutic intervention imbued with cultural conventions, gender-sensitive issues, and veiled power games. It can sometimes trigger deep-seated emotional experiences, such as previous physical trauma, that can quickly become overly activated (Heller & LaPierre, 2010). While most high-risk youth have experienced such abuse, most are open to being touched once the worker has established some credibility; in fact most are desperate for it.

Children want and need to be touched emotionally and physically. Many children – many of our high-risk youth – have never received "the repeated, patterned physical nurturing needed to develop a well-regulated and responsive stress response system. They had never learned that they were loved and safe. They were starving for touch" (Perry & Szalavitz, 2006, p. 95). Physical contact is not only critical in developing attachments, but compassion and emotional warmth is conveyed through touch and it can be a powerful means of providing support and soothing stress (Brendtro et al. 2009; Kagan, 2004; Ungar, 2009). Withholding close bodily contact in children accounted for anxious and avoidant attachment patterns and with older children such a pattern can be reinforced if professionals continue to be hesitant in showing affection. This can also contribute to how a neglected child can use sex to secure substitute attachments. Touch is confused with sex, love with intercourse (Ungar, 2009). Perhaps if they received appropriate touch and could learn that healthy touch does not have to be sexual in nature, their view of healthy relationships might not be so skewed.

We all seek a sense of intimacy but the way we interpret how this works can depend on our early experiences. If children become youth with an unhealthy perspective of touch and intimacy, and then become adults and parents, we are likely to see much confusion around touch, violence, love, intimacy, and sex carried from generation to generation. This is sadly illustrated by residential school survivors who were subjected to horrific physical and sexual abuse. I have read and heard many Aboriginal survivors who are in their 60s, 70s, or 80s say they were unable to hug their own children or tell them they loved them because their perspectives were all distorted through the abuse and the messages they received of what love, trust, intimacy, and touch meant. Their children lived their legacy, missing out on loving and intimate parental words and touches. This is what lack of boundaries by people in positions of authority does. As the residential school system shows us, it can take many generations to heal such gross violations of trust, eradicate the sense of shame, and work through the utter confusion about what is appropriate and inappropriate touch. Some of these Aboriginal youth bearing the burden of such injustices make up some of the high-risk youth who give up looking and bury their need for nurturing and contact. They may find other ways to externally trigger a release of the pleasure or 'feel-good' chemical dopamine that nurtured children and youth take for granted. Perhaps this is alcohol and drugs, cutting, sex, excessive eating, or other high-risk behaviours; anything that helps them ignore the pain of abandonment[7] (Maté, 2008; Ungar, 2009). Touch therefore can also be an important piece of the healing process in overcoming addictions. Our youth have missed critical healthy physical contact during very sensitive periods in their development, so there is a need to interact with these children and youth not based on their age, but based on what they need. We need to show them what healthy touch and relationships are about; "we need to hug our children" (Perry & Szalavitz, 2006, p. 96).

Ungar (2009) asks, "What damage do we risk if we raise children in a vacuum of no-touch policies and zero tolerance worlds that leave them without role models of how to touch and be touched?" (p. 102). We have become so afraid of unhealthy touch that we may actually make it more likely by failing to meet the needs of children for healthy physical affection. This makes it even easier for predators to thrive by picking out those who seek out affection (Perry & Szalavitz, 2006). These children can end up not only being sexually abused, but groomed for child sexual exploitation (prostitution).

Dr. John Seita, a former troubled youth and now a resiliency expert, contends that the "preoccupation with maintaining boundaries is often little more than a rationalization for detachment from young persons." Rules such as *treating all kids equally, don't create dependency, keep emotional distance to avoid burnout, don't risk sexual abuse allegations,* and *maintaining a social distance* are built into programs, creating an authoritarian wedge between workers and youth (Brendtro et al., 2009). Programs with many rules around avoiding physical contact, therefore, are less likely to reach their potential.

The ethical fears, prohibitions, and even taboos that surround therapeutic use of touch, particularly in Western society, reveal an overall lack of knowledge about its use (Brendtro et al., 2009; Heller & LaPierre, 2012). Human touch has been tabooed in Western society. We have created a "culture of untouchables, strangers to one another who ward off all forms of unnecessary closeness," yet all young people require touch and kindness so they can appreciate that they are valued (Brendtro et al., 2009, p. 54). These authors point out, ironically, that those who spend the most time with children seldom have had the specific training in how to connect with youth in conflict and help them cope with problems. Such skills are needed by parents, foster parents, educators, child and youth care workers, social workers, psychologists, probation officers, community and faith-based mentors, police, and peer helpers. In addition to training, there must be ongoing supervision and open discussions about touch to increase the sense of safety for everyone involved. Workers need to learn how to balance emotional and physical safety while giving youth the experience of an important "implicit healing language" (Heller & LaPierre, 2012, p. 271).

Reamer (2012) outlines some precautions *(in italics)* that can be taken by workers: *1) the primary concern should always be the wellbeing of the service user. 2) If initiating physical contact, the worker should obtain the youth's informed consent before any touch occurs.* There should be a sincere belief by the worker that this will benefit the high-risk youth, and could perhaps even be a breakthrough moment in the relationship. *3) The worker must pay close attention to their own feelings toward the youth to ensure that any physical touch is not self-serving.* Again this relates to being thoughtful, mindful, and intentional in practice. *4) Never use any form of touch that would make the youth or you, as the worker, uncomfortable.* Gut feelings can count for a lot in these situations. For example, a worker should not hug a youth when the gut feeling is that a pat on the shoulder is appropriate for the occasion. *5) Be careful to explore the true meaning behind a youth's request for you to touch them.* This may be necessary when it appears the youth is acting out of character, or you as the worker are feeling uncomfortable. However, one must be careful to ensure such probing will not embarrass the youth and make the situation awkward, causing them to be reluctant to take such an important risk in the future. *6) The worker must decide whether their decision to not touch a youth in unique circumstances would be inhumane.* It could be a male worker is so fearful of a false allegation they could reject a genuine hug from a youth who is seeing the physical contact as a needed reassurance from a fatherly figure.

Again, creating the right environment, such as having colleagues around or using a side hug, can help manage an emotional situation. If the circumstances are not appropriate, it is critical to explain such fears while reinforcing to the young person that it was not wrong to initiate a hug and that you hope it will not prevent him or her from giving or accepting hugs from safe people in the future.

We expect our youth to take risks when engaging in a relationship, so we need to be mindful that we also may need to take a risk too rather than generalizing and seeing every youth as waiting to make a false allegation. I have never run into a situation in which there was a concern about a false allegation myself in well over 27 years working with children and youth (and adults). Perhaps this is a combination of being thoughtful and intentional, communicating effectively, taking precautions, and luck! I say *luck* as we have no way to predict how all youth will behave in all situations given their life experiences. While there are no risk-free guarantees, I believe physical contact is an essential part of our work and we must take the *opportunity* for thera-peutic touch.

The uneasy relationship with love

> Troubled children are in some kind of pain – and pain makes people irritable, anx-ious and aggressive. Only patient, loving, consistent care works; there are no short-term miracle cures. This is true for a child of three or four as it is for a teenager.
>
> Bruce Perry and Maia Szalavitz[8]

"I'm sure Peter loves me . . . as part of his caseload or whatever." This struck me as sweet rather than a lack of boundaries. The first time I heard this on a video about the High Risk Youth Initiative,[9] my first reaction was that there is a lot of truth to her statement. It feels like a different love than I would describe in relation to my own kids, yet it is far, far more than her just being one of a number of youth who happen to be on my caseload. Even writing this, *love* is an awkward word, but to acknowledge that I had a love for the youth I have worked with over the years is a truth within me; by this I mean it feels right for me personally. I would not pontificate and say workers should all profess to love the youth they are working with if they truly want to do good work. I have no basis for this, but I think it is healthy to wrestle with this notion. This work goes well beyond just being a job. If it does not, the youth are painfully aware of this and it is likely to stunt the growth of the relationship. We can do great work with our youth if we appreciate them, really like them, enjoy spending time with them, or love them "as part of [our] caseload." At the same time, it is important to be mindful about our perception, thoughts, and feelings, and to maintain appropriate and healthy boundaries.

Perry and Szalavitz (2006) tell us that healing and recovery are impossible without lasting, caring connections to others. What young people need most is a rich social environment, one where they can belong and be loved. There needs to be consistent, patient, and repetitive loving care. Of course it is not all on us, but helping create a *rich social environment* is part of our responsibility when children and youth are in the child welfare system and when we enter their lives in a helping capacity. What is essential is that we are part of those *quality relationships*. As is the case with touch, it feels like a significant boundary crossing to talk about 'loving' a young person who is on a government or agency caseload. Possibly, fear of scandal has left workers feeling unable to get close to children and youth (Turney, 2010). Some high-profile gross boundary violations we hear within the system, or through the media, give us even more pause. We may start to keep our distance from our high-risk youth, perhaps becoming even less emotionally available without being overtly conscious of the subtle messages we are delivering. We start building walls around us while at the same time encouraging the youth to take risks and tear down their own walls.

In the past few years it has become more common to hear colleagues acknowledge that they do have love for their youth. It is typically followed by a qualifier such as adding "in a professional sense." I am also hearing more questions as to why we are too uptight to admit that we love the children and youth on our caseloads. We may not love them all the same way perhaps, and we do not tell them we love them, but it is perhaps something we need to acknowledge. Conversely, others may say bringing love into our work is getting overly involved, setting the youth up for grief and loss when we are no longer working with them, and that it is not our role. Admittedly, sorting this out is a work in progress for me, but I admire people I know with very solid boundaries who have no problem declaring that they do love their clients. I also believe that children and youth should never have to go through life feeling unloved and never knowing how to genuinely love another. This being the case, and knowing how these young people need to see and hear what love is, where does my practice fit and how do I reconcile this as a person who has gone into the human service field to help others and hopefully make a difference in their lives? Is love something that exists in our work but we deny its existence? Is it wrong to say it or feel it? Is caring the same as love? Is love the same thing as giving someone *unconditional positive regard*? (Rogers, 1961). These are questions to grapple with as individuals and discuss among colleagues, yet we hesitate to make this part of our practice conversation.

When speaking about love, surely this is the role of the foster parent – until the behaviour of the youth means the placement breaks down. It is the group home worker's responsibility – until the youth breaks the rules and is kicked out. It is the extended family that needs to show their love – until family conflicts arise and the youth keeps running away. We are better at telling our high-risk youth what love is not. When they are in an abusive relationship – and a vast majority experience this – we point out that extreme jealousy is not love, that a loving boyfriend or girlfriend would not beat them, threaten them, or destroy their personal belongings. A loving partner would not have sex with them in anger, make them turn tricks (i.e., prostitute) to get money, or have them recruit girls to be sexually exploited. Youth understand that our words make sense, but it does not tell them how to recognize love when they see, hear, and feel it. There are no easy answers, but being kind and being open to talking to youth about our own perspective of love when they inquire can be a good start.[10] We should not avoid the subject, as it is essential to the human condition even though it may take time to become comfortable discussing it. I believe we can do good work with youth just by *caring*, but I do not know if this is enough given the gaps, trauma, attachments, and skewed view of love that our high-risk youth have experienced, almost universally. Maté (2003) writes that "one learns love not from instruction but from being loved. . . . Emotional contact is as important as physical contact" (p. 203).

Turney (2010) acknowledges that, indeed, it does perhaps feel slightly odd to be mentioning love in the context of professional relationships, especially given there can be a presumption that close adult-child relationships are intrinsically suspect and should be discouraged. Turney (2010) adds that we assume adoptive parents will learn to love their adopted children, but we are ambivalent about the idea of love being part of a professional rather than a private/family relationship. He asks whether workers should be allowed, or even expected, to love the children or adults they work with. And how close can these relationships be? As stated earlier, we know there have been disturbing boundary violations, so one wonders how a young person can ever bounce back from losing their own parents and then having their lives undermined by exploitive and invasive relationships with adults who were in a position of trust and responsibility. This has partly led to some calling the child welfare system an extension of the residential school system (Kundougk & Qwul'sih'yah'maht, 2009; Lafrance & Bastien, 2007). Given the publicity such scandals have created, the possible misuse of professional relationships has prompted regulations to be developed to forbid closeness. This anxiety and confusion can leave workers virtually unable to relate to the children in their care (Turney, 2010).

These thoughts are echoed by psychologist Camila Batmanghelidjh, who works with high-risk youth in London, England. She refers to the damage caused by the unwillingness of care staff to respond humanely and with love despite the fact that a worker's ultimate task is to help the client to access love and meaning in their lives:

> The committed individual is perceived as too involved, as if feeling is somehow an indicator of incompetence, of inferiority or weakness. Our structures are failing children because we're scared of love. The expression of our humanity terrifies us into political cowardice. . . . We need, as individuals, to reclaim our portion of the action, to make a personal difference. . . . Children need our protection, and they need our love.
>
> (Batmanghelidjh, 2006, p. 157)

Turney (2010) points out that this work is about a caring love (from the Greek word for love, *agape*, or Latin word, *caritas*, aligned with altruistic love in which an individual can care for a complete stranger – a fellow human being – as if they were family) as opposed to a romantic or sexual attraction. Therefore, rather asking whether a worker should love those they work with, this should be reframed as, *can they not love them?* The ability to manage boundaries sensitively and in the child's interest is critical. However, the importance of close and caring relationships which allow children to form secure and lasting relationships has not changed and needs to find a place in our more bureaucratized and risk-averse care systems. Reclaiming the notion of love may start to offer a way forward. This can, once again, help our youth to avoid compensating for the lack of love and finding poor substitutes through addictions (Maté, 2008). Maté (2008) echoes others when he writes that when working with street-involved people, and those with addictions and a history of trauma, "there needs to be love, in a pure way that is not unadulterated with judgment, vindictiveness or a tone of rejection" (p. 380). Further, and critically, workers must be mindful of how their thinking, words, and feelings impact on service users. We all need love but we must be always conscious of whose needs are being met. Our youth are already struggling enough about what love means due to negative life experiences without having workers adding to the confusion and blurring boundaries further.

The role of gender in worker-youth relationships

Gender issues between the workers and the youth within the HRYI do surface occasionally, and this must be considered if identified by a young person. If there have been concerns by the youth about having a male or female worker, we typically have been able to work through such challenges. Feedback from the youth in general is that they value a worker who is non-judgemental, genuine, and honest ahead of whether they are male or female. However, there are always exceptions and the life experiences of these few youth can impact whether they are more comfortable with a particular sex. If a youth has been victimized by a male or female, there can be value in having a worker of the same sex to demonstrate that not all males or females are dangerous. This requires the youth to be open and willing to try working through these dynamics while feeling emotionally safe. If they do not feel safe, developing a relationship will be very difficult and the youth may feel they are not being heard or that their trauma experiences may be repeatedly triggered, thereby keeping the young person chronically fearful. Consideration must also be given to LGBTQ+ (or queer)[11] youth who have also been victimized, as their life experiences may cause them to have specific preferences about the gender of their worker, especially if they have not come out or fear being judged and consequently not being able to access services.

Conversely, some male workers can be hesitant to work with female youth or may limit face-to-face contact unless there is a colleague present. There may be reluctance to being alone with a female service user, including in a vehicle even though there is often a need to drive them places. This comes from fear and anxiety about false allegations, which can be fair given it is certainly not unheard of for some youth to have a history of making false claims of sexual impropriety. However, if these fears are preventing a relationship from developing, the youth's file should not be assigned to such a worker in the first place.

Female workers, in my experience, do not have as much fear of false allegations, but more fear around saying things that could be misinterpreted by a male youth on a sexual level. Female workers may have stricter rules about accepting hugs from male youth than they would from female youth. However, being diligent about false allegations is prudent for female workers as well as women have also been charged for sexually exploiting youth. I was involved in a situation as a supervisor in which a 16-year-old male was exploited by a female worker at a residential treatment centre. The worker was charged as the youth was under 18 and she was in a position of authority. Another female youth worker from a different agency was supporting this youth through the court process, the media attention, and explaining how he was exploited in the sexual relationship. It was questioned as to whether this worker should be male under the circumstances but the youth insisted he was connected to his current female youth worker. Later it was discovered they were also involved in an intimate relationship. While he was 18 by then, the youth worker was still in a position of authority and perhaps even more culpable given it was her role to help him through the first abuse. While it is critical to be intentional about what messages workers give to their youth, such intentionality can also be used for exploitation as a way for workers to meet their own emotional and sexual needs.

Workers should also be aware of the basic psychodynamic view of transference and counter-transference when working with youth, especially those who have experienced trauma. Youth can transfer feelings into their current circumstances even though such emotions are part of previous relationships (i.e., *transference*), typically templates (memories of early patterned and repetitive experiences, initial experiences; see Chapter 3) of parental connections, which can also influence gender concerns with workers. Thus, it can be difficult for youth to accept help from certain workers, as there can be a generalized expectation of further abuse prompting a hostile response toward their worker. The worker may also unwittingly react to being seen as a punitive parent by unwittingly falling into the role and acting precipitously or harshly (i.e., *counter-transference*). On the other hand, the opposite reaction may be to respond to the youth's hostility by overcompensating and making too many concessions and not addressing the hostility. The challenge is that these examples of counter-transference can develop unconsciously, so an awareness of it occurring in the moment can be limited. Again, reflection and self-awareness can help workers become conscious that they are being drawn into transference and counter-transference scenarios (Ruch, 2010b). Failure to do so can skew boundaries and prevent appropriate connections from evolving.

As noted earlier, it is hard to know how a youth will make sense of the relationship, as they may see workers as parental or extended family figures, likely compensating for relationships they have missed. These perceptions can be explored with the youth, as this might contribute to helping them find a place in the world. However, workers are responsible to deal decisively at the first hint of the youth hoping for a romantic connection or to sexualize the relationship,[12] even though such resistance can result in the youth becoming quite angry. In group care settings, some youth have attempted to sexualize the relationship by prompting a need to be restrained (Okamoto, 2002). Sex can be confused with love (Howe, 2011; Maté, 2008), so again, we need to be able to help youth gain a healthy perspective and understand that sex and love do not always have to go together.

In addressing these concerns, there needs to be a balance between supporting the youth, giving them the opportunity to have a relationship, and common sense. If a youth has made allegations in the past, being alone should be avoided, especially, for example, when talking to the youth about their past abuse, when having to confront them, when pushing them to take responsibility for their actions, or when having to tell them something you know they do not want to hear. When getting to know a youth, meet in more public places or where colleagues can see you. Particular caution is advised with initiating hugs or even supportive touches during the engagement stage. Whether a male or female worker, it is critical to be cautious and not say or do anything that could be misinterpreted, but it is also critical to not allow this fear and anxiety to be consuming to the point it prevents an appropriate level of youth-worker intimacy. We cannot simply make assumptions or generalize about worker-youth relationships. As Okamoto (2002) concludes in his research, "the female client's experience with an emotionally supportive and caring male appears to be extremely powerful intervention itself" (p. 245). Experience in the HRYI demonstrates that the reverse is true as well.

The goal of interdependence

We are absolutely interdependent. Our essence is to be able to form and maintain relationships.

Bruce Perry[13]

Being too close or overly involved can make the worker overloaded with concerns (Turney, 2010). This can also create dependency by transferring to the youth the idea that we are the only ones that can save them or we are the only ones that truly understand them. As discussed in Chapter 6, a big reason for engaging in the community is to build a *network of support* for the youth so they do not become dependent on one person being there for them or having all of the answers. Such involvement with youth is crossing an unhealthy boundary. A worker can have a close relationship with a youth, but feeling they cannot function in life without the worker can be detrimental. Just as handholding can be essential early in the relationship to help navigate systems, overcome fear, and teach life skills (how to ask for help, deal with landlords, open a bank account, search for jobs, register for school, find and doctor and dentist, etc.), so is knowing when to nudge the youth forward and let go when the time is appropriate. Failure to do so may speak more to the needs of the worker than it does the needs of the youth.

Common discourse tends to speak in terms of helping a youth become 'independent.' It is important for case workers, community workers, colleagues, and supervisors to all discuss how to avoid creating dependency, but independence is not the goal either. Humans are social creatures and need others to get by in life. Our goal, therefore, is *interdependence* (see Box 10.5) which again speaks to the need for youth to have many supportive people in their lives, typically transitioning from formal supports to informal supports as they get older. One thing we can impress on youth is to not fear reaching out for help from community supports, or family, no matter what age they are. This is what self-sufficiency means. We need to dispel the notion that self-sufficiency means independence, but rather appreciate that it relies on establishing relationships and receiving guidance throughout the transition to adulthood (Gaetz, 2011, 2014a). Therefore, helping a youth be self-sufficient, or interdependent, means we have a responsibility to build relationships with youth as they learn that not everybody, and not everybody in a position of authority, is out to harm them, and to recognize there are many people ready to lend a helping hand. Perhaps they can learn that actions and behaviours that promote interdependence can help cement relationships and help create a sense of belonging and wellbeing (Howe, 2014). In addition, I have seen repeatedly youth who quite naturally end up being that helping hand for other youth, a sign that a young helper has reached a level of interdependence.

Box 10.5   Dependency versus independence versus interdependence[14]

Dependent

Relying on someone or something else for aid, support, etc.

Independent

1   *Not influenced or controlled by others in matters of opinion, conduct, etc.; thinking or acting for oneself; an independent thinker.*
2   *Not subject to another's authority or jurisdiction; autonomous; free.*
3   *Not influenced by the thought or action of others.*

4   *Not dependent; not depending or contingent upon something else for exis-tence, operation, etc.*

5   *Not relying on another or others for aid or support.*

Interdependent

Mutually dependent; depending on each other.

It is not healthy to create a sense of dependency with the youth, as they can feel they are not able to function on their own, feel betrayed when the worker leaves, or sabotage progress to repeatedly bring helpers back into their lives. Discussing this on an ongoing basis as a team or in supervision is important. However, I have also heard workers being overly sensitive to this, when, in fact, there is a time and a place when youth need their support team to be right beside them. As we all do, sometimes youth need hand-holding! This is not to create dependency, but to help youth overcome some deep fears and anxiety around, for example, being poked and prodded by dentists and doctors when they are most vulnerable and have been violated as children. We can also help them deal with authority figures, as so many youth have had negative experi-ences. This hand-holding can be the difference between youth being negatively triggered, thus reinforcing that such professionals are unsafe, and having a positive experience in which they may better attend to their physical needs, be accepted into programs, and avoid resisting arrest or assault charges. Hand-holding is far from being a waste of time. It is powerful to be supporting a youth when they feel vulnerable and it demonstrates how anxiety-inducing situations can have a positive outcome. Gradually, the youth can become self-reliant in attending appointments and bring with them strategies they hope-fully learned during the hand-holding phase. We don't often send our own teenagers or young adults to appointments on their own. Should we expect our high-risk youth to navigate their medical appointments on their own with all their added fears and anxieties? We can try, but often they won't go, even if they are in considerable discomfort. While we often talk about youth being independent, interdependent is a worthier goal, as it implies they are using relationships without be dependent. Independent is what they were when they were shutting everybody out of their lives. While we do not want to create dependency, we don't want this level of isolating independence in which youth feel excluded and marginalized either.

When is a worker 'too involved'?

A frequent belief is that getting too involved with the youth will lead to burnout; however, it is difficult to determine what 'getting too involved' means. As discussed above this can be different for each worker, and each youth and the dynamics of each relationship has its unique characteristics. Sometimes we may be more in a place to feel we can be quite involved with the youth, while at other times, depending on what is going on in our lives, we may be more hesitant and fragile. Once again, this comes down to being self-aware and knowing our own limits at a certain place in time, and communicating this to the youth, being careful of how much we disclose.

We as workers have to be aware of how emotionally healthy we are to be taking on the traumatic stories that we hear from our youth so frequently. Youth have disclosed being violently raped, beaten by their partner, drugged and sexually assaulted, stabbed, shot at, hit by a bus, or forced to prostitute. Our youth have been driven out of the city and left in a field in sub-zero temperatures. Some youth have been so unhealthy there was a fear of their organs shutting down. A few have had cigarettes butted out on their skin, lost a baby, had their child apprehended, have been physically and emotionally abused by system carers, told they were 'sick' because of their sexual identity, and have repeatedly been emotionally shattered after once again being rejected and abandoned by their parent(s). Where do these stories go within us? How do we manage the accumulation of traumatic stories? When do we know we are taking on the burdens of the youth to the point we diminish our ability to be helpful?

Walker (2012) discusses how we can be impacted by our work with a traumatized population. He states that we are unique, in the same way emergency response personnel are unique: we are essentially running toward the crises and trauma while the natural instinct might be to run away from it. We do not, or cannot, avoid it, but it can come at an emotional cost to us; thus the frequent talk of self-help, looking after ourselves, and taking the time for ourselves. This work is tough and we need to stay healthy for our own sake, but also that of our youth. It is critical that we have a solid support system as well, including a healthy work environment and a supervisor who can understand and help us cope with the trauma to which we become a witness. A personal support system is also essential. Additionally, it is important to note that not all outcomes are negative either, as many workers do stay emotionally healthy and perhaps even thrive on the experiences they encounter. Walker (2012) identifies five possible effects of working with traumatized service users:

1   *Vicarious Traumatization* generally refers to the cognitive changes in us as a result of our work: More or less optimistic about the world, more or less fearful about life, more or less trusting of other people, and/or more or less present to your family and partner. Though widely used, this term is less well defined in research and the literature.

2   *Secondary Traumatic Stress* is a syndrome of symptoms similar to Post-Traumatic Stress Disorder that we may experience as a result of being in relationship with our traumatized clients. The worker may experience intrusive thoughts, avoidant responses, physiological arousal, distressing emotions, and/or insomnia.

3   *Compassion Fatigue* or *burnout* involves chronic exhaustion, growing frustration, chronic anger, and/or depression.

4   *Compassion Satisfaction* involves the pleasures that you derive from finding satisfaction in your work from making a difference in the lives of your clients, feeling competent in your job, enjoying learning and integrating new skills, enjoying working with colleagues towards a common good, and/or being part of a social movement creating a more just world.

5   *Post-Traumatic Growth* is the personal growth that can result from experiencing, directly or indirectly, deeply disturbing events. This may include an increased sense of both vulnerability and strength, an increased compassion for the suffering of

others, feeling more deeply connected to others, greater freedom to be one's true self, increased clarity regarding one's core values and priorities, and/or greater spiritual or spiritual meaning in life.

It is important to be aware of which area we are fitting into at any given time, and either reach out for support and guidance, or keep thriving. This challenging work is not for everyone, but those who are ready and go into it with both eyes wide open are able to maintain strong boundaries, avoid getting overly involved, avoid creating dependency, and find a good level of *compassion satisfaction* and *post-traumatic growth*.

Confidentiality

Confidentiality is bound by legislation, but it is also a mark of respect. Within the HRYI, a challenge arises in that many of the youth know each other and know each other's circumstances. While they are free to talk about each other it can strike them as odd that we cannot join the conversation. However, once they appreciate that we cannot disclose information about any youth to another youth, they understand why this is important and appreciate that this trust is maintained. An exception might be to approach a peer when a youth is uncharacteristically missing, is with people who might put that youth in danger, or is suicidal and there is reason to believe there are serious safety issues involved. This is less about sharing information about a youth and more about being able to help a youth who might be in distress. It is not uncommon for a youth to come to their case worker or community worker because they are concerned about their friend. This shows they hold confidence that we can help.

Rightfully so, youth get frustrated and angry when they feel that this confidentiality has been breached. On occasion, they request that their case worker or community worker have no communication take place with others involved with their lives. This is honoured but it can create a sense that there is an unwillingness to work together. Despite this, the requests of the youth must be honoured, unless it involves a mandatory reporting to ensure the safety of the youth and others, or if there is a crime involved. If over the age of 16, young people might ask that their worker share no information with their parents. Again, this is respected, though it can frustrate parents who may feel the worker has no right to withhold information. The worker is left to try and encourage the youth to communicate with their parents directly.

Connecting through technology

Outside of face-to-face contact, over 90% of the contact with high-risk youth is made through texting and social media. Telling a youth that I tried contacting by calling them at home on a land line is apt to bring on gales of laughter and highlight to the youth that I am old. Thanks to our high-risk youth, my thumbs can keep up with the best of them. Calling a youth on a cell phone does not always go over well; why would they waste valuable minutes talking to their social worker when they could be using them to make plans with a friend? "Not to be rude but could you text me instead" is something I have heard a few times, which is understandable despite the fact that I may be (through my role) providing them with the phone and the minutes in the first place!

Communicating with youth has obviously shifted over the past few years. I have heard complaints within the system that giving cell phones to youth is too costly, that the youth need to earn such a privilege, and that it is not our role to be supplying cell phones and minutes. However, this started out as a way to increase safety for youth, a number of whom were being sexually exploited, were in violent relationships, would party and get themselves into potentially dangerous situations, or were pregnant. In addition, almost all youth in society have a cell phone, so high-risk youth having a cell/mobile phone helps 'normalize' their lifestyle and prevents a situation in which non-system youth have cell phones while system youth do not have access. It also prevents them from jeopardizing their personal safety to get money to buy a cell phone and minutes.

An interesting development in the HRYI is, now that our youth have cell phones, far fewer youth are recorded as missing. They may not be in the placements we have found for them, but they are maintaining contact. Some may not tell us where they are, but they assure us they are safe and doing okay. That is significant as there is enough of a relationship that they keep open communication rather than taking off and hiding from us. And, if they are not texting their workers directly, they may update their situation on social media (typically Facebook).[15]

This is the way youth communicate so systems need to accept it, deal with it, and get on board. Part of the challenge is that the technology roared ahead faster than governments and agencies could keep up. While there are many mediums to communicate with youth, policies have been lagging behind. Government systems have had to play catch-up with respect to policy, resulting in significant confusion as to what workers could and could not do when using technology. Bureaucrats were being cautious while workers were trying to stay relevant in their communication methods. The dust is starting to settle now and workers using texting and social media is becoming commonplace. Documenting is required, as with any other form of communication, and more efficient ways to log these conversations are emerging.

Not shockingly, social networking has been abused, with a few workers crossing serious boundaries and communicating on personal social media pages for unethical purposes. However, this is more to do with the worker than the form of communication and one advantage is that, notwithstanding personal settings to avoid wider audiences, there can be a trail of evidence left behind. In one situation, this not only exposed a worker for initiating a sexual relationship with a youth, but his comments to the youth revealed how frequently he used abusive and threatening language.

Again, most workers use technology to keep their practice focused on best meeting the needs of high-risk youth. A number of case workers and community youth specialists have set up work-related Facebook pages that the youth can access. And they do. Accepting a youth as a 'friend' on a work Facebook page is obviously very different to accepting a youth from one's caseload on a personal page. The same would apply for sharing a work email address as opposed to a personal email address (Reamer, 2010). Using social networking sites can be used to help teach youth about protecting themselves and using proper privacy settings that can otherwise put the youth at even more risk. Facebook and other social media has helped locate youth and reach out to them. It has allowed workers to show concern when youth are going through a difficult time and avoiding, typically because they are embarrassed that they have relapsed or feel they have disappointed their support team. Young people have also used social media to show concern for friends who are not doing well. They post pictures to mark life events, share funny stories, or to show how well they are doing. Sadly, some youth have used various sites to advertise that they are available to 'hook up.' On the bright side, workers have been able to locate youth on these websites before they are sexually exploited. Of course, a worker must be able to justify why they are accessing such unsavoury sites on the internet, especially during work time on a government computer.

In the High Risk Youth Initiative, youth have access to all work cell phone numbers of the case workers and community youth specialists. While this is not too unusual for agency workers, especially outreach workers, it is more unusual for government workers. Historically, work cell phones have been to allow workers to maintain contact with their supervisor or colleagues, but given the focus in the HRYI is building relationships, the youth have quick access to their support people. A common question focuses on the assumption that this would make the youth demanding, causing them to abuse this access. While some youth in the testing phase of the relationship may call repeatedly at times, generally the youth are respectful. Once the worker sets the limits and boundaries, the youth do appreciate that workers are not available 24/7. There are times when a worker may make a special arrangement with a youth if that youth is going into labour, is suicidal, or is leaving an abusive relationship, though this is rare. My experiences is that when a young person texts or calls in the evening or weekends, they leave a message not expecting an immediate answer but perhaps as a reminder that they have an appointment or a significant issue to discuss. In short, taking a strength-based view of this access is much more productive than assuming the youth will not be able to manage the responsibility.

Conclusion

> It is impossible to imagine how one could conduct one's business in child protection without confronting and appreciating the multitudes of moral questions that are a daily occurrence.
>
> Bob Lonne, Nigel Parton, Jane Thomson, and Maria Harries[16]

While this chapter (by design) does not provide clear answers as to how to manage ethics and boundaries, it does emphasize how the work we do remains, and belongs, in the grey. Human relationships are never black and white and each connection is unique to the two people sharing the experience. As noted there are some clear-cut boundary violations that do much damage and relate to the absolute abuse of authority and the power of one person over another. When workers engage in such actions, it is the extreme in oppressive behaviour. However, a vast majority of boundary issues are *crossings* rather than gross *violations*. Therefore, we must be consistently on our guard, not allow ourselves to be lulled into complacency, and be aware of our thoughts and feelings toward any boundary crossing. When deciding to touch, share, express affection, or cross any kind of boundary with such a vulnerable population, we must remain:

- *Thoughtful*: How will this help my relationship with this youth? How will the youth be impacted? How will I be impacted?

- *Mindful*: Whose needs are being met? Do I ensure the needs of the youth are always paramount? How does this make me feel? Am I conveying healthy messages?
- *Intentional*: I believe crossing a boundary is helpful to the youth. I will talk to my supervisor and colleagues. I will document this interaction.

This process, which should be evident in all interactions with youth on a daily basis, shows caring and respect for the youth. It reduces misunderstandings, avoids hurt feelings, and keeps the communication in the relationship open and transparent. Our youth deserve nothing less and it helps protect us as well. We must be careful not to be in a state of fear, as this often leads to the implementation of strict boundaries that hinders making connections. Our children and youth do respond to kindness, as it helps them feel valued and models empathy (Brendtro & du Toit, 2005; Szalavitz & Perry, 2010). Batmanghelidjh (2006) tells us that "love is the only experience which can make traumatized children hopeful again" and "the ability to hope facilitates the fundamental will to live" (p. 109). How we navigate these areas is up to us, but we cannot ignore their positive impact.

Discussion questions to consider for Chapter 10

1 *Do you believe there is such a thing as positive boundary crossings?*
2 *How do you determine when a boundary crossing becomes a boundary violation?*
3 *What are your boundaries around touch? Is touch essential or does this fall outside the scope of working with children and youth in the child welfare system?*
4 *Would you ever respond to a youth that you 'love' them if the youth expressed this sentiment to you first? Would you ever initiate telling a youth you loved them? Would you tell this to a youth who maintained contact with you after their formal file has closed?*
5 *What are your thoughts about maintaining contact with a youth, even for a coffee chat periodically, after their file has closed?*
6 *How does a worker demonstrate healthy touch and manage boundary crossings simultaneously?*
7 *If a worker has experienced some of the same challenges in life as a high-risk youth, at what point does self-disclosure cross the line?*
8 *How comfortable are you incorporating social networking into your practice?*
9 *Share an example of when you had a positive experience with crossing a boundary. Share a negative experience.*
10 *SCENARIO: A close colleague comes to you and states that they have gone on a date with a former client who is a legal adult. The worker had not talked to or seen this person for five years but they bumped into each other recently. How would you respond? Would you report this to your professional association or is this circumstance ethically safe?*

Notes

1   I am not in a position of commenting on the practices of other helping professions outside of social work. Therefore, social work will be my reference point, but I would think much of the material would be relevant to other professions and associations that also have members doing child welfare practice directly or who are working with the same service users through community agencies.

2   The quote used by Reamer (2012) is from: Kagle, J. D. & Giebelhausen, P. N. (1194). Dual relationships and professional boundaries. *Social Work*, 39: 213–320.

3   This definition was taken from Dictionary.com.

4   From the book, *We Generation: Raising Socially Responsible Kids* (2009, p. 102).

5   It is recognized that those government or agency workers involved with the child welfare system, or in the High Risk Youth Initiative, are not all social workers or child and youth care workers and are not all bound by the Code of Ethics of the Canadian Association of Social Workers or the guidelines of the Child and Youth Care Association of Alberta. However, these are two of the largest groups that are expected to adhere to their professional code of ethics. This is presented to show the importance of having ethical guidelines when working with this vulnerable population.

6   These italicized categories are taken from Reamer (2012) who is referencing: Zur, O. (2007). *Boundaries in Psychotherapy: Ethical and Clinical Explorations*. Washington, DC: American Psychological Association.

7   As discussed in Chapter 3, many high-risk youth experience the multi-generational trauma of colonialism, residential schools, and the Sixties Scoop. During this dark time in Canada's history, children were, of course, not abandoned by their parents any more than the general population (though children trying to make sense of being in a residential school not seeing family could have felt this way), but children were removed from the care of their parents by church officials and government employees, at times assisted by police (Truth and Reconciliation Commission, 2015).

8   From the book, *The Boy Who Was Raised as a Dog and Other Stories from a Child Psychiatrist's Notebook* (2006, p. 243)

9   The documentary *The Word on the Street* was produced by the Child and Youth Advocate (2007), Alberta. Three youth, all labelled 'high risk' due to the life circumstances and the dangers that threatened them emotionally and physically, and three social workers (including this writer) were interviewed independently about their experiences in working together under the practice framework and philosophy of the High Risk Youth Initiative.

10 This is illustrated in the motion picture *Good Will Hunting* (1997), as the therapist, played by Robin Williams, talks to a young client with severe attachment issues (played by Matt Damon) about his experience with love to make a point about how shutting people out and not taking a risk can make for missing out on the important aspects of life.

11 For explanation of LGBTQ+ and 'queer,' see endnote 14 in Chapter 1.

12 Under the Canadian Association of Social Workers's (CASW) *Guidelines for Ethical Practice* (2005), Section 2.6 covers the area of 'No Romantic or Sexual Relationships with Clients': Social workers do not engage in romantic relationships, sexual activities or sexual contact with clients, even if such contact is sought by clients (2.6.1).

   Social workers who have provided psychotherapy or in-depth counselling do not engage in romantic relationships, sexual activities or sexual contact with former clients. It is the responsibility of the social worker to evaluate the nature of the professional relationship they had with a client and to determine whether the social worker is in a position of power and/or authority that may unduly and/or negatively affect the decisions and actions of their former client (2.6.2). Social workers do not engage in a romantic relationship, sexual activities or sexual contact with social work students whom they are supervising or teaching (2.6.3).

13 From a lecture by Dr. Bruce Perry in Edmonton, Alberta, on November 15, 2010.

14 These definitions are taken from Dictionary.com.

15 Some case workers and/or community workers have a 'professional' Facebook page that follows government or agency guidelines. Using their personal social media sites would be a problematic boundary crossing.

16 From the book, *Reforming Child Protection* (2009, p. 117).

Chapter 11

Conclusion

A reason for optimism

> Connectedness has been described as a spiritual process that enhances our sense
> of self.
>> Betty Bastien, Sohki Aski Esquao (Jeanine Carriere) and Susan Strega[1]

The *Get Connected* model is just about that – making connections. This book has
emphasized how connection is about helping youth find out who they are, and where
they belong, and letting them know that their past traumatic experiences are not their
fault. It is not about *doing to* them and thinking we know best how to direct their
lives, but journeying *with them* and along the way hoping they might be able to let
go of their shame, guilt, and sense of failure. Rather than youth feeling that there
are authority figures trying to control their lives, they hopefully discover people who
genuinely care about them. Hopefully they accept that others (professionals or informal supports) can actually worry about them without seeing this as a weakness or a
threat. These early connections can lead to deeper relationships which, having taken
the risk of allowing a healthy adult into their lives, may lead to taking more risks and
building up a support network of people who are willing to talk, support, help, refer,
advocate, reassure, go for coffee, and/or share a hug. The youth may learn that their
old scripts that adults typically fall into are not resulting in the expected rejection and
abandonment scenario, thus forcing them to see that there is perhaps another world
that it not as lonely, frightening, and painful. However, if there is no long-term commitment to such relationship-based practice and the child welfare world returns to
being entrenched in more traditional punishment-consequence or compliance-based
approaches, high-risk youth – and all youth – are not likely to be exposed to different ways of relating to case workers, community workers, and other supports. This
will result in a system that continues to inadequately meet the safety, emotional, and
physical needs of this very vulnerable population.

The good part is that there is a shift occurring. It is slow, but there are signs of
change. Letting go of traditional ways of practicing is not easy. Letting go of power
and control is not easy either. Coming to the realization that risk management cannot
eliminate risk can be a challenge for government institutions, but if we truly want
to serve youth – and children and families too for that matter – in the best possible
way, we must get out of our comfort zone, make service users part of the decision-
making and policy-making process, and help them navigate through the risks and
opportunities they encounter in their lives. There are many examples of case workers

and community workers doing truly intentional and thoughtful work with youth and helping them feel capable, valued, and included (see Boxes 11.1 and 11.2). However, these cannot just be examples, or practice anomalies, that get passed around as heart-warming stories. These stories must become the way practice is done; standard practice reflected in policy and legislation. It can no longer be 'exceptional' practice for workers to do this relational work themselves rather than delegate it to others. It has been thoroughly demonstrated in child welfare practice that the "endless drive to create rules and imperatives" has not served the helping professions well (Simmonds, 2008, p. xxii). While there are signs of a renewed focus on relational practice, there remains work to be done to ensure that "corporate parenting is personalized and given a human face" (Luckock & Lefevre, 2008, p. 2).

Box 11.1   Tracy's story: the forgotten birthday

'Tracy' is now 29. She tracked down her former worker, Arlene, as she had a story to tell her – an event that took place when she was in care at age 13. Tracy said she thinks about this story frequently, such was the impact it had on her. She was in a group home and it was her 13th birthday. She went to school and met with her friends but no one mentioned her special day. She remembers feeling sad and lonely, especially as her parents were not around to celebrate this occasion with her. Dejected, she found her way back to the group home. The staff did not appear to remember it was her birthday either. However, when she got to her bedroom there was a birthday card and some candy from Arlene. While a small gesture, Tracy tracked down Arlene 16 years later to tell her how transformational this had been for her. It showed somebody actually cared about her. This was influential in Tracy returning to school to study social work. She wants to help girls who are in the situation she found herself in when becoming a teenager. She believes she can make a difference in their lives, the same way Arlene had made a difference in her life.

Box 11.2   Erin's story: the right to vote

'Erin' is a passionate case worker and passionate about working with high-risk youth. She believes in the goodness of the youth on her caseload, no matter their circumstances or their attitude. Erin refuses to give up on any youth. Erin is an Aboriginal worker and the youth on her caseload are also Aboriginal. She takes many of them to cultural events and talks to them about Aboriginal issues to help get them interested in their culture and to share their history, both the tragedy and the resilience of their people. Erin is a mentor and a role model. She accepts this humbly but clearly she is a person who youth would look up to.

With three of her youth, Erin was engaged to the point of talking about social issues, social justice, and the dark legacy of residential schools and colonialism. She also talked to them about the political system in Canada and how they can

> *get involved, particularly by exercising their right to vote. During the election in Alberta (2015) Erin offered to take the girls to vote. On the day, she picked them up and took them to three different voting stations around the city corresponding to where they were registered. The young women were proud to cast their ballots for the first time in their lives. This turned out to be a great experience for Erin and a positive memory for the three youth. It helped get them involved in social issues, which can be empowering while reducing the sense of feeling excluded and marginalized.*

If more workers and resources are required up front, there must be a realization that this can be made up by significant savings in the future[2] by dealing with trauma, pain, poverty, physical and mental health needs, addictions, and criminal behaviour that often continues through generations (Levy & Orlans, 1998; National Scientific Council on the Developing Child, 2010a). While more and more funding is not a panacea, it can allow child welfare systems to do better. It goes beyond just a social return on investment, but can help prevent young people on an emotional, psychological, and spiritual level from entering adulthood feeling isolated, marginalized, and inadequate, which serves to increase the potential they repeat the cycle with their own children. To do this, government systems and agencies need to take risks and encourage workers to take risks. Workers already push their youth into areas of emotional discomfort, especially the risk of engaging in a relationship. Yet, we still tend to be risk averse ourselves. Siegel (2013) writes, "Risk breathes new life into rigid ways of doing things" (p. 109). We push youth so they can break free from their past lives and move forward. It is time that the child welfare system takes such leaps to move forward as well. This can start by questioning oneself as to why the same interventions are done over and over when they are clearly not working. Workers need to ask themselves if relationship is the priority when working with youth or whether one is simply relying on policy. This is part of recognizing that current policies and practices do not put relationships first and that current systems in place to help children and youth are not particularly helpful (Lonne et al., 2009; Perry & Szalavitz, 2006). As Munro (2011), in reviewing the British child welfare system, concluded:

> Children and young people . . . have said that, above all, they want a trusting and stable relationship with an adult who provides them with help and information when they need it. Yet for too many this was not achieved. . . . The child was not seen frequently enough by the professionals involved, or was not asked their views and feelings.
>
> (p. 129)

Thus it bears repeating: Until relationship-based practice is standard practice for all children and youth we will miss the key catalyst for change (Herbert, 2007).

This book is intended to share ideas and thoughts about doing practice differently. It's not the magic wand that workers wish they had. If it gives hope, that is magic in itself. The *Get Connected* model is just one way of working with youth that has produced a positive response, resulting in youth feeling more engaged and connected to adults. This is a big deal coming from a population of youth who can go to extraordinary lengths to test and sabotage relationships when they feel it is too unsafe or risky. Workers must be tuned in to this and demonstrate patience and understanding rather than assuming youth do not want help and support. As social workers, child and youth care workers, or workers from other educational backgrounds, this should be the natural way to work given we chose to enter the helping field.

I am quite convinced that people do not enter the world of child welfare or youth work so they can gain career satisfaction by engaging in power struggles with youth, putting youth in their place, locking them up, denying them privileges, ordering them into programs, or closing a youth's file because they will not comply with rules and expectations and do what is presumed to be in their best interest. So, as was similarly asked in the introduction, how did we end up becoming so reliant on punishment-consequence approaches when all we wanted to do was help people? Are we so stuck in or dependent on a system that we have no choice and cannot practice the way we would like, or even follow our professional code of ethics? Perhaps this is an excuse, perhaps it is not, but when we are one-on-one with a youth we can choose to follow relationship-based methods and focus on building connections rather than enforcing compliance. This does not increase risk, it lowers it by opening up communication and demonstrating that people worry because they care. Youth might be uncomfortable with this and see it as a threat to their control, but experience demonstrates they need and want it. This is not me thinking I know better (that would be contrary and oppressive) but rather because this is what youth consistently tell me. As humans we are social creatures and we need to know at least one person on this planet gives a damn about us, enough to worry when we are not safe.

Be humble

Working with high-risk youth requires workers to be thoughtful and humble about their practice and to break down why youth might be acting or speaking the way they are, rather than quickly reacting and falling into tired patterns of power and control. When in such a place it is hard to bow out gracefully, yet workers need to learn to put the emotional needs of youth ahead of their pride by saying, "Sorry, I was out of line." Child welfare expert Eileen Munro (2008) calls admitting you may be wrong the "single most important factor in minimizing errors" (p. 125) in the child welfare system. Workers may think they fully understand the high-risk youth on their caseload but even with the best intentions, and the best training, a worker's understanding of what goes on in someone else's mind, and our own ability to see the future, is limited (Munro, 2008). The challenge is people are resistant to changing their mind once they have formed a judgement. Workers judge youth based on what they have read on file and hold such thoughts when meeting with him or her. This is not lost on the youth. Workers can become locked in and find evidence to reinforce their judgement while ignoring evidence to the contrary. In a power-and-control mindset, changing one's mind can be seen as a weakness, though according to Munro (2008) it is a "sign of intelligence to revise a judgement when given new information that shows it was misguided" (p. 125). When invested in building relationships with youth, acknowledging mistakes and apologizing gets easier over time (trust me!) Of course it is okay that they see us as fallible, and critically, as human (not the unfeeling robots that youth accuse us of being at times.) I have also learned that saying sorry to a youth makes it easier for them to apologize to workers – "sorry for losing my shit on you," I was once told.

When talking about the punishment-consequence approach, I do, of course, believe that consequences are necessary. The youth need to learn from their mistakes, though it can be hard not to intervene in an effort to protect them from the extremely harsh emotional lessons they tend to experience. The issue is that they are constantly having to bounce back from the intense consequences they face, from other youth, abusive parents, pimps, gang members, dealers, and/or violent partners. Some high-risk youth can learn, while others come from circumstances that do not leave them with the capacity to experience, learn, and adjust for the future. Workers should be trying to work *with* the youth in order protect them from the terrible punishment and consequences of their decisions. When they feel like crap and are down on themselves, the concern is that workers tend to heap more guilt, shame and feelings of being a failure onto the youth. Being available to pick up the pieces, talking about these experiences, and develop safety plans for the future is infinitely more helpful and relationship-based than having the warped satisfaction of telling the youth you were able to predict the future and knew such an event would happen to them eventually. This is a hollow victory and a worker may well receive a deserved consequence of "fuck you" from the youth as they put up more walls and push that person out of their lives.

Be a hero

> Without care the personal social services becomes impersonal, and that is deeply ironic and desperately sad.
>
> David Howe[3]

Firstly, the high-risk youth are the heroes for surviving and thriving. They are heroes for taking the risk of allowing somebody into their lives who, for all they know, may hurt them once more. They are heroes for thinking things can get better in the future despite experiencing so much grief and loss and helplessness and hopelessness. They are heroes for helping professionals learn to be better workers and better people. But, workers can be heroes too. Kagan (2004) appreciates the complexity of working with children and youth who have been damaged by negative life experiences and how heroes can be made from refusing to give up:

> I believe heroes are the people who keep on caring for others and helping others, even when they feel hurt, scared, lonely, or so mad they cannot think straight. It takes courage, the courage to do the right thing. And, it takes commitment to become someone a youth can depend on over time
>
> (p. 216).

Obviously, case workers, community youth specialists, and other service providers do not go into this work to be a hero. I have seen many workers in the High Risk Youth Initiative who give so much of themselves to wanting better for these youth who have had such a difficult start to life. I consider them heroes. These workers understand that, as Saleebey (1996) points out, the goal is not "heroic cure" but rather "the constancy of caring and connection and collaborative work toward improving the quality of day-to-day living" (p. 303).

By hanging in there with the youth, working through their anger, being sworn at and told disturbing things that one can do to themselves, hoping not to hear tragic news upon arriving to work in the morning, and empathizing with them through the sadness and pain they endure on a daily basis, workers can be heroes in the eyes of the youth. I have heard on many occasions youth talking about how their workers have helped turn their lives around – albeit sometimes underestimating their own resilience and strength – and I have had the privilege of youth sincerely thanking me for being involved in their lives. Though it is not uncommon to hear workers say youth should be more appreciative and less demanding, workers should not expect this or see the youth in a negative light because youth are not stroking their professional egos. However, it is profoundly rewarding that having fought to let anybody get close to them for very good reason, he or she has taken this risk and has come to see that there are adults who genuinely care about them.

Being mindful of this highlights how powerful connections can be and why there is a need to ensure youth feel safe in a relationship rather than ensure they are being compliant. Containing youth is easier for the worker in the moment, but helping youth form relationships can perhaps allow them to avoid future isolation and loneliness. It is powerfully significant that experiences with positive relationships can also change the future development of the mind (Howe, 2008, 2011; Szalavitz & Perry, 2010; Siegel, 2003). We can help create an environment in which these new relationships, with patterned, repetitive, and consistent messages can actually contribute to the creation of new neural pathways in the brain (Perry & Szalavitz, 2006). This is truly profound.

By being beside them as they navigate and negotiate their way through their adolescent years there is the opportunity for workers to be a catalyst. They can create the safety for youth to be able to step out of the dark and frightening place that has become their world, allowing for relational experiences and the creation of the space they need to take risks. This may sound dramatic or far-fetched, but I think this has more to do with coming from traditional punishment-consequence perspectives in which this kind transformative relationship is rare, and the fact that workers, even those who do take a more relationship-based approach, underestimate the impact they can have with the youth. Again, it is very disappointing to see how workers discount the influence they can have on youth or how much the youth want a connection. Recently, I heard a young mother tell a room full of case workers that they have no idea of the positive impact that they can have in the lives of youth. Workers must be tuned in to the youth, as it is our responsibility to establish safety and enhance positive risk-taking. If we are not tuned in and do not give them the safe place they need, we will continue to reinforce the feeling that nobody cares or run the risk of repeating the cycle of rejection and abandonment.

Change is not easy but it is happening anyway

When called to re-examine their practice, workers can be resistant by hiding behind policies and professional protocols, remaining in their comfort zone, or limiting themselves to one way of thinking about practice.[4] As stated in Chapter 1, John Maynard

Keynes recognizes the difficulty people have with letting go of the old ways of doing things. However, to be consistent in what we ask of youth, workers also need to take risks and go into places that might not be always comfortable.

Granted, the system itself does not always provide a safe environment to allow change, but traditional practices are more and more being called into question. The language is also changing and punitive policies and procedures, and denying youth services and basic needs because of non-compliance or testing behaviours, is being challenged. Kicking a youth out of a placement for not following expectations and with no plan for an alternative place to stay is now seen as causing a youth to be homeless. Threatening to close a youth's file due to poor cooperation or denying clothing, food, transportation, or visits with family or service providers until they do what they are told is now more likely to be seen as professional bullying – indeed it should be called for what it is. It has become more difficult to simply state that one is simply following policy. This is positive, as workers can start to practice in ways that fit better with their values. Hopefully they will feel more comfortable in being creative and flexible through a relationship-based approach because, after all, this is the best way to adequately meet the needs of the youth they are serving. It recognizes that all youth deserve caring attention and respect and that there is simply no such thing as a throwaway youth, high risk or otherwise.

A universal design perspective to working with youth

The *Get Connected* model has a 'universal design' approach[5] because it is designed for high-risk youth but can be effective for engaging and working with any youth in the child welfare system, or any youth in general as all youth value relationship, appreciate being consulted in decisions about their lives, and want help and support to be available when they need it. The universal design thinking is relevant in that building a program for the most complex and challenging youth is actually relevant for all youth.

As mentioned before, all youth are unique and have unique needs, but individualized practice can be adapted from a general practice model and philosophy. This can mean youth along the continuum from moderate needs (youth able to make connections, who have experienced minimal trauma, but who nevertheless find themselves in the child welfare system) to high-risk youth. One youth can perhaps benefit from using a few strategies (outlined in Chapter 9), while another may need a focused effort incorporating most or all of the strategies. Some youth may feel supported by an occasional check-in over coffee while for others it is critical to have a thorough understanding of how trauma impacts the ability to form relationships. Regardless, all youth can be captured through an understanding of the practice framework.

A concern I have had is that the *Get Connected* model has often been seen as applicable for a relatively small group of youth who are a significant challenge for the child welfare system. This has made it difficult to generalize the model for other youth who continue to be served by more traditional approaches. It has felt, at times, that the high-risk youth workers are separate and do different practice that does not apply to the rest of the system. When presenting or training on working with the high-risk youth population, I typically get asked why the practice framework and philosophy are only used for this sub-population of youth. I reply that while high-risk youth have been my focus, this model can be applied to all youth, as well as children and families, adapting it as circumstances present. I am glad to hear this question because it implies workers are thinking about how they can incorporate the principles into their practice and their varied caseload. As practice evolves into more relationship-based approaches, and as workers become more mindful about their work, the principles of this practice framework will start to be more generalized.

Reflect

In reflecting on one's practice, it should be less about how change impacts one as a worker (though still important) and more about the impact such change can have on the youth. As stated earlier, the youth have given us an excellent guideline in what does and does not meet their needs, so shifting practice to align with their needs does indeed honour their voices. Some may say relationship-based practice is vague, soft, and not easy to quantify (Howe, 2014), but youth are responding to it regardless. There needs to be accountability, of course, but this means going to the recipients of services and listening to what they believe they need rather than emotionally detached workers assessing them and telling them what they need and what to do. This does not provide safety for the youth and, without help to deal with the stresses of the external world, a youth is not going to be able to focus or deal with the trauma and chronic stress of their inner world (Howe, 2014).

Without the opportunity to learn coping skills and to take risks in allowing people to care about them and get close, what outcomes are we hoping to achieve? Through experience, we can somewhat guess the outcomes when workers have conflictual power-over interactions with youth. As authorities, workers can ultimately pull out the power trump card and close the youth's file, often resulting in youth becoming more entrenched in their addictions and in the justice system. Their own kids frequently become part of the child welfare system, and these children run the risk of repeating the cycle of becoming a challenge for the education, health, and mental health systems. I have seen this play out repeatedly. Nobody wins and the cost to society is high on many levels. Workers must detach themselves from oppressing the youth and truly understand that experiences of anxiety, stress, anger, and depression as a result of poor-quality caregiving or severe poverty and deprivation in early life can result in risky lifestyle habits (Howe, 2014). Howe (2014) continues:

> These lifestyle choices can represent inappropriate attempts to deal with feelings of hurt, pain, and confusion. These are people who are more likely to drink excessively, take drugs, and self-harm in their attempts to deal with painful memories and unmanageable feelings. But these are the same people who have compromised stress and immune systems as a result of epigenetic changes to their DNA. Thus, the least robust people, biologically speaking, face the biggest risks, environmentally speaking.
>
> (p. 107)

This is what we start to understand when we are in the community building relationships with the youth and their community supports. Systems cannot continue giving mixed messages about increasing face-to-face contact with youth while keeping case workers in front of their computers. Nor can systems build up caseloads so high the worker can do little more than respond to crises. This is simply paying 'lip service' to the value of caring relationships resulting in practice that runs the risk of being "not only insensitive but also ineffective" (Howe, 2014, p. 128). It is interesting that in an era of measuring outcomes, youth will recall that what made the difference for them is the belief a worker had in them or that someone cared about them. Too many youth remember having worker after worker, so while a long-term relationship with a worker is, sadly, rare, where it exists can be very precious (McMahon, 2010). Of course, such subjective and touchy, feely, yet heartfelt feelings are hard to measure and thus tend not to be the outcomes sought.

Challenge

> "The High Risk Youth Initiative is an opportunity to right a wrong. This is more than a project or program, it is a responsibility."
>
> Karen Bruno, Aboriginal Consultant[6]

While there continues to be far too many examples of oppressive practice and the use of punishment-consequence interventions to 'help' youth, practitioners can be more open in challenging such traditional thinking. The importance of relationship-based practice is being talked about more than ever and there is the opportunity to get the message out that youth need compassion, hand-holding, and love (Batmanghelidjh, 2006; Howe, 2014; Maté, 2008; Szalavitz & Perry, 2010). Experts say this because these are more effective ways to engage and work with youth. Child welfare systems must acknowledge that traditional approaches have failed youth and have kept them isolated and estranged from the help they so desperately need. There has been little encouragement for case workers "to be involved, to get in touch with the service user's inner world and the pain they will find there, and to make warm relationships" (McMahon, 2010, p. 162).

As Munro (2011) points out above, it has also become overwhelmingly obvious through my experience that high-risk youth want healthy connections with caring, empathic, and non-judgemental adults. Therefore, it is up to us to respond and take responsibility to accept their invitations or "bids for connections" (Brendtro et al., 2009, p. 48). No matter how much they test, frustrate, or try to hurt us, they are struggling more than we are, so let us stand up and be counted, take risks ourselves, and journey with the youth to help them see that their life trajectory can change rather than having a sense of being trapped with little hope for the future. If we can do this, there will undoubtedly be fewer youth, when asked about their experiences in the child welfare system, relating the following themes: We are vulnerable; we are isolated; we are left out of our lives; no one is really there for us; care is unpredictable; care ends and we struggle (Oneil, 2011, p. 7).

To help us think intentionally about practice we can continually ask ourselves, "What is happening in my relationship with this young person that does not work for them?" (Gaughan & Kalyniak, 2012, p. 100). As a way to think anti-oppressively, be aware of the impact we have on the youth, and being in a position of authority, we can also reflect on the questions shared by Cindy Blackstock:

1   What are the effects of your actions or inactions on other people?
2   How courageous are you prepared to be to stand up for what you think is important?
3   What are you prepared to sacrifice? (Galat, 2010)

It must be recognized that all people are more likely to tackle life's challenges and gain strength when feeling recognized, accepted, and understood. We need a deep day-to-day understanding that "practitioners who are skilled at weaving together love and work, empathy and structure, therapeutic alliances and technical know-how, are effective practitioners" and that people become motivated to change when their workers bring "warmth, recognition, hope, and purpose to the relationship" (Howe, 2014, p. 136). When youth are treated poorly and are being bullied and threatened by workers who feel justified in making demands of the youth before respecting them enough to build a relationship, we must be prepared to challenge colleagues for such practice. To let these incidents pass is an act of oppression itself and allows for some youth to be treated with dignity and respect while others, through no fault of their own, are emotionally harmed on a systemic level.

I firmly believe this shift in practice is building momentum and the child welfare system can help relationship-based approaches reach a tipping point. Resisting change could result in one day having to look back and acknowledge, once again, our mistakes of the past. To avoid repeating history, workers, agencies, and governments can challenge the loud and boisterous calls for action to repress youth as reflected in popular media and in society's neo-conservative view of children in which there is a call for a hardline, tough love, and old-fashioned values approaches, even though such a mentality, as youth have repeatedly demonstrated, is ineffective and polarizing (Ungar, 2004).

A colleague[7] passionately stated that making a meaningful connection with a youth is not just about being warm and fuzzy; it is well-researched and evidence-based practice that makes a difference in people's lives. As reflected in this book, it is this fact that should be driving the change that youth need to see, hear, and feel. We are in a position now to provide youth who engage in high-risk behaviours with more hope, to draw them in rather than push them away, and to collaborate in an effort to tackle head on the cycle of multi-generational trauma. Once on this path there is no going back to traditional approaches, as they do not make sense for the youth and they will no longer make sense for workers. An outreach worker once described a high-risk youth as a "wild child looking for peace." Rather than demonizing such youth, we must offer a way to make a connection and help them find this sense of peace.

Notes

1   Taken from the book chapter, 'Healing Versus Treatment: Substance Misuse, Child Welfare and Indigenous Families' by Betty Bastien, Sohki Aski Esquao (Jeannine Carrier), and Susan Strega (in *Walking This Path Together: Anti-Racist and Anti-Oppressive Child Welfare Practice*, edited by Susan Strega and Sohki Aski Esquao (Jeannine Carrier), 2009, p. 229).
2   While research would be required to build this case, my experience has shown that high casloads can be expensive. This leads to a worker being spread too thin and responding to crises rather than having the time to get to know children, youth, and families. If we have lower caseloads, and we can develop relationships, we can anticipate crises or the youth and

family can feel safe enough to reach out when a situation is building toward a crisis. When a situation erupts into a crisis, high-cost services tend to be implemented or the child/youth ends up coming into high-cost placements; this is also a more traumatic experience for family members. Being able to engage the family earlier can de-escalate the situation, offers an opportunity to work through circumstances and develop strategies for future challenges, avoids the use of emergency and high-cost band-aid services, and is better for the mental health of all involved.

3 Taken from the book, *The Compleat Social Worker* by David Howe (2014, p. 21).

4 The *Get Connected* model incorporates a variety of theories and models but opens itself to many approaches consistent with relationship-based interventions, including cognitive behavioural therapy (CBT), motivational interviewing (MI), narrative therapy, solution-focused intervention, ecological perspectives, structural perspectives, and models such as Signs of Safety and Circle of Courage, over and above what is highlighted in this book: harm reduction, strength-based/resiliency approaches, community collaboration, attachment theory, and neuroscientific perspectives on trauma and development.

5 Often, designers of products focus on the average user. In contrast, universal design (UD), according to the Center for Universal Design (CUD) at North Carolina State University, "is the design of products and environments to be usable by all people, to the greatest extent possible, without the need for adaptation or specialized design." Universal design can be applied to any product or environment. For example, making a product or an environment accessible to people with disabilities often benefits others. Automatic door openers benefit individuals using walkers and wheelchairs, but also benefit people carrying groceries and holding babies, as well as elderly citizens. Sidewalk curb cuts, designed to make sidewalks and streets accessible to those using wheelchairs, are more often used by kids on skateboards, parents with baby strollers, and delivery staff with carts. When television displays in airports and restaurants are captioned, programming is accessible not only to people who are deaf but also to others who cannot hear the audio in noisy areas. Universal design is a goal that puts a high value on diversity, equality, and inclusiveness (by Sheryl Burgstahler, http://www. washington.edu/doit/universal-design-process-principles-and-applications). Thus, by the same thinking, if a program – such as the High Risk Youth Initiative *Get Connected* model – is designed for the youth with the most challenging issues, all youth, as well as children and families, can potentially benefit from the practice framework principles and philosophy.

6 Karen Bruno is currently an Aboriginal leader, consultant, and mentor. She was involved with the High Risk Youth Initiative when employed at Boyle Street Community Services in Edmonton, Alberta, Canada.

7 David Rust has been an advocate for change in various government systems and community agencies for years, promoting how essential it is to form relationships with youth. The former foster parent is an advocate, mentor, trainer, public speaker, and true inspiration to many in the helping professions. David was a maverick in developing programs promoting harm reduction approaches and relationship-based interventions well before practice started to noticeably shift in that direction.

References

Abels, P., & Abels, Sonia L. (2001). *Understanding narrative therapy: A guide for the social worker*. New York: Springer Publishing Company.

Abramovich, A. (2013a). No fixed address: Young, queer and restless. In S. Gaetz, B. O'Grady, K. Buccieri, J. Karabanow, & A. Marsolais (Eds.), *Youth homelessness in Canada: Implications for policy and practice* (pp. 387–404). Toronto, Ontario: Canadian Homelessness Research Network.

Abramovich, A. (2013b). *There are no shelters for LGBTQ youth in Canada*. Canada Homeless Hub. Retrieved from: http://www.homelesshub.ca/gallery/there-are-no-shelters-lgbtq-youth-canada

Allen, B. (2011). The use and abuse of attachment theory in clinical practice with maltreated children, part 1: Diagnosis and assessment. *Trauma, Violence & Abuse, 12*(1): 3–12.

Altman, J., & Gohagan, D. (2009). Work with involuntary clients in child welfare settings. In R. H. Rooney (Ed.), *Strategies for working with involuntary clients* (pp. 334–337), Second Edition. New York, NY: Columbia University Press.

American Psychiatric Association. (2013). *Diagnostic and statistical manual of mental disorders*, Fifth Edition. Arlington, VA: American Psychiatric Association.

Anderson, G. R., & Seita, J. (2006). Family and social factors affecting youth in the child welfare system. In N. Boyd Webb (Ed.), *Working with traumatized youth in child welfare* (pp. 67–91). New York, NY: The Guilford Press.

Baines, D. (2007). Anti-oppressive social work practice: Fighting for space, fighting for change. In D. Baines (Ed.), *Doing anti-oppressive practice: Building transformative politicized social work* (pp. 67–82). Canada: Fernwood Publishing.

Baskin, C. (2013). Shaking off the colonial inheritance: Homeless and indigenous youth resist, reclaim and reconnect. In S. Gaetz, B. O'Grady, K. Buccieri, J. Karabanow, & A. Marsolais (Eds.), *Youth homelessness in Canada: Implications for policy and practice* (pp. 405–424). Toronto, Ontario: Canadian Homelessness Research Network.

Bastien, B., Esquao, Sohki Aski, & Strega, S. (2009). Healing versus treatment: Substance misuse, child welfare and indigenous families. In S. Strega & Sohki Aski Esquao (J. Carrière) (Eds.), *Walking this path together: Anti-racist and anti-oppressive child welfare practice* (pp. 29–44). Canada: Fernwood Publishing.

Batmanghelidjh, C. (2006). *Shattered lives: Children who live with courage and dignity*. London, UK: Jessica Kingsley Publishers.

Bender, L., Moore, C. (Producers), & Van Sant, G. (Director). (1997). *Good will hunting* [Motion Picture]. USA: Miramax Films.

Benoit, M. B. (2006). The view from the mental health system. In N. Boyd Webb (Ed.), *Working with traumatized youth in child welfare* (pp. 279–294). New York, NY: The Guilford Press.

Berger, C. (2005, November/December). What becomes of at-risk gay youths? *The Gay & Lesbian Review*.

Bernard, B. (2004). *Resiliency: What we have learned*. San Francisco, CA: WestEd.

Bigler, M. O. (2005). Harm reduction as a practice and prevention model for social work. *The Journal of Baccalaureate Social Work*, 10(2): 69–86.

Bishop, A. (2002). *Becoming an ally: Breaking the cycle of oppression in people*, Second Edition (pp. 334–337). Canada: Fernwood Publishing.

Blackstock, C. (2008). Reconciliation means not saying sorry twice: Lessons from child welfare in Canada. In *From truth to reconciliation: Transforming the legacy of residential schools* (pp. 162–75). Aboriginal Healing Foundation. Retrieved from: http://www.ahf.ca/downloads/from-truth-to-reconciliation-transforming-the-legacy-of-residential-schools.pdf

Bloom, S. (1993). The clinical use of psychohistory. *The Journal of Psychohistory*. 20(3): 259–266.

Blundo, R. (2001). Learning strength-based practice: Challenging our personal and professional frames. *Families in Society*, 82(3): 296–304.

Bolton, G. (2014). *Reflective practice: Writing and professional development*, Fourth Edition. London, UK: Sage.

Bowlby, J. (1969). *Attachment and loss, Volume 1: Attachment*. New York: Basic Books.

Bowlby, J. (1973). *Attachment and loss, Volume 2: Separation*. New York: Basic Books.

Bowlby, J. (1980). *Attachment and loss, Volume 3: Loss, sadness and depression*. New York: Basic Books.

Boyd Webb, N. (2006). The impact of trauma on youth and families in the child welfare system. In N. Boyd Webb (Ed.), *Working with traumatized youth in child welfare* (pp. 13–26). New York, NY: The Guilford Press.

Brendtro, L. & Ness, A. (1983): *Re-educating troubled youth*. New York, NY: Aldine.

Brendtro, L., Brokenleg, M., & Van Bockern, S. (1990). *Reclaiming youth at risk: Our hope for the future*, Revised Edition. Washington, DC: National Education Service.

Brendtro, L., & du Toit, L. (2005). *Response Ability Pathways: Restoring bonds of respect*. Claremont, South Africa: Pretext Publishers.

Brendtro, L., Mitchell, M., & McCall, H. (2009). *Deep brain learning: Pathways to potential with challenging youth*. Circle of Courage and Starr Commonwealth. Albion, MI: Starr Commonwealth.

Bretherton, I. (1992). The origins of attachment theory: John Bowlby and Mary Ainsworth. *Developmental Psychology*, 28: 759–775.

Brocato, J., & Wagner, E. F. (2003). Harm reduction: A social work practice model and social justice agenda. *Health and Social Work*, 28(2): 117–125.

Burgstahler, S. (2015). *Universal design: Process, principles, and applications – How to apply universal design to any product or environment*. Retrieved from: http://www.washington.edu/doit/universal-design-process-principles-and-applications

Canadian Association of Social Workers. (2005). *Code of ethics*. Retrieved from: http://www.acsw.ab.ca /pdfs/2005_code_of_ethics.pdf

Canadian Association of Social Workers. (2005). *Guidelines for ethical practice*. Retrieved from: http://www.acsw.ab.ca/pdfs/casw_guidelines_for_ethical_practice.pdf

Canadian Medical Association. (2008). *8th annual national report card on health care*. Retrieved from: http://www.facturation.net/multimedia/CMA/Content_Images/Inside_cma/Annual_Meeting/2008/GC_Bulletin/National_Report_Card_EN.pdf

Canadian Mental Health Association. (2015). *Fast facts on mental health*. Retrieved from: http://www.cmha.ca/media/fast-facts-about-mental-illness/#.VSy5GvldXfg

Canavan, J. (2008). Resilience: Cautiously welcoming a contested concept. *Child Care in Practice*, 14(1): 1–7.

Child Trauma Academy. (2002). *Bonding and attachment in maltreated children: Lesson 1, introduction*. Child Trauma Academy. Retrieved from: http://www.childtraumaacademy.com/bonding_attachment/lesson01/page02.html

Child and Youth Care Association of Alberta. (2014). *Code of ethics*. Retrieved from: http://www.cycaa.com/about-us/code-of-ethics

Choi, S. K., Wilson, B. D. M., Shelton, J., & Gates, G. (2015). *Serving our youth, 2015: The needs and experiences of lesbian, gay, bisexual, transgender, and questioning youth experiencing homelessness*. The Palette Fund, True Colors Fund, and the Williams Institute. Retrieved from: http://truecolorsfund.org/news/new-study-sheds-light-on-problems-facing-lesbian-gay-bisexual-and-transgender-homeless-youth

Clare, D. (2009). Snakes and ladders: The ups and downs of self-harming behavior. *International Journal of Narrative Therapy and Community Work, 2009*(2): 60–71.

Cook, A. (2008). Knowing the child: The importance of developing a relationship. In B. Luckock & M. Lefevre (Eds.), *Direct work: Social work with children and young people in care* (pp. 223–233). London: British Association for Adopting & Fostering.

Cunningham, P., & Page, T. (2001). A case study of a maltreated thirteen-year-old boy: Using attachment theory to inform treatment in a residential program. *Child & Adolescent Social Work Journal, 18*(5): 335–352.

Dame, L. (2004). Live through this: The experiences of queer youth in care in Manitoba. *The Canadian Online Journal of Queer Studies in Education, 1*(1). Retrieved from: http://jqstudies.oise.utoronto.ca/journal/viewarticle.php?id=2&layout=html

Dennis, K. W., & Lourie, I. S. (2006). *Everything is normal until proven otherwise: A book about wraparound services*. Washington, DC: CWLA Press.

Douglas Mental Health University Institute/McGill University. (2009). *Press release.*Retrieved from: http://www.mcgill.ca/channels/news/childhood-trauma-has-life-long-effect-genes-and-brain-104667

Eaton-Erickson, A., Campbell, T., & Smyth, P. (2011). *Younger youth, higher risk: Position paper* (Unpublished report). Edmonton & Area Child & Family Services (Region 6), High Risk Youth Operations Committee. Edmonton, Alberta.

Elovich, R., & Cowing, M. (1993). *Recovery readiness: Strategies that bring treatment to addicts where they are*. National Harm Reduction Working GroupReport from October 21–23, 1993, Meeting.

Esquao, Sohki Aski, & Sinclair, R. (2009). Considerations for cultural planning and Indigenous adoptions. In S. Strega & Sohki Aski Esquao (J. Carrière) (Eds.), *Walking this path together: Anti-racist and anti-oppressive child welfare practice* (pp. 29–44). Canada: Fernwood Publishing.

Farmer, R. L. (2009). *Neuroscience and social work practice: The missing link*. Thousand Oaks, CA: Sage Publications, Inc.

Felitti, V. J. (2002). The relationship of adverse childhood experiences to adult health: Turning gold into lead. *Z Psychosom Med Psychother, 48*(4): 359–369. Retrieved from: Norlien Foundation website: www.norlien.org

Felitti, V. J. (2003). The origins of addiction: Evidence from the adverse childhood experiences study. *Praxis der Kinderpsychologie und Kinderpsychiatrie, 52*: 547–559. Retrieved from: Norlien Foundation website: www.norlien.org

Felitti, V. J. (2009, May, 4). *Adverse Childhood Experiences (ACE) and their relationship to adult well-being and disease*. Lecture conducted from Edmonton, Alberta, Canada.

Fenton, L. (2014). *Frederick Douglass in Ireland*. Cork, Ireland: The Collins Press.

Fonagy, P. (2000). Attachment and borderline personality disorder. *Journal of the American Psychoanalytic Association, 48*: 1129–1146. doi:10.1177/00030651000480040701

Fontana, V. J., & Gonzales, M. P. B. (2006). The view from the child welfare. In N. Boyd Webb (Ed.), *Working with traumatized youth in child welfare* (pp. 267–278). New York, NY: Guilford Press.

Fosha, D. (2003). Dyadic regulation and experimental work with emotion and relatedness in trauma and disorganized attachment. In M. F. Solomon & D. J. Siegel (Eds.), *Healing trauma: Attachment, mind, body, and brain* (pp. 221–281). New York, NY: W. W. Norton & Company.

Gaetz, S. (2004). Safe streets for whom? Homeless youth, social exclusion, and criminal victimization. *Canadian Journal of Criminology and Criminal Justice*, 46(4): 423–455.

Gaetz, S. (2009). Chapter 3.2: Whose safety counts? Street youth, social exclusion and criminal victimization. In D. J. Hulchanski, P. Campsie, S. Chau, S. Hwang, & E. Paradis (Eds.), *Finding home: Policy options for addressing homelessness in Canada (e-book)*. Toronto: Cities Centre, University of Toronto. Retrieved from: www.homelesshub.ca/FindfingHome

Gaetz, S. (2010). The struggle to end homelessness in Canada: How we created the crisis, and how we end it. *The Open Health Services and Policy Journal*, 3: 21–26.

Gaetz, S. (2011). *Plans to end homelessness in Canada: A review of the literature*. Toronto, Ontario: Eva's Initiatives.

Gaetz, S. (2014a). *Coming of age: Reimagining the response to youth homelessness in Canada*. Toronto, Ontario: The Canadian Homelessness Network Press.

Gaetz, S. (2014b). *A safe and decent place to live: Towards a housing first framework for youth*. Toronto: The Canadian Homelessness Research Network Press.

Gaetz, S., & O'Grady, B. (2013). Why don't you just get a job? Homeless youth, social exclusion, and employment training. In S. Gaetz, B. O'Grady, K. Buccieri, J. Karabanow, & A. Marsolais (Eds.), *Youth homelessness in Canada: Implications for policy and practice* (pp. 243–268). Toronto, Ontario: Canadian Homelessness Research Network.

Gaetz, S., O'Grady, B., Buccieri, K., Karabanow, J., & Marsolais, A. (2013). Introduction. In S. Gaetz, B. O'Grady, K. Buccieri, J. Karabanow, & A. Marsolais (Eds.), *Youth homelessness in Canada: Implications for policy and practice* (pp. 1–13). Toronto, Ontario: Canadian Homelessness Research Network.

Galat, J. M. (2010). Cindy Blackstock: It's not intentions – It's results that count. *The Advocate*, 35(1): 24–25, Alberta College of Social Workers.

Gaughan, K., & Kalyniak, S. (2012). The centrality of relationships. In S. Goodman & I. Trowler (Eds.), *Social work reclaimed: Innovative frameworks for child and family social work practice* (pp. 94–110). London, UK: Jessica Kingsley Publishers.

Giller, E., Vermilyea, E., & Steele, T. (2006). Risking connection: Helping agencies embrace relational work with trauma survivors. *Journal of Trauma Practice*, 5(1): 65–81.

Gold, M. (2006). Stages of change. *Psych Central*. Retrieved on June 30, 2014, from: http://psychcentral.com/lib/stages-of-change/000265

Goldblatt, A. (2007, February). *Should we dance: A resource for effective partnering*. Based on Discussions of the Partnership Dialogue, Edmonton, Alberta. Sponsored by Inner City Connections, Community Partnership Enhancement Fund.

Government of Alberta. (2010). *Protection of sexually exploited children and youth*. Edmonton, Alberta: Government of Alberta. Retrieved from: http://humanservices.alberta.ca/documents/PSEC-manual.pdf

Graybeal, C. (2001). Strengths-based social work assessment: Transforming the dominant paradigm. *Families in Society*, 82(2): 233–242.

Hammond, W. (2010). *Principles of strength-based practice*. Calgary, Alberta, Canada: Resiliency Initiatives. Retrieved from: http://www.mentalhealth4kids.ca/healthlibrary_docs/PrinciplesOfStrength-BasedPractice.pdf

Hammond, W., & Nuttgens, N. (2007, November 14). *Resiliency: Embracing a strength-based approach to service provision*. Presentation at Joint Professional Development Day, City Centre Education Project, Edmonton, AB.

Hartman, L., Little, A., & Ungar, M. (2008). Narrative-inspired youth care work within a community agency. *Journal of Systemic Therapies*, 27(1): 44–58.

Harvard University, Center on the Developing Child. (2011). *Serve and return interaction shapes brain circuitry*. National Scientific Council on the Developing Child. Retrieved from: http://developingchild.harvard.edu/activities/council/

Hathazi, D., Lankenau, S. E., Sanders, B., & Jackson Bloom, J. (2009). Pregnancy and sexual health among homeless young injection drug users. *Journal of Adolescence, 32:* 339–355.

Heller, L., & LaPierre, A. (2012). *Healing developmental trauma: How early trauma affects self-regulation, self-image, and the capacity for relationship.* Berkeley, CA: North Atlantic Books.

Henton, D. (2009, November 23). Volunteer turns painful past into life of helping, healing. *Edmonton Journal.* Retrieved from: http://www2.canada.com/edmontonjournal/news/story.html?id=8c8111ab-ae09–48d0–9119–6059b5ed8c90

Henton, D. (2010, February 1). Hobbema shooting has many victims. *Edmonton Journal.* Retrieved from: http://www2.canada.com/edmontonjournal/news/story.html?id=3ab1721b-4b45–4c39–8aae-e8428a7572f1

Herbert, M. (2007). Creating conditions for good practice: A child welfare project sponsored by the Canadian Association of Social Workers. In I. Brown, F. Chaze, D. Fuchs, J. Lafrance, S. McKay, & S. Thomas-Prokop (Eds.), *Putting a human face on child welfare: Voices from the prairies* (pp. 223–250). Prairie Child Welfare Consortium. Retrieved from: www.uregina.ca/spr/prairiechild/index.html/CentreofExcellenceforChildWelfare; www.cecw-cepb.ca

Holmes, J. (2004). Disorganized attachment and borderline personality disorder: A clinical perspective. *Attachment and Human Development, 6*(2): 181–190.

Homeward Trust Edmonton. (2015). *Community strategy to ending youth homelessness in Edmonton* (Unpublished report). Edmonton, AB: Planning and Research, Homeward Trust Edmonton.

Horwath, J., & Morrison, T. (2007). Collaboration, integration and change in children's services: Critical issues and key ingredients. *Child Abuse & Neglect, 31:* 55–69.

Howe, D. (2005). *Child abuse and neglect: Attachment, development and intervention.* New York, NY: Palgrave, McMillan.

Howe, D. (2008). *The emotionally intelligent social worker.* New York, NY: Palgrave, McMillan.

Howe, D. (2011). *Attachment across the lifecourse: A brief introduction.* New York, NY: Palgrave, McMillan.

Howe, D. (2014). *The complete social worker.* New York, NY: Palgrave, McMillan.

Hudson, P. (1999, October). Community development and child protection: A case for integration. *Community Development Journal, 34*(4): 346–355.

Hunt, G., Joe-Laidler, K., & MacKenzie, K. (2005). Moving into motherhood: Gang girls and controlled risk. *Youth Society, 36:* 333–373.

Hunter, E. (2008, July). What's good for the gays is good for the gander: Making homeless youth housing safer for lesbian, gay, bisexual, and transgender youth. *Family Court Review, 46*(3): 543–557.

Hurley, D. (2013, May). Trait vs fate. *Discover Magazine.*

Inckle, K. (2011). The first cut is the deepest: A harm reduction approach to self-injury. *Social Work in Mental Health, 9:* 364–378.

Kagan, R. (2004). *Rebuilding attachments with traumatized children: Healing from losses, violence, abuse, and neglect.* Binghamton, NY: The Haworth Maltreatment & Trauma Press.

Kania, J., & Kramer, M. (2011, Winter). Collective impact. *Stanford Social Innovation Review,* Winter 2011: 36–41.

King, K. E., Ross, L. E., Bruno, T. L., & Erickson, P. G. (2009). Identity work among street-involved young mothers. *Journal of Youth Studies, 12*(2): 139–149.

Klain, E. J., & White, A. R. (2013). Implementing trauma-informed practices in child welfare. *State Policy Advocacy and Reform Centre.* Retrieved from: childwelfaresparc.org/wp-content/uploads/2013/11/Implementing-Trauma-Informed-Practices.pdf

Knowles, D. (2013, July 23). 'Crack baby' study finds poverty is worse for child development than exposure to drug in womb. *New York Daily News.* Retrieved from: http://www.nydailynews.com/news/national/crack-baby-study-overturns-common-assumptions-article-1.1407081

Kreitzer, L., & Lafrance, J. (2009). Colocation of a government child welfare unit in a traditional aboriginal agency: A way forward in working with Aboriginal communities. *First Peoples Child & Family Review*, 5(2): 34–44. Retrieved from: http://journals.sfu.ca/fpcfr/index.php/FPCFR/article/viewFile/91/156

Kundougk (Green, J.), & Qwel'sih'yah'maht (Thomas, R.) (2009). Children in the centre: Indigenous perspectives on anti-oppressive child welfare practices. In S. Strega & Sohki Aski Esquao (J. Carrière) (Eds.), *Walking this path together: Anti-racist and anti-oppressive child welfare practice* (pp. 29–44). Canada: Fernwood Publishing.

Lafrance, J., & Bastien, B. (2007). Here be dragons! Breaking down the iron cage for aboriginal children. In I. Brown, F. Chaze, D. Fuchs, J. Lafrance, S. McKay, & S. Thomas-Prokop (Eds.), *Putting a human face on child welfare: Voices from the prairies* (pp. 89–113). Prairie Child Welfare Consortium. Retrieved from: www.uregina.ca/spr/prairiechild/index.html/Centreof-ExcellenceforChildWelfare; www.cecw-cepb.ca

Lawler, M. J., Shaver, P. R., & Goodman, G. S. (2010). Toward relationship-based child welfare services. *Child and Youth Services Review*, 33: 473–480.

Lawryk, L. (2001). *Adopting children living with fetal alcohol spectrum disorder*. Calgary, Alberta, Canada: OBD Triage Institute.

Lee, B., & Richards, S. (2002). Child protection through strengthening communities: The Toronto Children's Aid Society. In B. Wharf (Ed.), *Community work approaches to child welfare* (pp. 9–25). Canada: Broadview Press.

Lee, F. W., & Charm, L. M. (2002). The possibility of promoting user participation in working with high-risk youth. *British Journal of Social Work*, 32: 71–92.

Lemma, A. (2010). The power of relationships: A study of key working as an intervention with traumatised young people. *Journal of Social Work Practice*, 24(4): 409–427.

Levy, K. N. (2005). The implications of attachment theory and research for understanding borderline personality disorder. *Development and Psychopathology*, 17: 959–986.

Levy, T. M., & Orlans, M. (1998). *Attachment, treatment, and healing: Understanding and treating attachment disorder in children and families*, Washington, DC, USA: Child Welfare League of America, Inc.

Little, A., Hartman, L., & Ungar, M. (2007). Practical applications of narrative ideas to youth care. *Relational Child and Youth Care Practice*, 20(4): 37–41.

Logan, D. E., & Marlatt, G. A. (2010). Harm reduction therapy: A practice-friendly review of research. *Journal of Clinical Psychology: In Session*, 66(2): 201–214.

Lonne, B., Parton, N., Thomson, J., & Harries, M. (2009). *Reforming child protection*. New York, NY: Routledge.

Luckock, B., & Lefevre, M., (Eds.) (2008). Introduction. In B. Luckock & M. Lefevre (Eds.), *Direct work: Social work with children and young people in care* (pp. xxvii–xxxii). London: British Association for Adopting & Fostering.

Madsen, W. C. (1999). *Collaborative therapy with multi-stressed families: From old problems to new futures*. New York, NY: The Guilford Press.

Madsen, W. C. (2007). *Collaborative therapy with multi-stressed families*, Second Edition. New York, NY: The Guilford Press.

Maté, G. (1999). *Scattered minds: A new look at the origins and healing of attention deficit disorder*. Toronto, Canada: Vintage Canada.

Maté, G. (2003). *When the body says no: The cost of hidden stress*. Toronto, Canada: Vintage Canada.

Maté, G. (2008). *In the realm of hungry ghosts: Close encounters with addiction*. Toronto, Canada: Alfred A. Knopf.

McCharles, T. (2011, October 1). *Vancouver's injection clinic gets Supreme Court blessing to stay open*. Toronto Star, Canada. Retrieved from: http://www.thestar.com/news/canada/2011/10/01/

McMahon, L. (2010). Long-term complex relationships. In G. Ruch, D. Turney, & A. Ward, (Eds.), *Relationship-based social work: Getting to the heart of practice* (pp. 148–163). London, UK: Jessica Kingsley Publishers.

Morgaine, K., & Capous-Desyllas, M. (2015). *Anti-oppressive social work practice: Putting theory into Action.* Thousand Oaks, CA: Sage Publications Ltd.

Mullaly, B. (2007). *The new structural social work.* Canada: Oxford Press.

Mullaly, B. (2010). *Challenging oppression and confronting privilege,* Second Edition. Canada: Oxford Press.

Munro, E. (1999). Protecting children in an anxious society. *Health, Risk & Society, 1*(1): 117–127.

Munro, E. (2008). *Effective child protection,* Second Edition. London, UK: Sage Publications Ltd.

Munro, E. (2011). *The Munro review of child protection (final report): A child-centred system.* Department of Education. Retrieved from: http://www.official-documents.gov.uk/document/cm80/8062/8062.pdf. Contains public sector information licensed under the Open Government Licence v3.0.

National Association of Social Workers, Delegated Assembly. (2008). *Code of ethics.* Retrieved from: http://www.socialworkers.org/pubs/code/code.asp

National Scientific Council on the Developing Child. (2004a). *Young children develop in an environment of relationships.* Working Paper No. 1. Retrieved from: http://www.developingchild.net

National Scientific Council on the Developing Child. (2004b). *Children's emotional development is built into the architecture of their brains.* Working Paper No. 2. Retrieved from: http://www.developingchild.net

National Scientific Council on the Developing Child. (2005). *Excessive stress disrupts the architecture of the brain.* Working Paper No. 3. Retrieved from: http://www.developingchild.net

National Scientific Council on the Developing Child. (2007). *The timing and quality of early experiences combine to shape brain architecture.* Working Paper No. 5. Retrieved from: http://www.developingchild.net

National Scientific Council on the Developing Child. (2008). *Establishing a level foundation for life: Mental health begins in early childhood.* Working Paper No. 6. Updated edition. Retrieved from: http://www.developingchild.net

National Scientific Council on the Developing Child. (2010a). *Persistent fear and anxiety can affect young children's learning and development.* Working Paper No. 9. Retrieved from: http://www.developingchild.net

National Scientific Council on the Developing Child. (2010b). *Early experiences can alter gene expression and affect long-term development.* Working Paper No. 10. Retrieved from: http://www.developingchild.net

National Scientific Council on the Developing Child. (2012). *The science of neglect: The persistent absence of responsive care disrupts the developing brain.* Working Paper No. 12. Retrieved from: http://www.developingchild.net

Neborsky, R. J. (2003). A clinical model for the comprehensive treatment of trauma using an affect experiencing-attachment theory approach. In M. F. Solomon & D. J. Siegel (Eds.), *Healing trauma: Attachment, mind, body, and brain* (pp. 282–321). New York, NY: W. W. Norton & Company.

Neufeld, G., & Maté, G. (2004). *Hold on to your kids: Why parents matter.* Canada: Alfred K. Knopf.

Nicholas, D. B., Newton, A. S., Calhoun, A., Dong, K., deJong-Berg, M. A., Hamilton, F., Kilmer, C., McLaughlin, A. M. . . ., & Shankar, J. (2015).*The experiences and perceptions of street-involved youth regarding emergency department services.* Alberta Centre for Child, Family and Community Research. Retrieved from: http://www.research4children.org/data/documents/2014-Feb-03_Scientific_Report_091015TOP-Nicholas.docx.pdf

Nicholson, D., Artz, S., Armitage, A., & Fagan, J. (2000). Working relationships and outcomes in multidisciplinary collaborative practice settings. *Child and Youth Care Forum, 29*(1): 39–73.

Noseworthy, S., & Lane, K. (1998). How we learnt that scratching can really be self-abuse: Co-research with young people. In C. White & D. Denbrorough (Eds.), *Introducing narrative therapy: A collection of practice-based writings* (pp. 25–33). Adelaide, Australia: Dulwich Centre Publications.

Noshpitz, J. D. (1994, Summer). Self-destructiveness in adolescents. *American Journal of Psychotherapy, 48*(3): 330–346.

Office of the Child and Youth Advocate. (2007). *Word on the street* (video). Available from the Office of the Child and Youth Advocate, Peace Hills Trust Tower, #803, 10011–109 St., Edmonton, AB, (780) 422–6056.

O'Grady, B., Gaetz, S., Buccieri, K. (2013). Policing street youth in Toronto. In S. Gaetz, B. O'Grady, K. Buccieri, J. Karabanow, & A. Marsolais (Eds.), *Youth homelessness in Canada: Implications for policy and practice* (pp. 445–468). Toronto, Ontario: Canadian Homelessness Research Network.

O'Hare, T. (2001). Substance abuse and risky sex in young people: The development and validation of the risky sex scale. *The Journal of Primary Prevention, 22*(2): 89–101.

Okamoto, S. K. (2002, August). The challenges of male practitioners working with female youth clients. *Child and Youth Care Forum, 31*(4).

Oneil. (2011). *My real life book: Report from the youth leaving care hearings.* Provincial Advocate for Children and Youth, Ontario. Retrieved from: http://www.provincialadvocate.on.ca/documents/en/ylc/YLC_REPORT_ENG.pdf

Perry, B. (2006). Applying principals of neurodevelopment to clinical work with maltreated and traumatized children: The neurosequential model of therapeutics. In N. Boyd Webb (Ed.), *Working with traumatized youth in child welfare* (pp. 27–52). New York, NY: Guilford Press.

Perry, B. (2009). Examining child and maltreatment through a neurodevelopmental lens: Clinical application of the Neurosequential Model of Therapeutics. *Journal of Loss and Trauma, 14*: 240–255.

Perry, B. (2010, November 15). *Introduction to the Neurosequential Model of Therapeutics (NMT): A collaborative day of learning.* Alberta, Canada: Lecture conducted from Edmonton.

Perry, B. (2014, April). *The impact of trauma and neglect on the developing child.* Alberta, Canada: Lecture conducted from Edmonton.

Perry, B., & Szalavitz, M. (2006). *The boy who was raised as a dog and other stories from a child psychiatrist's notebook.* New York: Basic Books.

Pipher, M. (1994). *Reviving Ophelia: Saving the selves of adolescent girls.* New York: Riverhead Books.

Poirier, J. M., Francis, K. B., Fisher, S. K., Williams-Washington, K., Goode, T. D., & Jackson, V. H. (2008). *Practice brief 1: Providing services and supports for youth who are lesbian, gay, transgender, questioning, intersex, or two-spirit.* Washington, DC: National Centre for Cultural Competence, Georgetown University Centre for Child and Human Development.

Province of Alberta. (2000). *Child, youth and family enhancement act* (current as of January 2014). Edmonton, Alberta: Alberta Queen's Printer.

Public Health Agency of Canada. (2005). *Fetal Alcohol Spectrum Disorder (FASD).* Government of Canada. Retrieved from: http://www.phac-aspc.gc.ca/hp-ps/dca-dea/prog-ini/fasd-etcaf/faq/pdf/faq-eng.pdf

Quinn, T. L. (2002, November/December). Sexual orientation and gender identity: An administrative approach to diversity. *Child Welfare, LXXXI*(6): 913–928.

Quintana, N. S., Rosenthal, J., & Krehely, J. (2010). *On the streets: The federal response to gay and transgender homeless youth.* Washington, DC: The Center for American Progress.

Retrieved from: https://www.americanprogress.org/wp-content/uploads/issues/2010/06/pdf/lgbtyouthhomelessness.pdf

Reamer, F. G. (2012). *Boundary issues and dual relationships in the human services*. New York, NY: Columbia University Press.

Reamer, F. G., & Siegel, D. (2008). *Teens in crisis: How the industry services struggling teens helps and hurts kids*. New York, NY: Columbia University Press.

Regehr, C., & Glancy, G. (2010). *Mental health social work practice in Canada*. Ontario, Canada: Oxford University Press.

Ricks, F., Charlesworth, J., Bellefeuille, G., & Field, A. (1999). *All together now: Creating a social capital mosaic*. Frances Ricks, Victoria British Columbia and Vanier Institute for the Family, Toronto Ontario. Victoria, British Columbia: Morriss Printing Company.

Rogers, C. (1961). *On becoming a person: A therapist's view of psychotherapy*. New York, NY: Houghton Mifflin Company.

Ruch, G. (2008). Developing 'containing contexts' for the promotion of effective direct work: The challenge for organisations. In B. Luckock & M. Lefevre (Eds.), *Direct work: Social work with children and young people in care* (pp. 295–306). London: British Association for Adopting & Fostering.

Ruch, G. (2010a). The contemporary context of relationship-based practice. In G. Ruch, D. Turney, & A. Ward (Eds.), *Relationship-based social work: Getting to the heart of practice* (pp. 13–28). London, UK: Jessica Kingsley Publishers.

Ruch, G. (2010b). Theoretical frameworks informing relationship-based practice. In G. Ruch, D. Turney, & A. Ward (Eds.), *Relationship-based social work: Getting to the heart of practice* (pp. 29–45). London, UK: Jessica Kingsley Publishers.

Saleebey, D. (1996). The strength-perspective in social work practice: Extensions and cautions. *Social Work*, 41(3): 296–305.

Saleebey, D. (1997). Introduction: Power in the people. In D. Saleebey (Ed.), *The strengths perspective in social work practice*, Second Edition (pp. 3–19). New York, NY: Longman Publishers.

Santa Maria, C. (2012, December 20). Insanity: The real definition, *Huffington Post, Huff Post Education*. Retrieved from: http://www.huffingtonpost.com/2011/12/20/insanity-definition_n_1159927.html

Sarri, R., & Phillips, A. (2004). Health and social services for pregnant and parenting high risk teens. *Children and Youth Services Review*, 26: 537–560.

Schore, A. N. (2003). Early relational trauma, disorganized attachment, and the development of a predisposition to violence. In M. F. Solomon & D. J. Siegel (Eds.), *Healing trauma: Attachment, mind, body, and brain* (pp. 107–167). New York, NY: W. W. Norton & Company.

Siegel, D. (2003). An interpersonal neurobiology of psychotherapy: The developing mind and the resolution of trauma. In M. F. Solomon & D. J. Siegel (Eds.), *Healing trauma: Attachment, mind, body, and brain* (pp. 1–56). New York, NY: W. W. Norton & Company.

Siegel, D. (2013). *Brainstorm: The power and purpose of the teenage brain*. New York, NY: Jeremy P. Tarcher/Penguin.

Silver, J. (2014). *About Canada: Poverty*. Halifax, Canada: Fernwood Publishing.

Simmonds, J. (2008). Direct work with children – Delusion or reality? In B. Luckock & M. Lefevre (Eds.), *Direct work: Social work with children and young people in care* (pp. xiii–xxvi). London: British Association for Adopting & Fostering.

Smith, T. J. (2004). *Guides for the journey: Supporting high-risk youth with paid mentors and counselors*. Public/Private Ventures. Retrieved from: http://www.nationalserviceresources.org/files/m2991-guides-for-the-journey.pdf

Smyth, P. (2004). Community integration: The next challenge for child welfare. *Journal for Services to Children and Families*, 1(1): 18–23.

Smyth, P. (2013). A different approach to high-risk youths. *Social Work Today, 13*(6): 10.

Smyth, P. (2016). Navigating through systems: The journey of young mothers to adulthood. *Canadian Social Work, 18*(1), 54–68.

Smyth, P., & Eaton-Erickson, A. (2009). Making the connection: Strategies for working with high-risk youth. In S. McKay, D. Fuchs, & I. Brown (Eds.), *Passion for action in child and family services: Voices from the prairies* (pp. 119–142). Regina, Saskatchewan: Canadian Plains Research Centre.

Smyth, P., Eaton-Erickson, A., Slessor, J., & Pasma, R. (2005). *The word on the street: How youth view services aimed at them* (Unpublished report). Edmonton. High Risk Youth Task Force, Edmonton and Area Child and Family Services, Region 6.

Steering Committee, High Risk Youth Initiative, Edmonton and Area Child and Family Services, Region 6. (2007). *More words on the street: A follow up report on how youth view services aimed at them* (Unpublished).

Strega, S. (2007). Anti-oppressive practice in child welfare. In Baines, D. (Ed.), *Doing anti-oppressive practice: Building transformative politicized social work*. Halifax, Canada: Fernwood Publishing.

Strega, S., & Esquao, Sohki Aski (Carrière, J.). (2009). Introduction. In S. Strega & Sohki Aski Esquao (J. Carrière) (Eds.), *Walking this path together: Anti-racist and anti-oppressive child welfare practice* (pp. 29–44). Canada: Fernwood Publishing.

Szalavitz, M., & Perry, B. (2010). *Born for love: Why empathy is essential – And endangered*. New York, NY: William Morrow, Harper Collins.

Taylor, M. (2010). *Essentials of harm reduction* (Unpublished). Power Point Presentation. Streetworks, Edmonton.

Terr, L. C. (1991). Childhood traumas. An outline and overview. *American Journal of Psychiatry, 148*, 10–20.

Thomas, N. (2008). Consultation and advocacy. In B. Luckock & M. Lefevre (Eds.), *Direct work: Social work with children and young people in care* (pp. 97–114). London: British Association for Adopting & Fostering.

Trocmé, N., Knoke, D., & Blackstock, C. (2004, December). *Pathways to the overrepresentation of Aboriginal children in Canada's child welfare system*. Social Services Review.

Trout, M., & The Infant-Parent Institute (producers). (1997). *Multiple transitions: A young child's point of view on foster care and adoption* (DVD). Retrieved from: http://www.infant-parent.com/collections/all

Truth and Reconciliation Commission. (2015). *Final report of the truth and reconciliation commission of Canada. Volume One: Summary*. Toronto, Ontario: James Lorimer & Company Ltd.

Turnell, A., & Edwards, S. (1999). *Signs of safety: A solution and safety oriented approach to child protection*. New York, NY: W.W Norton & Company, Inc.

Turney, D. (2010). Sustaining relationships: Working with strong feelings. In G. Ruch, D. Turney, & A. Ward (Eds.), *Relationship-based social work: Getting to the heart of practice* (pp. 102–117). London, UK: Jessica Kingsley Publishers.

TVO Parents (producer). (2012, May 29). *Gabor Maté: Attachment and brain development*. Retrieved from: http://www.youtube.com/watch?v=uKES1nyitAg

Ungar, M. (2002). *Playing at being bad: The hidden resilience of troubled teens*. Nova Scotia, Canada: Pottersfield Press.

Ungar, M. (2004). *Nurturing hidden resilience in troubled youth*. Canada: University of Toronto Press.

Ungar, M. (2005). Delinquent or simply resilient? How 'problem' behaviour can be a child's hidden path to resilience. *Voices for Children*. Retrieved from: http://www.resilienceproject.org/files/PDF/Delinquent%20or%20simple%20resilient.pdf

Ungar, M. (2006). *Strengths-based counselling with at-risk youth*. Thousand Oaks, CA: Corwin Press.

Ungar, M. (2007a). *Too safe for their own good: How risk and responsibility help teens thrive*. Toronto: McClelland & Stewart Ltd.

Ungar, M. (2007b). Contextual and cultural aspects of resilience in child welfare settings. In I. Brown, F. Chaze, D. Fuchs, J. Lafrance, S. McKay, & S. Thomas-Prokop (Eds.), *Putting a human face on child welfare: Voices from the prairies* (pp. 223–250). Prairie Child Welfare Consortium. Retrieved from: www.uregina.ca/spr/prairiechild/index.html/ CentreofExcellenceforChildWelfare; www.cecw-cepb.ca

Ungar, M. (2009). *We generation: Raising socially responsible kids*. Toronto: McClelland & Stewart Ltd.

Ungar, M. (2011). The social ecology of resilience: Addressing contextual and cultural ambiguity of a nascent construct. *American Journal of Orthopsychiatry, 81*(1): 1–17.

Ungar, M. (2013a). Resilience, trauma, context, and culture. *Trauma, Violence, and Abuse, 14*: 255–266.

Ungar, M. (2013b). The impact of youth-adult relationships on resilience. *International Journal of Child, Youth and Family Studies, 3*: 328–336.

Ungar, M. (2014, May). Counselling children, youth and families with complex needs: A social ecological approach to nurturing resilience across cultures and contexts. *High Risk Youth Conference*, Edmonton, Alberta. Power Point Retrieved from: http://www.hryc.ca/assets/ michael-ungar-workshop-handout.pdf

Ungar, M. (2015). *Working with children and youth with complex needs: 20 skills that build resilience*. New York, NY: Routledge.

Ungar, M., Brown, M., Liebenberg, L., Othman, R., Kwong, W. M., Armstrong, M., & Gilgun, J. (2007). Unique pathways to resilience across cultures. *Adolescence, 42*(166): 287–310.

Ungar, M., Manuel, S., Mealey, S., Thomas, G., & Campbell, C. (2004). A study of community guides: Lessons for professionals practicing with and in communities. *Social Work, 49*(4): 550–561.

Valios, N. (2001, October 4–10). Men at work. *Community Care*. Retrieved from: www. community-care.co.uk

van der Kolk, B. (2003). Posttraumatic stress disorder and the nature of trauma. In M. F. Solomon & D. J. Siegel (Eds.), *Healing trauma: Attachment, mind, body, and brain* (pp. 168–195). New York, NY: W. W. Norton & Company.

Walker, J. (2012, September 28). *Introduction to trauma informed care, part 1: Secondary trauma & other effects on workers* (Unpublished). PowerPoint Presentation.

Ward, A. (2010). The learning relationship: Learning and development for relationship-based practice. In G. Ruch, D. Turney, & A. Ward (Eds.), *Relationship-based social work: Getting to the heart of practice* (pp. 183–198). London, UK: Jessica Kingsley Publishers.

Washington, K. T. (2008). Attachment and alternatives: Therapy in child welfare research. *Advances in Social Work, 9*(1): 8–16.

Wharf, B. (2002a). Introduction. In B. Wharf (Ed.), *Community work approaches to child welfare* (pp. 9–25). Canada: Broadview Press.

Wharf, B. (2002b). Community social work in two provinces. Part 1: The neighbourhood house project in Victoria and the Hazelton Office of the Ministry for Children and Families. In B. Wharf (Ed.), *Community work approaches to child welfare* (pp. 47–62). Canada: Broadview Press.

Wharf, B. (2002c). Building a case for community approaches to child welfare. In B. Wharf (Ed.), *Community work approaches to child welfare* (pp. 181–197). Canada: Broadview Press.

White, M. (2007). *Maps of narrative practice*. New York, NY: W. W. Norton & Company Inc.

Winnicott, D. W. (1988). *Babies and their mothers*. London. UK: Free Association Books.

Winston, A. P. (2000). Recent developments in borderline personality disorder. *Advances in Psychiatric Treatment*, 6: 211–217. doi:10.1192/apt.6.3.211

Wolin, S. & Wolin, S. (1999). Project Resilience: Resilience as behavior. *Project Resilience*. Retirevied from: http://projectresilience.com/resasbehavior.htm

Worden, M. (1999). *Family therapy basics*, Second Edition. Pacific Grove, CA: Brooks/Cole Publishing Company.

Index